MARY GILLIATT'S

INTERIOR
DESIGN
COURSE

MARY GILLIATT'S
INTERIOR DESIGN COURSE

Contents

First published in 2001 by
Conran Octopus Limited
a part of Octopus Publishing Group
2–4 Heron Quays
London E14 4JP
www.conran-octopus.co.uk

Reprinted in 2002
This paperback edition published in 2005

Text copyright © Mary Gilliatt 2001

Design and layout © Conran Octopus 2001
Illustrations copyright © Conran Octopus 2001

Publishing Director: Lorraine Dickey
Senior Editor: Muna Reyal
Editor: Alison Wormleighton

Creative Director: Leslie Harrington
Designer: Mary Staples
Picture Editor: Jo Walton

Production Director: Zoe Fawcett
Production Controller: Alex Wiltshire

British Library Cataloguing-in-Publication
Data. A catalogue record for this book is
available from the British Library.

ISBN 1 84091 443 2

Colour origination by Sang Choy
International, Singapore

Printed in China

*For my three special children:
Sophia Gilliatt, Annie Constantine and Tom Gilliatt,
not forgetting my dear Sophie, David and Phoebe.
And for my four (so far) equally special grandchildren: Olivia, Georgia and Iona Constantine
and Freddie Gilliatt.*

	INTRODUCTION	6
	PART ONE: THE BASICS	8
SECTION ONE	General Planning	10
	Planning essentials	12
SECTION TWO	The Elements of Design	18
	Understanding light	20
	VOCABULARY OF LIGHTING TERMS	28
	Maximizing storage	30
	Using colour	42
	VOCABULARY OF COLOUR TERMS	53
	Playing with texture and pattern	54
	Controlling scale and balance	58
SECTION THREE	Style	60
	A sense of style	62
	The suitability factor	64
	Influences on style	70
	Chronology of style-periods	76
	VOCABULARY OF DECORATING STYLES	78

PART TWO: THE SPECIFICS   84

SECTION FOUR   Walls and Ceilings   86
Decorative options   88
A guide to paint   94
VOCABULARY OF PAINT TERMS   102
Wallpapers   104
Alternative wall coverings   112

SECTION FIVE   Floors   120
Flooring options   122
Carpets   124
Rugs   128
VOCABULARY OF CARPET TERMS   134
Hard flooring   136
Flexible flooring   144

SECTION SIX   Windows   146
Choosing window treatments   148
Curtains and top treatments   152
Blinds   162
Alternative window treatments   166
Problem windows   168
Fabrics for windows   172
VOCABULARY OF FABRIC TERMS   175

SECTION SEVEN   Furniture   178
Furniture arrangement   180
Upholstered furniture   184
Non-upholstered furniture   186
Beds   188
Period furniture   190
VOCABULARY OF PERIOD FURNITURE TERMS   198

SECTION EIGHT   The Finishing Touches   204
Finessing a room   206
Accessories   208
Arranging art   212
Plants in the home   216

INDEX   218
ACKNOWLEDGEMENTS   223

Almost everyone at one time or another has to create a home, whatever their circumstances or space …

Curiously, the basics of designing interiors and the art of making a home are rarely taught to anyone but aspiring professionals. For some reason it seems to be tacitly accepted that decorating or renovating a house or apartment should be done by intuition. But although some people seem instinctively to possess such useful abilities and a natural sense of style, the fact remains that even the greatest flair or aptitude has to be backed by practical knowledge and honed by experience.

Trial and error, which is the best way to gain meaningful experience in most fields, can be a depressingly expensive process when it comes to renovating, decorating and furnishing. In short, if you want to become competent enough to design your own home, whatever its size, in a pleasing and practical way with the minimum amount of stress, you will need to understand fully the fundamental tenets of the subject.

It is a truism that as far as possible your home should be an extension of your personality, or at least a solid expression of your tastes and preferences. But, more importantly, I think, your home also has to be a comforting haven, a place for relaxation. If a home, however elegant it is, however

visually stunning, however fashionable, is not welcoming, not really comfortable, not suited to your lifestyle, it can seriously undermine your whole outlook. In other words, learning how to create a home that is both good-looking and practical is important to your actual well-being.

To achieve this, you will need to have a good working knowledge of all aspects of decoration. How else can you really get to know the most efficient way to plan, how best to choose among the myriad choices, how to buy sensibly and what design and decorating standards to use? Even if you can afford to employ an architect or a designer (or both), it will still be necessary to brief them succinctly on what you want, what your ideal home includes, and the way that you hope to live in it.

In most cases, rooms or homes to be designed or redesigned already contain certain ingredients, like carpets, rugs, pieces of furniture, soft furnishings and accessories. Some of these will have to be incorporated into any new design, or at least rethought, refurbished or re-covered. Indeed, it makes the process easier, by giving you a starting point. On the other hand, it is exciting to be able to plan a room, or a whole home, from scratch.

HOW TO USE THIS COURSE

Whichever situation applies to you, it is obviously extremely useful to learn about imaginative ways to utilize a given space; effective lighting methods; potential (and practicable) decorating styles; possible treatments for walls, ceilings, floors and windows; furniture and soft-furnishing options; and the sensitive use of colour and texture, scale and balance, contrast and harmony.

That is why I have prepared this course, which, if followed step-by-step, should give you a thorough grounding in the whole subject of interior design. It is the distillation of all my own hard-won knowledge and various writings on the subject.

My hope is that the course will actually be followed from the first page to the last, and that it will then go on being useful as a reference source. The aim is to take you through the entire procedure of planning a room, or a complete home, in a simple and logical order – the order that any good designer or decorator would follow – and, in the process, give you as much knowledge of the subject as is practicable. Above all, I want this course to engender ideas that could act as a springboard to inspiration for your own home. If I can achieve that, I will have achieved much.

Good design is the art of making something work well and look good. Since one of the most creative and rewarding achievements in life is the satisfying design of a home, it is clearly important to try to succeed at this as well as one possibly can. This course is therefore structured in such a way that, by the end of it, if you have thoroughly absorbed and understood the content, you should feel confident enough to tackle or mastermind any style of room or apartment or house.

I have divided the course into two main parts: **The Basics** and **The Specifics**. Both of these main headings are broken down into separate sections, each leading logically into the next.

Thus, **The Basics** begins with *General Planning* (which will help to determine your needs, finalize the budget, get the framework right, draw up plans and specifications). This is followed by *The Elements of Design* (covering lighting, storage, colour, textures and pattern, scale and balance). *Style*, the third section, asks what is really meant by style, and goes into the distinguishing features of the most popular style-periods. In addition, a chronological chart puts each style into its historical context, giving dates, reigning monarchs and concurrent period-styles of other countries.

The second part, **The Specifics**, is just that. It starts with *Walls and Ceilings*, which goes into the finer points of decoration using paint, paper, fabric and alternative coverings. *Floors* includes the full range of hard, flexible and soft floorings, including antique carpets. The next section in this part, *Windows*, offers an extensive survey of curtain and window-blind styles, as well as how to deal with difficult window shapes. *Furniture* covers both modern and antique furniture, relating the latter to the style-periods covered in *Style*.

Finally, *The Finishing Touches* reveals how to acquire an eye for detail and accessorize skilfully.

Vocabulary pages appear throughout the book, explaining the technical terms for Lighting, Colour, Decorating Styles, Paints, Carpets, Fabrics, and Period Furniture.

As you progress through the course, you should always keep in mind the following three headings:
- function
- mood
- style

The first is to remind you of the function of a room (what it is needed for; how it will be used, and by whom). The second refers to what mood you need to create (calm, restful, stimulating, warm, cool and so on, depending upon the function of the room and the climate in which you live). The third refers to the style of the room or home (traditional, eclectic, contemporary, American country, English country house, French Provençal, Gustavian, etc).

I very much hope that this course will provide a useful grounding in design. Remember that although assimilating it all is going to be hard work, doing so will provide its own rewards – in particular, confidence in your own taste and the knowledge that you are making the right choices.

PART ONE

THE BASICS

SECTION ONE

Some people take years to plan the contents of their ideal home and know exactly how they want each room to look and feel. Too many of us, however, apart from having a few particular likes and dislikes, plunge unprepared into the process and have to learn on the way, mostly through expensive mistakes. That is why I have got into the habit of trying to plan a home like a campaign. Really thinking about all possible needs from the beginning, finding out about costs beforehand, making endless lists and drawing up plans – all this can be tedious when you are impatient to get on with the job. But it is worth putting up with for the long-term gain. Major redecorating jobs rarely come without their attendant upsets, but at least you should feel in control. And, in fact, much of the planning and anticipation can be both creatively satisfying and exciting. Best of all, you should not be disappointed with the result.

General Planning

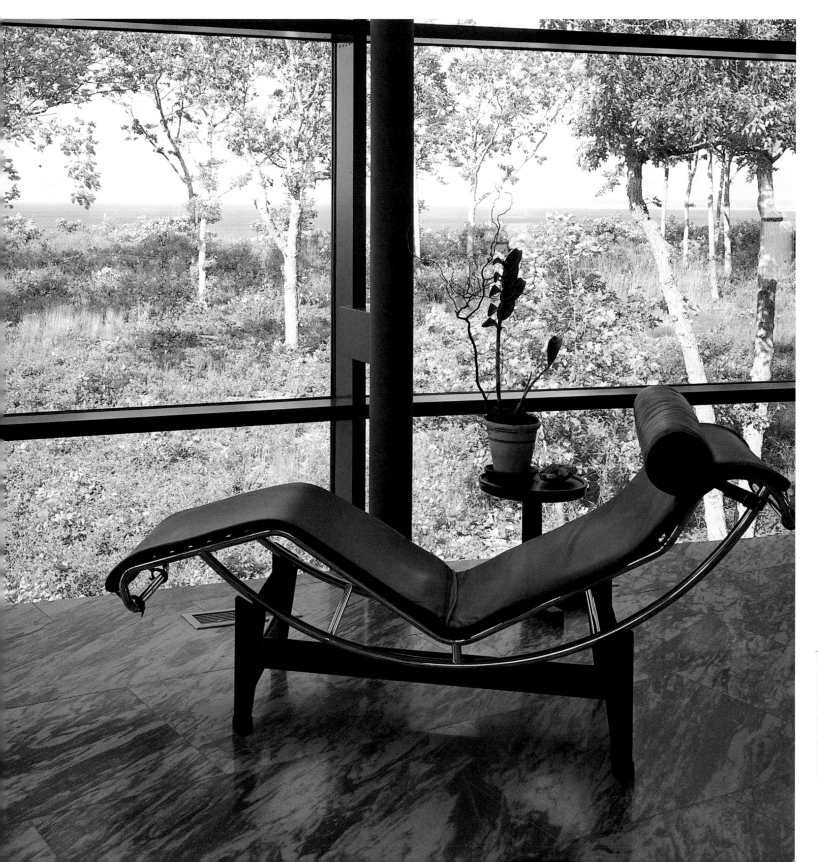

Planning Essentials

To ensure that the interior design of a room allows it to function to best advantage, you first have to go back to basics. This involves deciding how the space can be apportioned into different zones; what should be done about the wiring, lighting, ceiling, floor, walls and windows; what can be improved and how. The results of this analysis will form the framework on which you can add whatever mood and style you choose.

Good interior design is as much about practicality, comfort and detail as it is about mood and style. However beautiful the window treatments, however original the colour schemes, however splendid the furnishings, no one is going to thank you if the overall room is not comfortable to live in or does not function as it should.

QUESTIONS TO ASK

Any competent designer who is asked to improve a home or to plan one from scratch would start by finding out their clients' tastes and the factors that make them feel most at ease, how they live their lives, how they would *like* to live their lives in an ideal world and how much they are prepared to spend. To start with the optimum requirements and to work backwards from there, in the light of the money available for the project, is as good a way as any of getting priorities right.

When designing for yourself, you should take a similar approach and be equally clear about your budget. The questions listed on the right are what a designer would ask you, although they would vary according to whether the work involved redoing a room or a whole house or apartment, or completely starting from scratch. The questions cover the four main aspects of the work: function, practicalities, aesthetics and budget.

1 *A small table at the entrance to this kitchen is still large enough for a cup of coffee or snack, a chat with a friend or simply writing notes, and makes the space seem much more civilized.*

2 *Old moulds make a pleasant wall decoration in a dining room, which has been designed with both eating and working in mind.*

3 *A home office has been created in this small house. The winding stairs are simple but sculptural.*

Function

1 How long do you expect to stay in this home?

2 Are there, or are there likely to be, children in the household? If there are children now, how many are there and what are their ages? (This affects room planning.)

3 Are there any pets, and if so, what kind? (This affects the finishes and surfaces used.)

4 Are any elderly relatives living or staying with you, or likely to be?

(If so, you will need to think about good light for stairs, corridors, and hallways, non-slip bathroom floors, grip rails for bathtubs, showers, etc.)

5 How many people are at home for all of the day? (This might affect colours and lighting.)

6 What are the respective needs of each member of the household? Are these needs likely to change?

7 Where does the family feel most comfortable eating?

8 Who uses the living room most?

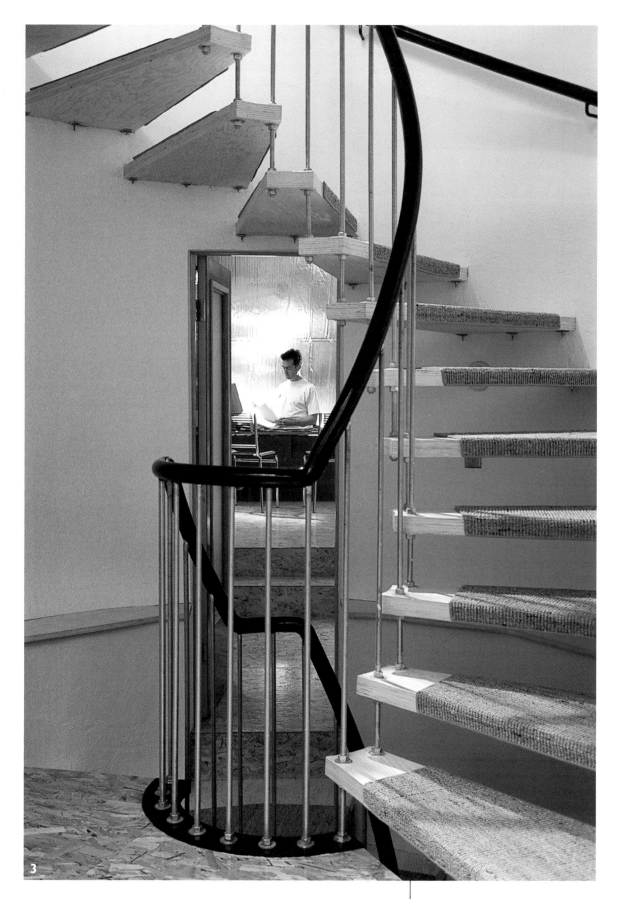

9   How often do you entertain and how?

10 How many people do you generally entertain at once?

11 In what rooms do you entertain the most?

12 If your children have friends in, where do they entertain them? (This affects space and surfaces.)

13 Do you feel that, in general, the overall space in the home is inadequate, or capable of being put to better use if you could only think how?

14 What is the minimum number of rooms you think you need? Can these be found from existing space (such as the attic, basement, or garage)?

15 Is the room in need of total rethinking as well as redecoration? Have family circumstances or interests changed since you first arranged it? Could your present facilities be improved? (To allow for the pace of technological change, you will need maximum flexibility, which affects wiring and lighting.)

16 Where do you and your partner like to sit most, and on what? Do you need different chair backs and seat heights? Where do you both like to work when paying bills, writing letters, etc?

17 If you are redesigning the bedroom, what kind of bed and mattress do you both prefer? Is bedroom lighting as good as it could be?

part one: the basics

Practicalities

1   What is the state of walls, windows, woodwork, ceiling and floors?

2   How up-to-date is the wiring? If you need to add any new electric sockets, will they overload the present system or be difficult to install? Does your wiring comply with safety requirements? Is it adequate for your present and future needs (again bearing in mind technological advances)?

3   Are there enough electric sockets in the right places?

4   Would it be an improvement to install long windows or French doors anywhere? (Obviously, they must not look odd or incongruous from the outside.)

5   Are any existing air-conditioning units unsightly, and if so, can they be improved, covered or even removed from windows and resited in the wall?

6   Do you need to put in burglar, fire or smoke alarms?

7   Does the existing hardware – such as door handles, light switches, finger plates, window catches or taps – need replacing, re-plating or re-brassing?

8   Can you fit in another bathroom, shower room or cloakroom? Do existing fittings need replacing, or can they be resurfaced? Is everything in good order and likely to last some years without need of repair or replacement?

9   Are there nice floorboards under the existing flooring? Can they be scraped and sanded? Do they need repairing or replacing? Would you like a different kind of floor, such as quarry tiles or marble?

If an answer to any of the previous questions will mean major work – such as rewiring or re-plumbing; re-flooring or stripping and sanding a floor; repairing damaged walls, ceilings or floorboards; knocking down walls or adding new ones; changing air-conditioning units or putting in a new window – this obviously must be done before any decoration can be undertaken and should be allowed for in the overall budget.

Aesthetics

1   Is your taste in decorating and furnishing eclectic, traditional, modern, romantic, minimalist or something else? Does it depend on the style of the house or room?

2   Do you and your partner share similar tastes or have decidedly different ones? Have you agreed to each have your own way in different rooms, or do you have to find some sort of compromise?

3   Do you know what colour scheme you want? Are you open to suggestion?

4   What colours are you and your partner happiest with? Are there any colours either of you particularly dislikes?

5   What styles do you admire? What style would you like for this room or house?

6   Is it possible to include existing furniture, if any?

1 *Steel doors and handles make an elegant contrast to the polished wood floor, as well as leading the eye to the piano and bust in the room down the hallway.*
2 *There is a deliberately cool and tranquil air about this hall. The two rugs and the few carefully chosen pieces work harmoniously together and are well lit at night.*
3 *Optimum use of space has been made in this two-level room. A sofa is tucked away against the wall while the tall steel filing cabinet doubles as a side table as well as visually balancing the steps to the book area.*

Budget

1 What is the maximum you can spend on your project, bearing in mind that you should always keep a contingency sum in hand?

2 Are you truly comfortable with this budget? Have you researched current prices for merchandise and services?

3 If you could list the ten luxuries that would make your home seem more attractive to you and/or work better, what would they be?

4 What must be spent? Where can you save? Can you form a long-term plan so that urgent things can be implemented now and others later?

5 Can you make sensible compromises on items that could be recycled to less important rooms if better things can be afforded in the future?

Once you have gone through all these questions a few times, you should have a clearer idea of your ideal home, of the jobs that most need doing and of what it will cost. Some of the questions might sound elementary, but in the enthusiasm or the confusion of the moment, with so many things to think about, it is all too easy to forget the most basic elements of a home. Nevertheless, I cannot stress too strongly how important it is to take the time to find out for yourself the essentials that will make a room or home look and work better.

part one: the basics

Floor and lighting plan

This rough floor and lighting plan is nevertheless drawn accurately to scale. This makes it easier to plan the space, as well as to allow an electrician to see exactly what lights and power sockets you want positioned where and what lights (like the central recessed spotlights) you want working from what switch. Such a plan will save much expense later, when far too many people realize, after the decoration has been done, that nothing has been planned for overall lighting and lamps or, for that matter, power sockets and telephone.

FLOOR PLANS

Drawing accurate floor plans is an important part of any designer's work, whether professional or amateur. Quite apart from the usefulness of floor plans for working out any changes, they are invaluable for deciding on the positions of new electric sockets (outlets), lighting and furniture.

To draw a floor plan, or sketch plan, first make a preliminary plan of the room. Using a well-sharpened pencil, roughly sketch the shape on plain paper, then use a good-sized retractable tape measure to mark the dimensions of the main structural elements on the sketch. These should include the length of walls, the width of doors and other openings, the size of windows and any fixtures, the thickness of partitions, and the distance of fittings from one another. Also mark

Furniture arrangement plan

The same accurately scaled plan will also save you from making furnishing mistakes, like impulse-buying pieces of furniture that are too big for the space or will not fit through doors. Lighting has been included again in this plan, to show, for example, how art placed on the walls can be lit by recessed spot-lights in the ceiling, and how the small side tables by the sofa can be left uncluttered by table lamps because of the swing-arm lamps on the walls above them.

✕ ✕	power sockets
⊕	recessed spotlight
⊢○	work light or picture light
■	TV socket
⊙	telephone socket
▮	switch

the positions of any existing electric sockets, telephone and television jacks, radiators, grilles, permanent heating appliances and air conditioners.

To draw up the plan properly, you will need some graph paper; if possible, choose the kind with invisible perforations, which help you to draw straight lines. If using metric measurements, choose metric graph paper with the 2cm squares divided into tenths, and make one of these 2mm squares equal to 10cm; a 2cm square will equal 1m. If measuring in inches and feet, choose graph paper with the 1in squares divided into eighths, and make two of these ⅛in squares equal to 1ft; a 1in square will equal 4ft. This scale will work for all rooms except kitchens, bathrooms and laundry rooms, for which a scale of twice this size is better.

With the sharp pencil, and also a ruler if the graph paper does not have invisible perforations, draw the perimeter of your room to the chosen scale on the graph paper. It is important to do this absolutely accurately.

Erase any door openings, marking their clearance (or swing, when opening) with an arc drawn to scale, then mark in fixtures or odd corners, windows, radiators, electric sockets, television points, phone jacks and air conditioners, incorporating the appropriate symbols shown in the key below and using the sample plan (see opposite) as a guide.

Make sure that everything is accurate, as the slightest deviation can have disastrous consequences. If you will be taking delivery of large pieces of furniture, make notes of the measurements of windows, door openings and staircases, especially at any turns, as well as the width, height and depth of any elevators, to make sure they will fit.

DECORATING SCHEDULES

Another essential aid to decorating is a decorating schedule for each room, which will serve as a reminder of exactly what is to be done. If you are employing any contractors, type up copies for everyone involved so that there can be no misunderstandings or mistakes. Decorating schedules can be prepared at the same time as sample boards and kept with them for daily reference.

Head the paper with the name of the room, and then down the side of the paper write the following headings, leaving enough space between them for clear descriptions:
• Walls
• Floor
• Ceiling
• Woodwork
• Mouldings

• Lighting and general wiring (phone jacks, television points, doorbell, stereo, etc.)
• Window treatments
• Hardware (switch plates, dimmers, door handles, taps, shower fittings and so on.)
• Bed treatments (if applicable)
An example of a similar decorating schedule, for part of a house rather than just a single room, is shown below. (It includes only five of the above headings because the other headings are not affected by the redecorating.)

If you prepare a mock decorating schedule for every room in your own home, it will soon become second nature to you – so much so that you will automatically conjure up those headings in your mind when looking at a room to be redesigned. This way you will never forget to cater for small but essential parts of the room.

SAMPLE BOARDS

The other essential aid to decorating is a sample board for each room. Also known as a colour board, this will help to clarify your scheme and act as an *aide-mémoire*. You will need several sheets of thick cardboard, preferably in a colour such as grey, dark blue, green, khaki or sludgy brown, since white or cream can distort the effect of colours. They should be cut to a size of at least 60cm (24in) square. A larger size – say, 75cm (30in) square, or 75 x 90cm (30 x 36in) – might be more useful, but the smaller size is easier to transport.

Gather together small samples of your proposed paint colours, wallpaper, fabric and flooring. Cutting them out with pinking shears will prevent loose threads and untidy edges, but ordinary scissors can be used. The samples should ideally be large enough to show the designs, but if necessary you can have back-up samples to show very large designs and also pattern repeats. You could make the size of each one roughly in proportion to its use in the room, to create a more accurate impression of the final effect, but this is not essential.

Arrange the samples on the board, using paste or double-sided tape to stick them down. With a black pen, caption them clearly, with their name and number, colourway, supplier and price. Print the name of the room at the top of the board.

If you wish, protect the board with a sheet of acetate the same width as the board but a little longer. Wrap it over the board, sticking it down at the back. Another attractive presentation, if you plan to keep your samples permanently, is to make the sample board out of two sheets of card bound together, with windows cut out of the top sheet to frame the samples.

SAMPLE DECORATING SCHEDULE

• All painted surfaces to be properly made good and prepared with primer or undercoat, and two coats of paint, or three where necessary.
• If applying wallpaper, walls to be properly prepared and lined.

HALL

Walls	Flat emulsion, off-white no. 552
Floor	Blue, wool/nylon blend twist pile carpet
Ceiling	Decorator's flat white emulsion
Woodwork	Decorator's white satin finish
Mouldings	White eggshell emulsion

LIVING ROOM

Walls	Pale terracotta rag-rubbed finish (see sample); undercoat of Gardenia eggshell oil
Floor	Brussels weave carpet no. 224
Ceiling	Flat white emulsion with tinge of terracotta
Woodwork	Decorator's white satin finish
Mouldings	White eggshell emulsion

MASTER BEDROOM

Walls	Wallpaper: no 9671 col. blue/white
Floor	Axminster carpet no. 66
Ceiling	Decorator's flat white emulsion
Woodwork	White satin finish
Mouldings	White eggshell emulsion

CHILD'S ROOM

Walls	Wallpaper: no. 5890 col. pink/orange/white
Floor	Stripped, varnished floorboards
Ceiling	Flat white emulsion
Woodwork	White gloss
Mouldings	White eggshell emulsion

In the context of this course, the elements of design are the factors that are part and parcel of every room – the aspects that give a room its initial character before the finishing touches are applied. These are lighting, storage, colour, texture and pattern, scale and balance. All of these elements, along with styles and specifics like paint, wallpaper, fabrics and window treatments (dealt with elsewhere in the book), have to be thought about in detail before any decoration can begin.

The Elements of Design

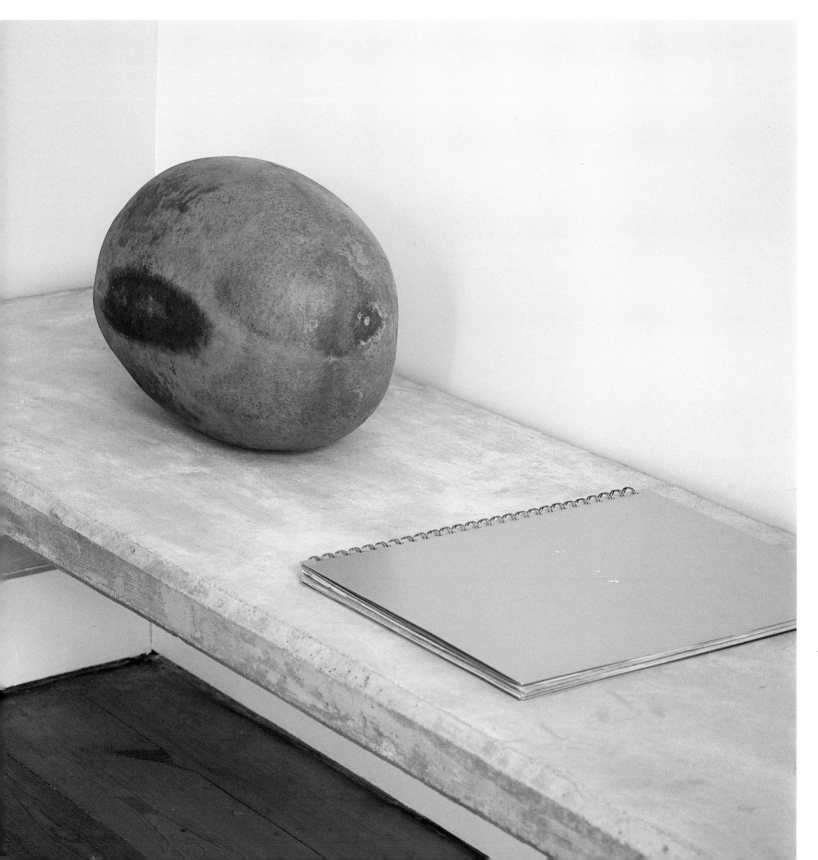

Understanding Light

Good lighting can alter the apparent size of a room, enhance good features or diminish ugly ones. It can add glamour, sparkle and drama or a warm, comforting glow, at the turn of the appropriate dimmer switch. Lighting is as essential to the success of a room as it is to theatre or film, yet it is often the least planned of all decorating elements. How often do people not even bother thinking about the lighting of a room until long after the decoration is underway and it is too late? If only they had considered it before, it might have been possible to install a useful and flexible system for comparatively little expense.

Many people think of artificial light as the counterfeit of daylight and treat them as completely separate issues. However, for an effective lighting system that will provide comfortable light at all times, a balance must be struck between the two types of light, with one discreetly boosting the other whenever necessary.

MAKING THE MOST OF DAYLIGHT

Daylight has, of course, all the advantages of variety. It alters in intensity through the seasons and even from hour to hour. And it changes in colour, from the intense blue of clear skies to the dull grey of overcast days; from the clear light of early morning to the lavender glow of dusk; and from the burnished golden light of high summer to the white dazzle cast up by winter snow.

During each phase, the interior of a building will look subtly different (which is why it is useful to see a room in as many lights as possible before deciding on a colour scheme and furnishings). Small windows should be left as uncluttered as possible, to make the best of what light there is, while large windows should have blinds or sheers that can filter any super-abundance of daylight.

Daylight does not, however, have great qualities of penetration. In an average room, about one per cent of the available daylight will reach the areas farthest from the windows, compared with as much as ten per cent near the windows. That is why, for large periods of the year, demanding visual tasks like working at a computer screen, reading, writing, drawing, painting or sewing can only be done close to a window.

Many rooms in buildings with a narrow frontage, or in buildings surrounded by other buildings, will have poor lighting at most times of the day. A good many rooms will therefore always need the boost of artificial lighting for some purposes, and in deep buildings, dark central areas that are used as kitchens, bathrooms and laundry rooms, as well as halls and passageways, will need constant artificial light.

USING ARTIFICIAL LIGHT

Artificial background light used during the day is much less depressing if you do not notice the source, so it is a good idea to conceal any booster lighting behind pelmets over windows, around the perimeter of a room or behind large pieces of furniture. In other words, try to keep it literally in the background.

Background lighting is just one kind of lighting, for lighting can be divided into three distinct types:
- general or background lighting
- local or task lighting
- accent or decorative lighting

Ideally, every room should be a combination, to a greater or lesser degree, of at least two of these, and they should meld into each other to form a harmonious whole.

1 The entire window wall in this bedroom has been hung with elegant, thin-slatted Venetian blinds to filter and soften the daylight that would otherwise flood the room.

2 Diamond-shaped panes set into this old arched window criss-cross and pattern the shafts of sunlight that glance through the glass. The role of artificial light should be to provide just such gentle drama.

part one: the basics

TYPES OF LIGHT BULB

The light bulb (or lamp, as it is somewhat confusingly called by the trade) is just as important a consideration as the type and position of a light fitting. The three main types of bulb used in the home – tungsten, halogen and fluorescent – vary in their energy efficiency, their average lifetime and the quality of colour they lend to whatever they illuminate.

Tungsten

The tungsten (also known as incandescent) filament bulb is the most common domestic light source. Compared with daylight, tungsten has a warm, yellowish tone and is good for interior use because it does not much alter colour relationships and it provides good tonal contrast. Tinted tungsten bulbs are also available in a range of colours, with pink the most popular.

Tungsten bulbs come in different sizes, wattages, and designs, to suit different kinds of fixtures. In addition to ordinary bulbs, there are strip lights, spots, globes, candle shapes and bulbs with silvered backs or crowns to alter the manner in which light is spread. Tungsten bulbs have a relatively short life, however, and they do not make efficient use of electricity, since they generate a lot of heat.

Halogen

This type of bulb is increasingly used in the home, giving a cool, crisp light that is whiter and brighter than tungsten. Like tungsten, halogen is effective at colour rendering and at revealing contrasts, but it also has a particularly attractive sparkling

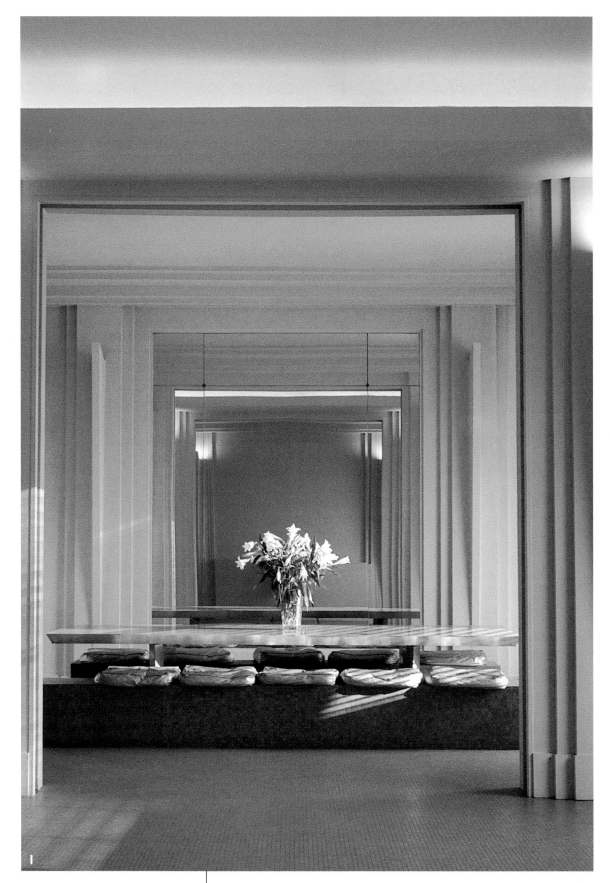

1 Coloured lights installed above these archways space, cast a roseate glow onto the ceiling, in warm contrast to the predominantly pale green scheme. 2 Recessed down-lights set into the partition wall illuminate the shelf below. Tiny low-voltage spots like these can also be tucked into comparatively small recesses between the ceiling and floor for additional illumination. 3 An elegant sculptural halogen floor lamp creates a dramatic curved light in this minimal living room.

quality, which makes it useful for up-lights, down-lights, spots and accent lighting in general. In a tall, sculptural floor lamp, it gives a great punch of light. A halogen bulb should ideally be used with a dimmer switch, and must never be touched with the bare hands or it will be ruined.

Fluorescent

Because fluorescent light is long-lasting and efficient, and therefore less costly to run than tungsten lighting, it is much used in commercial and industrial buildings. It has a bright, even light, and in the past was not very sympathetic for domestic use. Modern fluorescents, however, are improving all the time. Some produce a very passable imitation of daylight, and special diffusers are available to make the light quality more sympathetic.

ROOM-BY-ROOM LIGHTING

Every room has different lighting requirements. Here is a brief guide to the best lighting for each.

Living rooms, libraries and studies

General or background lighting will seem more subtle if it comes from

well-placed down-lights (or from wall-washers, track lights or wall lights, if ceilings are made of concrete or have scant recess space above). Use them either on their own or with floor-standing up-lights, which can be concealed behind plants, furniture or decorative objects like sculpture or urns. This kind of lighting will give a soft wash of light, which is far preferable to the bland and often harsh light that comes from the still ubiquitous central ceiling fixtures.

If you are going to rewire the room, it is a good idea to have all the portable, plug-in lights on a separate circuit, so they can be operated from the doorway. It obviates a lot of switching on and off, not to mention bending down to the floor to reach the switches. If this is impossible, try at least to have kick switches on each

tip

UP-LIGHTS PROVIDE THE BEST WAY OF MAKING DRAMATIC ROOM CHANGES WHEN IT IS IMPOSSIBLE TO CHANGE THE OVERALL WIRING OR TO PUT IN MORE ELECTRIC SOCKETS. ALL THEY NEED IS TO BE PLUGGED IN.

part one: the basics

up-light and separate dimming capability, though that will still mean having to crawl around.

Local, or task, lighting is provided by table lamps and floor lamps placed alongside sofas and chairs for comfortable reading or, if there is not much floor space, by swing-armed or other adjustable wall lamps set just above seating areas. Desk lamps are used for writing and general work. Very close work might benefit from a strategically positioned recessed down-light in the ceiling.

Accent or decorative lighting often comes from spotlights recessed into the ceiling, surface-mounted on it or mounted on lengths of track or tensioned 'barewire', which are angled to highlight paintings, objects, table tops, and so on. It also comes from pools of light cast by table lamps, concealed lights in bookshelves and cabinets, up-lights set in or on floors and good old-fashioned candles.

Dining rooms and dining areas

These look best, and more romantic, by candlelight, backed up by discreet, manoeuvrable background light. But candles should be either above or below eye level so that they do not flicker directly in the diners' eyes.

Supplement the candlelight with a down-light or two, controlled by a dimmer switch. A pendant rise-and-fall light with an opaque shade will cast a pleasant light on the table but, again, should be attached to a dimmer switch and placed so as to avoid uncomfortable dazzle.

The serving area should be lit separately, perhaps by a well-angled spotlight or down-light or by an incandescent (not fluorescent) strip discreetly concealed behind a pelmet on the wall above the serving area.

Halls and staircases

Far too many halls and staircases have hopelessly inadequate lighting. They should be well lit at all times, with light on the floor to show changes in level or surface, and light on the walls to show switches and door handles. The ideal is to have a separate circuit of low-level lights that can be left on at all times, but this is seldom achieved except when starting from scratch. Instead, you could plug in small night lights to prevent total darkness.

Bedrooms

Bedside lamps should be high enough to shine directly onto a book. The bottom of the light should be in line with your shoulder when you are in a semi-reclining position, and the lower edge of the shade at eye level. Swing-arm wall lamps are excellent: not only is the light in the right position, but they save space on bedside tables. They are also useful for beds with side curtains. Bedside lamps should be on a dimmer switch, to obviate glare as well as being kinder to a sleeping partner.

Light above a mirror used for make-up is, contrary to custom, less helpful than light placed at either side. Also, lights that are positioned to shine outwards are better than those that shine on the mirror itself. The same applies to full-length mirrors, where the light should be directed onto the viewer rather than onto the glass.

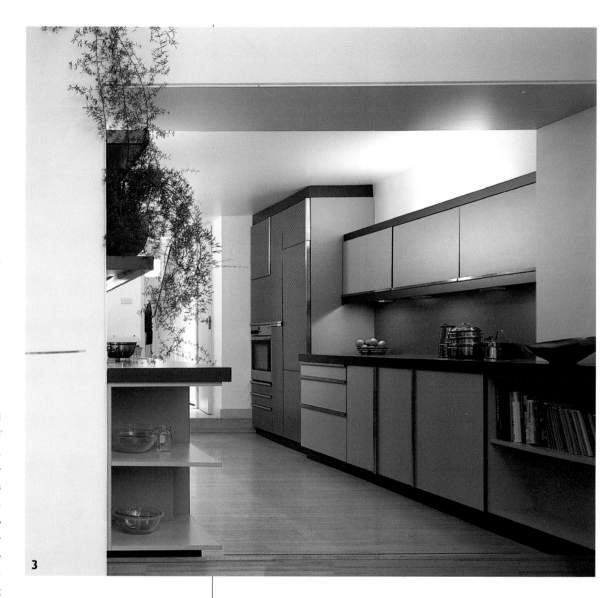

1 Lights placed at either side of a bathroom mirror give better lighting for applying make-up, as here. However, if the mirror is just used for shaving, a light above the mirror, or small lights recessed into the glass, might be preferable.

2 Down-lights illuminate stair treads in addition to lighting up the display niches around this sculptural staircase.

3 Lights set on top of cabinets as well as underneath them illuminate both ceiling and work surface in this well-planned kitchen, its spare lines softened by trailing plants.

Children's rooms

In the rooms of small children, all electric sockets should be childproof and all light fittings well out of reach, which means that table and floor lamps cannot be included. Wall lights are good, as they will give a softer light than ceiling fittings. For children who are afraid of the dark, dimmer switches are useful, as the light can be turned down to a low level; alternatives are the very low-wattage skirting fixtures designed to just cut the darkness. Older children need good light for homework, computer work, hobbies and reading in bed, so adequate lighting should be provided on work tables and above beds.

Bathrooms

Small bathrooms may need only one ceiling light and preferably that should be recessed. In a larger bathroom, a couple of down-lights are preferable, with one of them set over the bath or shower in a waterproof fitting. If a mirror is used for both make-up and shaving, lights should be fixed on each side, but if it is to be used only for shaving, a light should be positioned just above the mirror. An alternative is to recess small custom-made lights right into the glass.

Kitchens

All kitchens should have good overall light, plus booster light for any precise activity like reading cookbooks, chopping, mixing, assembling ingredients and rinsing or washing dishes. Well-placed general diffusing lights fixed flush to the ceiling, inset spots or a mixture of down-lights and angled spots produce a good background light. Supplement this with strip lights concealed under high-level cupboards to shine down on the work surface. Any fluorescent lights should be De Luxe Warm White, Ultralume 2000 or any new variety geared to making food look more appetizing (and complexions more attractive) than earlier fluorescent versions did. Try also to light inside storage cupboards.

part one: the basics

directional spot aimed from below. Up-lighting the painting in any of these ways will prevent reflection in picture glass or the glossy surface of an oil painting.

If you use a conventional picture light mounted on a frame to light the picture from above, it should have a rotating reflector. If the frame is thick, the picture light will need to be adjustable from the wall.

For wall hangings fixed near floor level, floor sculpture or plants, use up-lights or small adjustable floor spots, concealed behind the plants, in corners or next to the objects to be lit. These will bounce light up or graze the object with light. Again, for convenience, try to get such lights either switched from the door or fitted with kick switches.

FLOOR AND TABLE LAMPS

People are often beguiled by the look of a floor or table lamp into purchasing it without thinking much about what the lamp achieves in the way of light output. A lamp should be

LIGHTING ART

For a whole wall of pictures, prints, wall hangings or other art, the ideal is to use recessed wall-washers set into the ceiling about 60cm (2ft) from the wall. They will literally bathe the surface with light. If this is difficult, use a surface-mounted strip such as Plugmold, which can be bought in any length with any number of sockets on which to attach lights, or use track or tensioned 'barewire'. These make it possible either to light individual paintings or to wash a whole wall with light, depending on the desired effect.

The best spotlights for illuminating individual paintings and objects are framing projectors. They are extremely expensive but worth it for serious paintings. When their lenses and shutters are adjusted accurately, they will focus exactly on an object, painting or sculpture, with no overspill of light. Framing projectors should be recessed into the ceiling 90–105cm (36–42in) from the wall. Alternatively, surface-mounted fittings can be either used in conjunction with a track or mounted individually on a ceiling or beam.

Low-voltage halogen fittings give an excellent light. If it is difficult to install recessed lighting or surface-mounted lights and you want to illuminate a painting over a mantelpiece, up-light it from low-voltage halogen spots, which are very small and portable. Alternatively, conceal a halogen light in a vase or small canister on the mantelpiece, or use a

1 *In a series of display shelves, an adjustable spotlight is set right into one of the niches to highlight a photograph. Small down-lights can also be recessed into shelves to shine down on objects, or up-lights can be recessed to do the opposite.*
2 *A judiciously placed lamp shines down on the objects on this table as well as highlighting the handsome marble top.*
3 *An adjustable floor lamp set between a sofa and a pair of chairs can be swung either way for easy reading. It could also, of course, be angled upwards to shine on the painting. This type of floor lamp is nicely versatile.*

as functional as it is good-looking, providing generous light for tasks and reading, as well as adding a comfortable feeling to a room.

Another area in which many people go wrong is the height and position of lamps. A good rule of thumb for table lamps is that the lower edge of the shade should be at eye level when someone is seated on an easy chair: that is, about 97–107cm (38–42in) from the floor.

Floor lamps should be 102–123cm (40–49in) from the lower edge of the shade to the floor. For reading, the lamp should be placed behind the reader's shoulder. This obviously is not possible when a chair or sofa is against a wall, so in this situation use adjustable swing-arm floor lamps. Swing-arm wall lamps are also handy

for reading in small rooms where the seating is close to the walls, and in rooms where a pair of lamps is wanted and end tables are of unequal height.

In a table lamp for reading, use a soft white-pink bulb of at least 150 watts, and in a floor lamp a soft white bulb of 150–200 watts. (Make sure that

they do not exceed the maximum recommended wattages for the shades.) A table-top or flex dimmer can be fitted to vary the level of light.

part one: the basics

Vocabulary of Lighting Terms

Three small vases on the shelf of a recess are lit so well, as is the picture above, that they stand out three-dimensionally to quite dramatic effect.

Accent lighting: Used to highlight colour, form and texture in objects and art, accent lighting is a key element in any sort of creative lighting design. It can range from a narrow beam to a broad SPOTLIGHT or WALL-WASHER.

Ambient lighting: General or background lighting that is unfocussed, indirect and, hopefully, unobtrusive.

Amp: An abbreviation of ampere, the base unit of electrical current, measuring the speed at which it flows.

Baffle: The device attached to a light fitting to lessen or prevent glare. Baffles on DOWN-LIGHTS and SPOTLIGHTS are usually formed with concentric black grooves on the inside of the cowl.

Ballast: A part used in the control apparatus of a discharge lamp or bulb to prevent overheating.

Barewire: A pair of tensioned CABLES that support LOW-VOLTAGE, tiny TRACK LIGHTS which can be moved along the length of the cables.

Barn doors: The adjustable hinged flaps attached to the front of some SPOTLIGHTS to control the shape of the BEAM.

Batten fitting: A fitting designed to hold a FLUORESCENT BULB and its control gear. It has an enclosed channel.

Batten holder: A ceiling rose with a built-in holder for a TUNGSTEN BULB.

Bayonet bulb: A TUNGSTEN BULB with two lugs to attach it to its holder (as opposed to a screw bulb).

Beam: The spread of light from a FLOODLIGHT, SPOTLIGHT or REFLECTOR BULB.

Blended lamp or bulb: A light source consisting of an incandescent filament and mercury discharge tube in one bulb. It has

a longer life than an ordinary INCANDESCENT BULB – often as long as 6,000 hours.

Cable: A covered or sheathed bundle of insulated wires used to carry electrical circuits around the home.

Candela: The SI unit of light intensity.

Ceiling rose: Normally, a circular housing that projects from the ceiling and holds the connection between a PENDANT light fitting or a chandelier and the electricity supply.

Circuit: The path of an electric current which passes along the supply CABLES to light fittings and electric sockets.

Circuit breaker: A special switch in an electrical consumer unit that carries out the same function as a fuse. In other words, under abnormal or potentially dangerous situations, it will cut off the current flow of the CIRCUIT.

Colour rendering: The effect of a light source on the appearance of a coloured surface, normally judged by comparison with its appearance by daylight. Some bulbs are given a Colour Rendering Index rating (CRI) between 1 and 100. The higher the number, the truer the colours.

Contrast: In lighting terms, this is the difference in brightness between two points of a visual field – that is to say, the

area that can be seen in front of us when our heads and eyes are still.

Control gear: The way in which the current passing through a FLUORESCENT BULB or a DISCHARGE BULB is controlled.

Cool beam bulb: A type of PAR BULB that reflects visible light but transmits infrared radiation so that the heat of the BEAM it transmits is greatly reduced.

Diffused light: Light that is filtered through a translucent material like a fabric shade.

Diffuser: Some sort of translucent screen used to shield a light source, soften it and distribute light evenly.

Dimmer switch: A control switch that allows the lighting levels of bulbs to be lowered or raised. Most lights benefit from this sort of control.

Direct lighting: Lighting provided directly from a light fitting without bouncing off surfaces like ceilings or walls.

Directional lighting: Lighting designed to illuminate a surface or a task from a particular direction. This is generally provided by SPOTLIGHTS or desk lights, which are normally adjustable.

Discharge bulb: A bulb whose light is produced by an electric discharge through a gas, a metal vapour or a mixture of gas and vapour.

Down-light: A fitting that is usually ceiling-recessed, ceiling-mounted, track-mounted or wall-mounted and that throws light vertically (or at least steeply) downwards. It may be either TUNGSTEN or HALOGEN.

Earth: A necessary connection between an electrical CIRCUIT and the earth. Its purpose is to conduct electricity out of harm's way if there is a fault in the wiring, such as a break in a circuit cable or insulation, which would otherwise make a light fitting or an appliance casing become lethally live.

Eyeball spot or down-light: An adjustable recessed SPOTLIGHT that looks rather like an eyeball.

Filament: A thin wire in a TUNGSTEN BULB that emits light when it is heated to incandescence by an electric current.

Fitting: See LUMINAIRE.

Flex: The cord of insulated wires that connects a light fitting or appliance to the electrical supply.

Floodlight: A spotlight containing a tungsten REFLECTOR BULB to produce a powerful, wide BEAM.

Fluorescent bulb: A kind of DISCHARGE BULB where the light is produced by the excitation of fluorescent phosphors by ultraviolet radiation. More energy-efficient than a TUNGSTEN BULB or a HALOGEN BULB, it is much cheaper to run and lasts longer. It now gives a wide variation of colour rendition, although in the past it had too harsh a white light for most domestic situations.

Framing projector: Also known as a profile spot or pinhole projector, this is a spotlight designed to illuminate a painting, sculpture or other work of art. Its attachments allow absolutely precise control over the shape and focus of the BEAM. Though expensive, it is the best and most accurate way to light art.

Glare: The discomfort and interference with vision that arise when some parts of the visual field are much brighter than their surroundings.

GLS bulb: General Lighting Service bulb – the term used in the trade for the ordinary TUNGSTEN BULB.

Halogen bulb: A special type of TUNGSTEN BULB containing halogen, which extends the bulb's life. Also known as a quartz halogen or tungsten halogen bulb, it gives a brighter punch of light than an ordinary tungsten bulb of the equivalent-wattage.

HID bulb: A High Intensity DISCHARGE BULB, used for outside lighting.

Incandescent bulb: A light source produced by an electric current heating a FILAMENT to the point where it gives off light. This is the original light bulb that was designed by Thomas Edison. TUNGSTEN BULBS and HALOGEN BULBS are both incandescent.

Indirect lighting: Lighting reflected off a ceiling or walls.

ISL bulb: An Internally Silvered Lamp, usually known as a REFLECTOR BULB.

Lamp: The trade term for a light bulb.

Low voltage: A low-voltage bulb is an excellent choice for lighting art and accenting objects, but it must be used in conjunction with a transformer. Available as either TUNGSTEN or HALOGEN BULBS.

Lumen: The SI unit of luminous lux, which means the amount of light given off by a source or received by a surface.

Luminaire: The trade term for a light fitting – the housing designed for a bulb and bulb holder to protect the light source, to provide a means of connection to the electrical supply and to direct and control the flow of light.

Lux: Lumens measured by the square metre or yard. The SI unit of illuminance, which is a measure of the light leaving a surface in a particular direction.

MCB: Miniature CIRCUIT BREAKER.

Neon bulb: A bulb containing neon, or inert gas, at low pressure which throws off a red or pink glow when VOLTAGE is applied.

Opal finish: An internal coating of silica on the glass exterior of a bulb which gives it a milky or opalescent appearance.

Overspill: See SPILL LIGHT.

PAR bulb: A Parabolic Aluminized Reflector is a sealed beamed bulb with a front of tough, heat-resistant glass. The back of the bulb is parabolic in cross-section, and the bulb is internally aluminized to throw off a powerful BEAM of light. Especially useful outdoors as it needs no protection from the weather.

Pendant: A light fitting designed to hang from, or project from, a ceiling.

Phosphor: A substance that can emit visible light when bombarded with electromagnetic radiation. It is used for the inner coating of FLUORESCENT BULBS.

Polar curve: A special diagram used to show the exact profile of light output from a bulb or light fitting.

Quartz halogen bulb: Alternative name for a halogen bulb.

Reflector bulb: A bulb with an internally silvered surface, used for SPOTLIGHTS or FLOODLIGHTS.

SI: Système Internationale d'Unités, an internationally agreed system of scientific measuring units.

Side-lighting: The technique of lighting from one side, usually to emphasize the modelling or texture of an object.

SON bulb: A high-pressure sodium bulb.

Spill light: Light that spills over from the main profile of a BEAM, as in the light that seeps outside a painting lit by a SPOTLIGHT or WALL-WASHER. A FRAMING PROJECTOR can be set to light a painting exactly, so there is no overspill.

Spotlight: A REFLECTOR BULB with a directional beam, used for accent or decorative lighting. It may be surface- or track-mounted on wall, ceiling or floor.

Spur: A CABLE used to extend a CIRCUIT so that electricity can be supplied to an additional fitting or appliance or used for an additional switch.

Task lighting: Lighting specifically used for facilitating a task like reading, writing, painting or sewing.

Tensioned barewire: See BAREWIRE.

Throw: The distance between a REFLECTOR BULB and the farthest object it can light.

Track lighting: Straight or curved track that can be mounted on the ceiling or walls, and supports SPOTLIGHTS which are either fixed in position (but can be angled and swivelled) or free, allowing them to be moved along the track. Both fixed and free types can be mains- or LOW-VOLTAGE.

Transformer: A device to transfer electric current from one CIRCUIT to another, usually with an increase or decrease in VOLTAGE. It is essential to the installation of any LOW-VOLTAGE bulb but is usually small enough to be hidden in the fitting.

Tungsten bulb: The ordinary, domestic electric light bulb known in the trade as a GLS. Its full name is a tungsten filament bulb, because it contains a filament of tungsten which is a metallic element with a high melting point. It casts a warmer light than most fluorescent bulbs.

Tungsten halogen bulb: See HALOGEN BULB.

Up-light: A light fitting that throws light up to be reflected back from the ceiling or walls. Floor up-lights are extremely useful both for back-lighting objects and

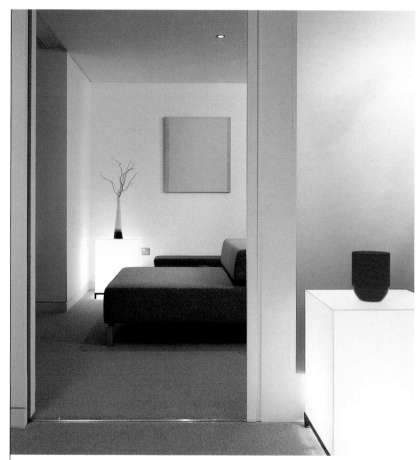

plants and for providing indirect light when you cannot install recessed lighting. Up-lighting can also be provided by floor and wall light fittings and by directional table lamps.

Visual acuity: The ability to distinguish fine detail when concentrating on a task.

Voltage: The pressure of electricity flowing through an electrical CIRCUIT – the greater the pressure, the higher the number of volts. Mains voltage varies from country to country; in Britain it is 240 volts, in Europe 220 and in the United States 120. For LOW-VOLTAGE lighting, a TRANSFORMER reduces the power, usually to 12 volts.

Wall-washer: A DOWN-LIGHT that bathes the wall in light, usually mounted on the ceiling (on track, on the surface, or

Lit from within, boxes made from Lucite (a thick, clear plastic similar to perspex) provide dramatic display areas as well as punctuating the space with arresting cubes of light. A directional low-voltage down-light highlights the painting on the far wall.

recessed), 45–90 cm (18–36in) from the wall, depending on the desired effect.

Watt: A unit measuring the rate at which electricity is consumed and indicating the power of the light source. Every light fitting you buy will specify a maximum wattage.

part one: the basics

Maximizing Storage

There are three unassailable facts about storage: you can never have enough of it; more space should be allowed for the purpose than you could possibly imagine; and any sort of storage should be as much in keeping with the basic feeling, style and proportions of a room as is viable.

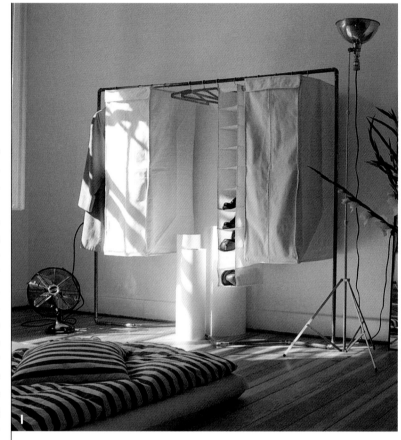

PLANNING AHEAD

Most people find that their possessions, however limited they are to begin with, inevitably expand with the years. It is therefore important that you plan for this expansion. Even if you do not wish to pay for extra storage now, you should at least think where you would like to put it later on, and have an idea of how much it would cost. If you intend to move at some time in the future, you need to decide whether you will want to take with you any storage that you buy now, and then choose accordingly.

For anyone who intends to start a family, planning ahead means thinking where you would keep a pram, push-chair, portable cot, toys – especially large-wheeled and oversized ones – and all the other impedimenta you will need. Determine how best to use the space you have, and how much extra storage you can squeeze in – your foresight and organization will save you a great deal of irritation and time later on. If you already have a young family, cast your mind forward to imagine all the bicycles, skis and other sports equipment, CDs, videos, books, files, clothing, luggage, linens and duvets the children will accumulate, and also the extra bathroom and kitchen storage needs.

If your children have grown up and you thought you had left all the detritus of a young family behind you, don't forget grandchildren (or incipient grandchildren). You may need to accommodate some apparatus for when they visit you, especially if you have moved to a smaller home. For example, you might want a separate large table top to protect your dining table, covered by a tablecloth, or you might need extra chairs for when you have to entertain all the family.

1 This temporary storage provided by canvas clothes bags suspended from a rack has a certain raffish charm of its own and fits in well with the striped futon on the floor.
2 Sliding doors resembling shoji screens conceal a variety of belongings in a neat and airy way. This is an excellent idea for dedicated minimalists determined to hide their possessions as aesthetically as possible.

ASSESSING YOUR NEEDS

The best plan is to analyse your storage needs room by room, to see not only how best to fulfil them but also how to fit in the storage as aesthetically as possible. Clear your mind by asking yourself these questions:

1 If you live in a small apartment that you are likely to move out of, do you have anything against using the same ready-made storage systems in each room? They would be easy to take with you and reassemble in a different configuration in your future home.

2 Do you like traditional storage behind closed doors in cupboards and in chests of drawers, bureaux and bookcases? If you possess this sort of storage already, can the interiors be improved or at least be better organized? If you do not have it, can it be built in fairly easily and affordably? Do you have any recesses, corners or old fireplaces that could be annexed for storage?

3 Have you considered a storage wall or entertainment units, or both, in your living room, to hold books, files, papers, computer, television, video recorder, music system, tapes, CDs and so on? How many of these storage units will have to be bought, and how many can be improvised? (For suggestions for improvised storage, see pages 39–41.)

30

APPROPRIATE STORAGE

It is important that new storage doesn't look out of place. Before you choose it, take a hard look at the room, noticing proportions and architectural details particularly.

Bedrooms

In an old building, bedrooms with high ceilings and good-looking mouldings might be best served with old free-standing armoires or wardrobes. Big pieces, often beautifully fitted inside, or capable of being specially fitted, can often be bought gratifyingly cheaply nowadays, since so few people have the space for them. Be sure to check the depth, however: many old pieces are too shallow for clothing to be hung in the conventional way. Ideally, they should be 60cm (24in) deep.

If you decide that you want built-in storage in a room that has fine proportions and mouldings, you must first determine where it can be sited without spoiling the harmony of the space. Ensure that any built-in storage that takes up a whole wall will not make the room seem too narrow for its height. If the bedroom has a fireplace with natural recesses on either side, the storage could perhaps be fitted in the recesses. One way of building in a lot of cupboards without losing a sense of perspective or depth is to fit them around doors or windows (see page 35 for more about this).

You will almost certainly need to spend money on an excellent carpenter, who should continue the same mouldings and skirting boards around the newly built pieces. It is of prime

2

importance to avoid an unsightly gap between the top of built-in wardrobes and the ceiling in such a room, unless your carpenter builds a pediment or you can place objects on top.

Rather than investing in custom-built storage, you could buy ready-made unfinished-wood units. Have them fitted by a carpenter, who could then add mouldings if necessary, to help them blend in. If you want to disguise them altogether, get flush doors with magnetic catches and either paint them or wrap any wallpaper or fabric around the doors.

1 Maximum storage advantage has been taken of the capacious bed platform in this splendidly spacious bedroom. Sliding-door cupboards above are balanced by deep drawers below. They are offset by bookshelves as well as recessed shelves in the room to display a diverse collection of objects.

2 This old chest of many drawers stores an enormous amount of odds and ends as well as hosting a generous sink.

part one: the basics

1 *Interesting doors in this bedroom conceal cupboard space as well as the bathroom beyond. The top of the cupboards provides a good spot for a collection of wicker baskets used for storing smaller objects.*

making sure they will still close. To prevent the paper tearing or the fabric fraying, you could install 'reeding' (a thin piece of moulding) around the edges of the doors. If the doors are panelled, they could be linked to the rest of the room with paint, paper, fabric or trim. To make the cupboards seem more like pieces of furniture, you could ask a paint specialist to 'grain' them in a wood finish. It is amazing

how handsome and realistic graining can look if done by skilled hands.

A good way of fitting maximum storage into a bedroom without robbing it of a sense of space is to build wardrobes on either side of a bed and a row of cupboards running over the top of the bed to join the two. If there is no space for bedside tables with this arrangement, build in shelves at the sides of the wardrobes and

install lighting underneath the top cupboards. This creates a sleeping recess and will provide a practical function as well as giving a sense of perspective and depth.

If you have a large bedroom, you could perhaps cut a chunk out of it to create a walk-in wardrobe. Or you may be able to do this by slivering off extra space from a less valuable room or corridor adjacent to the bedroom. Another way to provide storage space is to build a half-height partition at one end of a bedroom then add a cupboard on one side for storage and use the other as a bedhead. With any of these ideas, the skirting board, cornice and other detailing should match the rest of the room, so you may have to have them custom-made.

In a room where you do not need to pay attention to architectural detail, you could create storage space by building a bed on top of a platform of low cupboards. When a bedroom is small or awkwardly shaped, however, the best option might be to fit cupboards just outside the door in a corridor or on a landing, in order to leave more space in the room itself. Another way to avoid cluttering up a room is to incorporate a dressing table or a desk, or a piece that can double as both, into a wall of storage.

Living rooms and libraries

Much the same rules apply to living rooms and libraries as to bedrooms, especially where the rooms are handsomely detailed – if you want built-in storage, it is important that it does not ruin the room's proportions and that the detailing matches. For recesses on either side of a fireplace,

2 *Glass-fronted drawers look elegantly airy but require disciplined tidiness. The empty frame set among the pictures on top of the chest echoes the serried panes of glass below.*

3 *Rows of numbered pockets set into this practical curtain provide a place for special toys and objects in a child's room as well as looking both educational and decorative. Such inexpensive storage solutions are enormously useful for children's rooms, but similar holdalls are also handy for the backs of wardrobe doors and in the kitchen, utility room and bathroom.*

you might find very tall old bookcases that will fit in well. These recesses are also natural places to build breakfront bookcases, as are the walls on either side of windows. Each bookcase can have a deeper shelf at waist height with cupboards underneath. If the shelf is deep enough and tall enough, it can take a television on a turntable, a video recorder and a music system. The top of the bookcase can have a pediment or be finished off with the same moulding or cornice as the rest of the room.

Alternatively, a large bookcase could be purchased for a long wall, or you could build in shelves running the length of the wall, again incorporating

a deeper shelf with cupboards underneath for storage. Depending upon the size of the wall and the style of the room, the shelves could either have the cornice running in front, as in the rest of the room, or have a pediment, maybe with a light behind to cast a mellow glow at night.

If you want to create the look of wall-to-wall bookshelves, positioning the uprights for the bookshelves either side of the windows and doors will make these openings look recessed and the shelving seem an integral part of the walls.

In a narrow room, glass shelves with up-lights or down-lights, or both, will add sparkle and take up little visual space. You can also set glass or wooden shelves across windows, to create further shelving for display and save the cost of a window treatment.

You may wish to consider a storage wall, or entertainment units built around the television screen. Remember that if you want to incorporate in the wall unit various appliances like a television, computer, video recorder, music system or perhaps even a small refrigerator and miniature sink unit for making drinks, you will need to ensure that they fit flush with the rest of the units. The more expensive versions will incorporate most of these items anyway, or will at least specify what appliances, televisions or other equipment will fit. Don't forget that the wall will have to be wired to provide power for these devices before the installation takes place.

In a living room that is really short on space, look to the windows: you may be able to provide extra seating and storage, as well as improving the look of the windows. Place uprights that are 45–60cm (18–24in) deep on either side of a window. If there are two or three windows on one wall, so much the better. Suspend a hinged seat between each pair of uprights, and

build a cupboard underneath. Put tailored seat cushions on top of this lift-up window seat, and add scatter cushions. On the other side of each upright, build tall, shallow cupboards.

Children's rooms

Children's storage needs, for both clothing and equipment, seem to grow as fast as the children do, so it is a mistake to start off with child-sized storage. You can always use low hanging rods for clothes initially and raise them by degrees as the child grows.

Deep drawers under beds or bunks are useful, and there may also be room for a chest of drawers in the

part one: the basics

bedroom. My stock solution for cheap storage for the bedroom of any child from nought to late teens – and for a master bedroom or a home office, come to that – is to buy two or three unfinished-wood chests of drawers, or a mixture of chests of drawers and low cupboards. Set them a kneehole apart, and top them with a long laminated top, to serve first as a play area and later as a desk. The units can be stained or painted.

Fragile toys and games are best kept on deep shelves behind closed doors or in deep drawers, so that toddlers cannot easily pull them out and dump them on the floor. Sturdier toys can be stored in big boxes or chests for easy access. Inexpensive or robust books can be kept on window sills and on low shelves within reach, but more precious books should be set on higher shelves which small hands cannot reach.

Kitchens

Keen cooks will want everything they frequently use to be within grabbing distance. Wooden spoons, spatulas,

I *Storage doubles as decoration here with the curved shelves holding a miscellany of storage jars and scales, balanced by the herb box fixed below. Note how serving spoons, spatulas and even a good old-fashioned mincer are clamped or otherwise attached to shelves and wooden brackets. The three striped egg cups and Thermos on the surface below make a nice counterpoint to the various strong stripes set above.*

2

3

4

2 *Simple dowels hold a series of glass goblets from their bases, at the same time forming an airily decorative frieze againt the wall.*
3 *A practical wooden rack for storing crockery is fitted above the butler's sink in a tiled recess of this well-planned kitchen.*
4 *A series of rods set above a long window behind the sink supports a batterie de cuisine as well as decorative bunches of drying herbs.*

slotted spoons and similar tools can be kept in earthenware pots or jugs. Saucepans can hang from an overhead rack or rod or be stacked on shelves within easy reach of the stove, their lids slipped into wooden or steel racks. Measuring jugs and spoons, sieves and colanders can hang from racks, from hooks on pegboard or from hooks fixed to the underside of wall units. Chopping boards must be near to hand, as should sharp knives, which can be stored in a wooden knife rack.

Less dedicated cooks, however, will probably want all kitchen impedimenta behind closed doors. There is an enormous choice of storage to suit all spaces and all budgets. Once again, unfinished-wood cupboards are a viable option, as they are inexpensive and can be stained, painted or lacquered to match any decor.

Storage for a kitchen/dining room depends on whether the style of the room veers towards the rustic or the fairly sophisticated. For the rustic

look there are still all sorts of handsome old dressers to be found, rescued and rehabilitated. These will usually hold and display a great deal. For a more sophisticated look, the whole area could be fitted with wall-to-wall, floor-to-ceiling cupboards.

Dining rooms
If you have a dedicated dining room, you will need practical, but attractive storage for glasses, china, linen, cutlery and possibly wine bottles, as well as

after-dinner drinks, and probably some sort of display unit or units. The traditional sideboard, or its equivalent, can easily provide much of this, as can shelving units with cupboards and drawers underneath, depending upon the style of the room.

If, however, the dining room doubles as a library, study or home office, playroom or guest room, then imaginative dual storage is clearly the answer. Screens, I find, are a good solution for such rooms. Not only do they look

part one: the basics

- Make a desk by securing an unpanelled door to two, or even three or four, filing cabinets, leaving one or two kneeholes.
- If you do not want actual filing cabinets, use the fittings to line window seats, or old trunks or chests, to hold suspension files.
- Neat wooden file frames on wheels can be pushed under tables or desks or into wardrobes; and rattan boxes or plastic, lattice-sided crates, which also hold suspension files, can be stacked in wardrobes, under tables or even under beds.

For a home office in a bedroom, a fall-front desk is useful, since you can use the drawers partly for clothes, partly for papers, and then hide away any paperwork when you close up the desk portion. There are also all kinds of cunning desktops and work surfaces that pull or slide out from wall units, as well as doors that fold down to reveal complete computer systems; when they are closed, the walls seem merely panelled. In this way, you can go from the functional to the serene in mere minutes.

decorative, but if they are sturdy enough they can have pegs or hooks at the back for clothes, should the room be used for occasional guests. Exercise equipment, luggage, baskets of toys and all manner of other items can also be hidden behind them.

Studies and home offices

Since many home offices are part of another room rather than entities in themselves, much of the storage has to be disguised. The chief problem has to be filing cabinets. They can at least be painted to fit in with the general

Desk, file drawers, computer and a hamper for files or papers are all tucked nicely below the stairs, turning an unused corner of a living room into a pleasant home-office area. The space under stairs is invariably useful, either for general storage, perhaps with doors, or for the odd desk or table.

surroundings (I have even had them painted to look like copper) and can be made to look decorative, with designs and patterns. There are also a number of ways to hide them:
- Conceal the filing cabinet under a skirt (see page 40).
- If you are building bookshelves with cupboards underneath, make sure the cupboards are tall enough and deep enough to take filing cabinets on small wheels or tracks.
- With the help of a good handyman or carpenter, adapt ready-made units to incorporate filing cabinets.

Bathrooms

Vanity units provide useful storage space underneath the basin and sometimes come with drawers down the side as well. Or you can have them made to your own specification.

Bathroom cabinets of various sizes and degrees of grandeur are widely available, or you could fix shelves across any useful recess and then add a door with a mirror on it.

Glass shelves across a window will provide decorative storage as well as a degree of privacy.

IMPROVISING STORAGE

With a little thought, it's possible to improvise storage solutions that are as effective and good-looking as more expensive systems.

Baskets

Baskets in various shapes and sizes are useful for any number of small, and not so small, items. In one client's living room where space was at a premium, I fitted glass shelves lit by up-lights — the shelves were used for storing books, and large-handled baskets underneath them held mixer drinks and other bottles.

- Shallow, square, round or rectangular baskets are excellent for magazines and catalogues.
- Shallow, rectangular ones are good on large desks or work tables, or under side tables for work papers and files; on a hall table for hats, gloves, sunglasses or letters; and on a kitchen worktop for a surfeit of spice and herb jars.
- Laundry baskets can be used to store anything from blankets, linens or winter clothes to children's toys or cleaning materials.
- Deep, round baskets can be hung from pegs or hooks in a country-style bathroom to hold neatly rolled towels.

2 *Elegant shoe storage in this dressing-room-cum-bathroom with its stylish glass basin is nicely offset by a series of baskets filled with oddments like hair dryers, brushes, small electrical appliances and other grooming impedimenta.*

part one: the basics

Hooks and racks

Many people forget that the backs of doors can be used for storage. I always fix one or two double hooks to the backs of bedroom and bathroom doors on which to hang dressing gowns, nightclothes and items just back from the dry-cleaner, as well as wardrobe cases when packing or unpacking.

- In a small room or a holiday home, rows of large hooks on wooden or plastic backs, fixed high on a wall, can be amazingly handy for clothes storage when there is simply no room for wardrobes.
- Movable cloakroom coat racks are also useful for clothes storage, especially in holiday homes and in halls and corridors.
- Small cup-hooks can be fixed to the edges of shelves and to the underneath of wall-mounted cupboards to hold cups and small jugs, thereby freeing up space in cupboards for something else.
- Hooks on a pegboard are good for hanging up not just kitchen utensils (see page 37) but also home-office paraphernalia.
- Very large hooks can be used for suspending folding chairs.

Skirted tables

There is almost always space in a room for one or two skirted tables, which can hide any number of things. They do not, of course, have to be round. Rectangular tables covered in fabric, rugs or throws look good as side tables, too, and hold more underneath.

- Use them in bedrooms to conceal electric fans, baskets of clutter and even small pieces of exercise equipment such as weights.
- Fit a divided skirt to a table with a platform underneath, to hide the television. In order to see the screen, part the two sides of the skirt and hook them up.
- Conceal firewood under a skirted table in the living room.
- Hide a filing cabinet under one. If you want the table to be round, place a circular piece of MDF (medium-density fibreboard) on top, under the skirt.
- Stash luggage or other bulky objects underneath a large skirted table.

Shelves

Obviously shelves of different sizes are prime storage areas for almost anything, but there are a lot of places to put shelves that people do not think about.

- The space above doors is one good area. Depending on which room the door is in, use the shelf for display, books or storage baskets.
- Run a shelf 15–30cm (6–12in) below the ceiling, all around the perimeter of a room. This was often done in the late nineteenth and early twentieth centuries to show off plates, trophies and collections.
- Mount shelves or racks on the backs of wardrobe or pantry doors to hold all manner of things. It is advisable for the shelves to have lips in order to prevent things from sliding off when the door is in motion; or mount wire basket shelves. Do the same on the backs of cleaning-cupboard doors to hold polishes, dusters and general cleaning paraphernalia.
- Use wire shelves on the backs of wardrobe doors to hold handbags, scarves and other small, light items.

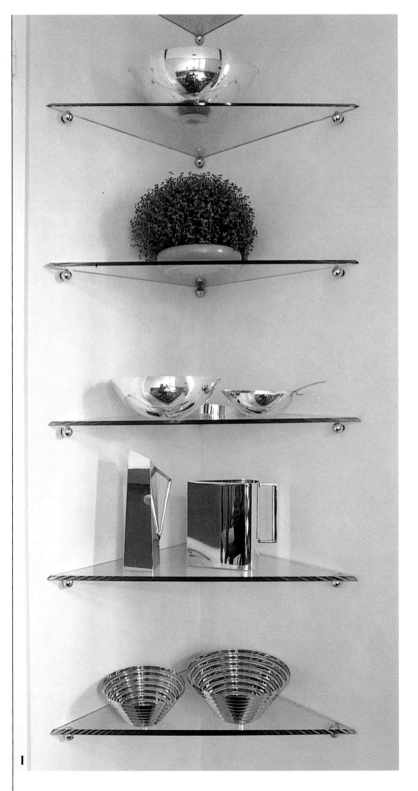

- Mount miniature shelves on the backs of kitchen-cupboard doors to hold jars of spices, herbs and condiments and also small packets.
- Make your own corner cupboard by fixing shelves across a corner, with or without a cupboard section underneath.

Under the bed

Do not underestimate what you can fit under a bed. In fact, if you are prepared to raise it a little higher than normal, you can store luggage, skis and other sports equipment, baskets, file boxes, blanket boxes or out-of-season clothes. Many beds can be bought with fitted drawers underneath, but if you do not have them already, you can get them made – say, one or two for each side of a large bed, so that you do not have to be perpetually crawling around to drag things out from the middle. Alternatively, simply buy a couple of large, shallow plastic boxes that are designed to slide underneath.

Under the stairs

Under-stair storage has always been practical and, if well organized, can be used for any number of purposes.

- Put a desktop mounted on filing cabinets there, with a chair on wheels to push under the desktop, and then build shelves all around the walls.
- If the temperature is fairly constant, use this space for wine storage. It is possible to buy wine racks specially designed to fit under the stairs, but any type could be adapted.
- Buy, build or adapt a honeycomb of storage boxes to fit the space.

- Build bookshelves into the space, with or without some cupboards underneath.
- Turn it into a cupboard with shelf and hanging space, or just shelves, with doors to shut it all away.

If you are fortunate enough to have a wide flight of steps going up to an attic, or down to a basement, you can use one side of the steps to stash baskets or plastic crates, clearly labelled with their contents so that you do not have to keep searching through every container to find what you want. These are excellent places to keep office supplies, extra stationery, spare paper goods (paper towels, toilet paper, tissues, paper napkins, paper plates for parties), tool boxes and any supplies you have bought in bulk.

Using fabric

Since curtains and blinds take up less space than doors, and certainly look less solid, they can be suspended across alcoves to create good clothes storage. Use them to conceal a movable clothes rack, a hanging rod or shelves full of shoes.

Attractive tent wardrobes, which look rather like old-fashioned bathing tents, can be placed in corners or alcoves and are as practical as they are decorative.

I once saw a guest bed that was built on a platform under a window on a landing. Privacy was created by inner curtains across the window and outer curtains on the other side of the bed, both of which could be either looped back or left loose. It had drawers underneath and the walls at either end of the bed were mounted with shelves.

1 *Good-looking triangular plate-glass shelves are fitted neatly into a corner to provide a generous display area with barely any loss of space in the room. Such shelves could be lit from recessed down-lights above, and some sort of up-light below, to provide maximum dramatic effect and sparkle – always a plus in any space.*

2 *Curtains hanging from a pelmet turn an alcove fitted with a bank of shelves into an attractive storage area. The curtains match those at the window in this small bedroom. An equally effective storage area could be created by suspending a curtain rod across a corner.*

part one: the basics

Using Colour

Colour is to rooms what light is to day – and is both the most noticeable and the most malleable element in decorating. Different combinations of colour can make the same room and the same furnishings seem warm or cool, restful or stimulating, harmonious or jarring, welcoming or impersonal. It can even affect the apparent proportions of a room. In short, the choice of colours is a fundamental part of decoration. For that very reason, it is the source of a great deal of worry to most people, not least because the range of possible combinations is so vast, and the results when it goes wrong seem so conspicuous.

INSPIRATION

Some rare individuals can carry a colour around in their heads and match it exactly. They look at a room and know instantly what will suit it, and how it will look in this colour combination or that. Most people, however, have to work at developing a colour sense. The easiest and most effective way is to get into the habit of looking hard at any combination of colours that appeals, and to analyse the build-up of colour within it.

Most painters develop the habit of patiently observing colour, noting all the nuances in their subject. It is an interesting experiment to take a single item – such as a rug, a painting or a piece of china or fabric – and to write down the various hues and tones in it. First note those that predominate and then the various ancillaries that, together, form the whole.

Once you have got used to looking at and analysing colour, you can draw inspiration from almost everything that visually pleases you, particularly, of course, from nature. Think of the colours of the countryside, forest, sea

or sky, or the build-up of tones in a Mediterranean village or a cottage garden. Most rural scenes contain innumerable shades of green, all harmoniously blended and with accents provided by bright flashes of colour from flowers, blossom, berries or crops.

Similarly, an old-fashioned rose garden can show how to successfully blend pinks, yellows and peaches with greens or terracottas. They create a scheme of equal tones against a background of the green tones of trees

or the rose-terracotta tones of an old brick wall – or the greys of a crumbling old stone wall, come to that.

Another way to build up ideas for a scheme is through emotional response. People often have extraordinarily violent reactions to different colours for no logical reason. 'I loathe green', they say – or, 'I just can't tolerate anything pink'. To make this intense response work in a positive way, take a favourite colour and think of it in depth. Think, say, of yellow, remembering everything

1 The chunks of primary colours like the red wall in the foreground of this room and the bright chrome yellow by the window show up with almost psychedelic intensity against the deliberate pallor of the rest of this room.

2 The pitting of vibrant strokes of colour against otherwise pale tones is also demonstrated in the room opposite. In this case, the yellows of the abstract painting seem to give a warm glow to the otherwise quite neutral colour scheme.

floral and yellow, from the palest creamy yellow of honeysuckle or freesias to the vivid velvet of rose petals, through narcissi to daffodils, to crocuses, to marigolds, nasturtiums and the centres of daisies. Or picture straw and dried hay, sand, heavy cream, the gold of stripped and waxed wood floors, lemons, honeydew melons and thick honey.

If you consider blue in the same way, you might think of forget-me-nots and periwinkles, the fresh sweet blue of hyacinths and bluebells, the intensity of delphiniums, irises and lobelia, and the gentle faded quality of dried hydrangeas and lavender. Then there are all those blues of the sky: the pale, blue-grey dawn, the azure of a clear summer's day, the grape blue of impending storms, the luminous blue of dusk, and the deep damson blue of a warm night. Think, too, of sun-dazzled water and of precious and semi-precious stones like aquamarines, sapphires, turquoise and lapis lazuli.

Imagine other colours in the same kind of depth, and it should be easy to translate all these subtleties and variations of tone into interesting monochromatic schemes. Remember that the ingredients which make up a room – wood and wool; cotton, velvet and tweed; paint and paper – will all give varying depths of colour.

If you are still unsure of the colours that you find comfortable to live with (and many people have a hard time with this), you should resort to the old trick that I recommend for colour as much as for style. Buy as many decoration books and magazines as you can. Mark pictures in the books and cut out pages in the magazines illustrating rooms that appeal to you. Put them aside for a few days, then look at them all at once. You will almost certainly notice that the same colour combinations reappear over and over. This will indicate, as nothing else does, the colours that are the most comfortable for you.

MATCHING COLOURS TO STYLES

It may be, of course, that you have set your heart on a particular style of decoration, or your home seems to demand a specific style, but you are concerned that the colours you like best are not appropriate. Again, don't worry. Specific colours are certainly connected with particular periods (for example, dark plums, reds and greens with late Victorian style; bright green with the Empire period; orange, green and cream with the 1930s). Indeed, colours are sometimes named after a period or style, such as Imperial purple, Pompeian red and Adam green. But there is no need to feel rigorously bound by them – after all, many reputable fabric companies frequently change the colourways of their archive designs.

The textile ranges of both Liberty and Sanderson, for example, include recoloured William Morris designs, which look good today without in any way sacrificing the William Morris late-1800s style. And many extra-ordinarily pretty chintzes have been revamped from old designs by Colefax & Fowler, Bennison, Pierre Frey and Braquenié, Cowan & Tout, Scalamandré, Boussac, Sanderson, Beaumont & Fletcher and others. It is all a question of balance and propor-tion, and as far as your home is concerned, success will depend on the way you personally manipulate the style to suit your own taste.

BALANCED COLOUR SCHEMES

Thinking up colour combinations for a particular style of room is one thing, but achieving the right balance is quite another, and preparing schemes for a whole house or apartment is the most intricate exercise of all. There are, however, various ways to achieve an interesting balance.

One approach is to keep most of the room in shades and variations of one colour, by using that colour – say, a warm but pale cream – for walls, window blinds and carpet or rugs. Mix it with another colour – such as rose – for upholstery and curtains.

Then add accent colours – perhaps white (for chair frames), green (in plants and a stencilled design on the walls) and burnt umber (in a dried flower bouquet).

Another approach is to keep walls, curtains, floor and furniture in one colour – perhaps white – and to ring the changes by varying the tones and textures. Alternatively, to the same basically white room, green and white cushions and masses of plants could be added to great effect.

A third approach is to use, say, a soft blue for walls, a slightly darker shade for a dado, crisp white paint for the woodwork, and touches of pale lilac. A variation here would be to add to these colours a chair, or even a carpet, in olive green.

It is important to vary surfaces and textures in the colours you choose, in order to make a play of light and shade and pattern. Picture, for example, a room papered in a blue and white wallpaper above a dado of dragged dark blue paint over a lighter blue. Woodwork could be white, or a blue from the paper, in a semi-gloss finish. A dark blue and white throw could be placed over a sofa covered in off-white canvas or heavy cotton. Arm-chairs could be a mid-blue velvet or corduroy, or even damask.

*1 Tonal variations are pale but interesting in a corner of this yellow room. Lemon-painted walls are offset by the row of clear yellow flowers on the shelves, as well as the framed yellow-green ferns. The touches of silver, the pottery, even the pale wood of the chair, all aid the subtlety of the colour build-up.
2 The room shown opposite illustrates a build-up of a much warmer yellow. The colour of the walls is repeated in the rug and nicely grounded by the wide planks of the polished floor. The lampshade is yet another yellow.*

1 Blocks of red-oranges, yellows and umber are teamed with – or, more precisely, calmed by – white and various natural wood tones in the cupboards, bed and floor of this spacious bedroom. The overall feeling is one of interesting vivacity, rather than the hectic discord one might otherwise associate with such a deliberately unrestful scheme.

2 A basically all-white room is relieved here and there by flashes of colour in cushions, a painting and the frame of the coffee table; the black of the hearth and floor lamp; and even the laid-back silver of the television set.

COLOUR PLANNING A HOME

The way you go about colour planning a whole house or apartment depends very much on the size of the home. If it is large, you can afford to have different schemes in every room, as long as you remember to take care with the meeting points of floor and wall finishes between rooms. You will also have to pay particular attention to corridors and open doors between rooms to make sure that differing colours, textures and patterns work well together.

If the home is small, then it is sensible to create a harmonious whole, with an overall palette of colours that can be used in differing proportions through all the rooms.

For example, suppose you were particularly happy with apricot, dark blue, burnt umber and green. You could use these colours throughout, varying the pace to prevent monotony.

In one room apricot walls would be combined with white painted shutters, a dark polished wood floor, a golden Afghan rug and upholstery in dark blue and plain cream, accented with green plants and old needlepoint cushions in shades of yellow, apricot and umber.

In another room you could have basically blue walls, overlaid with a dark apricot-umber glaze, and an apricot and blue paisley fabric at the windows and on chair seats.

Yet another room could have apricot and off-white wallpaper, used with plain deep blue upholstery.

A fourth room could be basically off-white, with an apricot and blue border or stencilling, polished floor-boards with a blue and apricot dhurrie or needlepoint rug, off-white blinds with a double border of apricot and dark blue petersham, and a mixture of blue, off-white and apricot upholstery, or blue or apricot bedspreads.

In this way, each room would seem entirely different and individual, but each one would also meld into the overall impression of the home without any discord.

MANIPULATING SPACE THROUGH COLOUR

It can be seen from the foregoing example that a small apartment or house will seem more spacious if the same colours are used in different juxtapositions throughout. This is all the more true if the rooms have the same floor covering or polished wood floor. Similarly, the way in which you use colour can alter the apparent proportions of a room.

- Strong or warm colours, like red or burnt orange, will make walls appear to close in and the space seem smaller.
- Cool colours will appear to stretch space, to push the walls out, particularly if the floor, walls and ceiling all relate to each other and seem a harmonious whole.
- A corridor will look less long and narrow if the end wall is painted or covered in a warm colour.
- A small space will seem larger if all the surfaces are painted the same light colour and the walls washed with light.
- A high ceiling will seem lower if it is painted a darker colour than the walls. This is the case even if the difference is slight.
- A ceiling will look higher if it is painted a lighter colour than the walls, or if a cornice is fixed all around the perimeter of the ceiling and painted a darker colour than the ceiling.
- A too-high ceiling can be made to look lower by adding a chair rail at waist level all around the walls and painting the wall beneath it a darker shade than the walls above, creating a dado effect.

part one: the basics

COLOUR
AND ATMOSPHERE

Colour will also immediately change the feel of a room, so when choosing a scheme, consider what atmosphere you want to achieve.

- Rooms painted in deep, warm colours like rust-red will seem cosy and comfortable and are perfectly appropriate in town or country, in any location with long winter months to get through.

- The same room painted white, pale yellow, blue or light grass-green will seem airy and cool in a hot climate, especially if filled with plants and white wicker furniture, with perhaps yellow, blue or green and white cushions or upholstery.

- A dark, rich room can be brightened by accents of more intense colour and either lightened by white woodwork or given a jewel-box atmosphere by painting the woodwork in the same colour as the walls.

- A light, somewhat bland room can be given more character by staining the floorboards a very dark brown and adding large plants in over-scale (very large) baskets or terracotta pots. Large pieces of furniture will look smaller if covered in a fabric of the same colour as the walls; a smaller piece of furniture, covered in an accent colour, can then balance it.

1 *Apricot and cream* trompe l'oeil *panelling adds warmth and interest to a pale and airy room. The same shades are picked up in cushions on the chaise longue and in the flowers,*

2 *'Greenery-yallery' curtains and a matching cushion are an interesting contrast to the checked bed linen. Note how they are brought into sharp focus by the yellow jug.*

3 *Warm, rusty red-orange walls in an attic bathroom cheer up a somewhat awkward space, as do the large mirror and the nice-looking old ceiling fitting.*

COLOUR IMPRESSIONS

- Dark, warm colours make rooms seem not only comfortable but also distinguished. In addition, they have the knack of making a room look more furnished, or finished, than it actually is.

- Use light, airy colours in a light, airy room. If the room is small as well, the light colours will seem to push out the walls and make the room feel far more spacious.

- It is a fallacy that white, or very light, walls will make a dark room look lighter. In fact, they usually just end up making it look gloomier. Choose rich, warm colours, or creamy yellow, apricot or a singing soft blue instead.

- If you have white cornices, they will stand out better if you paint the ceiling a much paler version of the walls.

- If the walls and ceiling are light, paint the mouldings a contrast colour. Alternatively, in a subtly coloured room, drag the top of a dry brush, lightly dipped into a brighter colour, over a white base coat so that you get just a hint of colour. For example, if the walls are painted a honeysuckle-yellow and the ceiling is cream, you could drag the mouldings with grass-green.

part one: the basics

HOW MANY COLOURS CAN YOU PUT TOGETHER?

People often worry about whether they are using too many or too few colours. I feel that *major* areas of colour (walls, floors, window treatments) should be restricted to three, at most, but that there need be no limit to the number of *accent* colours that can be used (for cushions, trims, mouldings, accessories, flowers, etc.).

For example, in a room with glazed yellow walls, the carpet could have a creamy yellow ground with odd touches of blues and rose-terracotta. The curtains could be in a yellow and white striped fabric, with under-curtains in creamy white. One sofa and one armchair could be cream, another sofa yellow, and a second armchair could pick up the blue in the carpet. Two other occasional chairs could have frames painted in soft terracotta and seats in faded blue-green, again to pick up some of the colours of the carpet. Strewn around the various upholstered pieces could be old needlepoint cushions, which match a third chair. A final colour would be provided by the greens of plants.

MIXING AND MATCHING COLOURS

When you are still finalizing a colour scheme, it helps to collect together samples of all the 'ingredients' you might use in a room (such as the flooring, wall covering, paint, curtains, blinds, tie-backs, trims, tablecloths, bedspreads and valances). Put them on a table, if possible in the room in which you are going to use them, and have a good squint at them with narrowed eyes. By squinting at all those assembled colours and textures, you will see what colours go best with each other and in what proportion, what stands out too harshly and what patterns and textures provide the most harmonious whole.

Sometimes you might have a colour in mind for walls or window treatments that you cannot find in any shop. The best thing to do is to keep an eye out for it in magazine features and advertisements, station-ery, wrapping paper, clothing, fabric scraps, etc. As soon as you see the colour, take it along to a paint shop to get the shade mixed. Or you could show it to a decorative painter, who might be able to achieve exactly the same subtlety by tinting a glaze and over-painting a wall, or by painting in different layers and rubbing the paint off by various methods until the desired effect is achieved.

Similarly, you might find precisely the right colour for a curtain fabric in a dress-fabric department. It will be a

1 Purplish lilacs in the painted cupboard, checked upholstery, cushions, lampshades and some of the ceramics make a harmonious contrast to the various yellows in the room, highlighted by the odd but telling touches of red.
2 Blue and yellow have always been a happy combination. Here, the floor tones beautifully with the blue walls and upholstery of the living area, with the blue cupboards of the kitchen and with the yellow walls in the zone between these two areas. Note the rug and cushions which, along with the floor, unite the three spaces.

part one: the basics

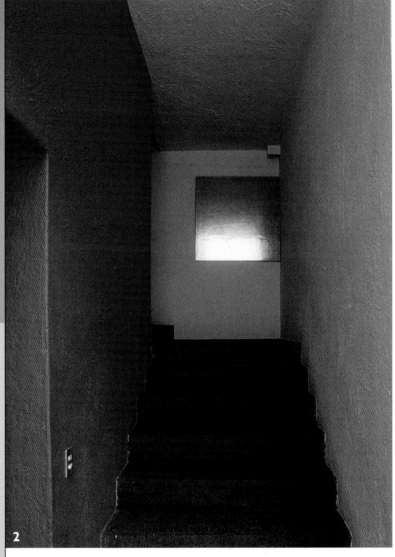

narrower width, and probably also a lighter weight, but it may well be worth it to you to get the exact shade you want. Do not forget about antique textiles and old fabrics in general. It is often possible to find beautiful old curtains and linens in charity shops as well as antique shops.

Finally, do not neglect serendipity – happy accidents – or think that once a room is done to your satisfaction, it is finished. Rooms develop and hopefully mellow, like people. A jacket left over the back of a chair might provide a colour juxtaposition that you had not thought of, which could be produced simply by adding a throw or some flowers. You might suddenly see a new (or old) fabric that seems to go perfectly with an antique rug. All you have to do is make a cushion with it, or an over-cloth for a table, and again the room has a new dimension.

tip

YOU DO NOT HAVE TO TAKE INFINITE PAINS OVER MATCHING COLOURS EXACTLY. THEY ARE NOT, AFTER ALL, CAREFULLY MATCHED EDGE TO EDGE IN NATURE. ALL YOU HAVE TO DO IS THINK IN TERMS OF FAMILIES OF COLOUR, AND, AGAIN, HARMONY. IN THIS WAY, YOUR ROOMS WILL HAVE THE MELLOWNESS THAT IS SO ENVIABLE TO OTHER PEOPLE AND COMFORTABLE FOR YOU.

1 *Another blue and yellow combination, this time allied to white and made even airier by the white-painted open screen room divider at the back.*

2 *An otherwise rather nebulous staircase space has been made warm and interesting by a play on roses: a darker rose on one wall is offset by a paler rose on the other, while the carpet is a greyed-down plum shade.*

Vocabulary of Colour Terms

Accent colours: Used in a scheme to add a little sparkle and variety, accent colours are often chosen from the opposite side of the SPECTRUM to the main colour of the room. They are used only in small areas, for example cushions, lampshades, flowers or picture mounts.

Advancing colours: These are warm colours, such as reds, yellows, apricots and oranges, and they appear to bring surfaces closer. Advancing colours may also make objects look bigger, and they are useful in large rooms to bring in walls and to lower ceilings. Dark shades of other colours have similar effects.

Colour wheel: The seventeenth-century physicist Isaac Newton developed the original colour wheel when he was studying the effects of a beam of light shining through a prism. A prism splits the light into the colours of the rainbow, and the colour wheel is the prismatic spectrum set out in circular form. It comprises twelve colours, from which all of the other identifiable hues are derived, and is based on the three PRIMARY COLOURS (red, yellow and blue), spaced equally around the circle. Between these are the SECONDARY COLOURS (violet, green and orange). The remaining six colours in the wheel are TERTIARY COLOURS. All other colours are variations of these basics, mixed either with each other or with black or white.

Complementary colours: Each PRIMARY COLOUR has a complementary colour, or complement, produced by mixing the other two primaries in equal amounts. Complementary colours are opposite each other on the COLOUR WHEEL. The complement of red is green (a mixture of blue and yellow), the complement of blue is orange (red and yellow) and that of yellow is violet (red and blue). When equal amounts of two complementary colours are mixed, they form grey. In design terms, however, the phrase 'complementary colours' generally means colours that go well together.

Contrasting colours: Technically, a contrast is what you get when you put a SECONDARY COLOUR against a PRIMARY. But in common usage the term means colours that are not near each other on the COLOUR WHEEL. Contrasting colour schemes include complementary schemes (using COMPLEMENTARY COLOURS) and triadic schemes (using colours equidistant from each other on the colour wheel). They generally work best if one colour (usually the RECEDING COLOUR) predominates. Small amounts of a contrasting colour are often useful as ACCENT COLOURS in a room scheme.

Cool colours: See RECEDING COLOURS.

Equal tones: Successful decorating schemes are often formed from a mixture of colours of equal tone – in other words, colours having approximately the same brightness, depth and lightness or darkness. Pastel pinks, yellows and peaches, therefore, look harmonious and well balanced together, as do combinations of strong reds, yellows and blues. In nature, the quality of the light often has the effect of reducing colours to equal tones – the pale colours of early dawn, the soft colours of dusk – while in decorating, white, grey or black is often added to colours to produce a similar effect.

Harmonious colours: These colours are close to each other on the COLOUR WHEEL and so are close in warmth or coldness. For example, a harmonious MONOCHROMATIC SCHEME might be composed of a light tone like pearl grey, moving through middle tones such as flannel grey and ending with a deep tone like charcoal.

Hue: A pure colour to which neither black nor white has been added.

Monochromatic scheme: This type of scheme utilizes one basic colour in a variety of TONES, though it will usually benefit from the addition of one or two ACCENT COLOURS. Textural interest is also important here.

Neutral colours: These range from black to white, taking in greys from the palest silver to charcoal, and also including off-whites and browns, from creams and camels to tans and nutmegs. (Theoretically, however, black and white are non-colours – see SPECTRUM.)

Palette: This refers to the assortment of colours used by an artist or designer for a particular picture or room scheme.

Pastel colours: Pastels are soft, gentle colours that are produced by adding a great deal of white to other colours and their many hues: for example, pink (from red), lilac (from purple) or apricot (from orange).

Primary colours: The three primary colours – red, yellow and blue – are pure colours and cannot be produced by mixing others. All other colours are derived from them.

Receding colours: Blue, violet and green, or colours to which these have been added, are known as receding colours. Also referred to as cool colours, they can make rooms seem larger, because they make surfaces appear to move away from the eye.

Saturation: The intensity, brightness or purity of a colour. The opposite of a saturated colour is a muted colour, often referred to as 'dirty' or 'knocked back'. Sometimes in a muted scheme it is a good idea to add the odd spot of saturated colour, which will almost sing out. However, it is not necessarily a good idea to add knocked-back colour to a saturated colour scheme.

Secondary colours: An equal mixture of two PRIMARY COLOURS produces a secondary colour: red and yellow make orange, blue and red make violet, and yellow and blue make green. Each secondary colour is a COMPLEMENTARY COLOUR of the primary colour not used in its making.

Shades: These are the TONES produced by adding black to a HUE. In common usage, the term can also mean the colours produced by adding grey or white or small amounts of other hues to a colour.

Spectrum: A beam of light when shone through a glass prism is broken up into its constituent wavelengths, represented by bands of red, orange, yellow, green, blue and violet, just like a rainbow. Studying this phenomenon led the physicist Isaac Newton to develop the

The blue-painted frame and deep recess turn this window into a kind of painting, showing off the leafy landscape outside.

COLOUR WHEEL. White is produced by a balanced mixture of all the colours of the spectrum, while true black is a total absence of colour.

Tertiary colours: These are the colours made up of equal parts of PRIMARY COLOURS and SECONDARY COLOURS – for example, lime green is composed of yellow (primary) and green (secondary).

Tints: The TONES of a colour produced by the addition of white. Tints are often only marginally different from the principal colour in a scheme.

Tones: These are the gradations of a colour from its weakest intensity to its greatest – for example, the range from pale pink to dark red.

Warm colours: See ADVANCING COLOURS.

part one: the basics

Playing with Texture and Pattern

Texture and pattern are much more crucial in a room's make-up than you might think. Colours are so radically changed by differences in texture and pattern that a monochromatic, or one-colour, room can be as lively and as memorable through its subtlety as a vividly contrasting room.

TEXTURAL CONTRASTS

Textures need to be considered as carefully as the process of colour building. They may not elicit such emotional reactions as colour, but they are just as evocative. The name of a known texture can conjure up an almost tangible surface. Just as thinking about one colour can evoke many depths and variations, so, too, do different textures engender their own imagery.

Bamboo
Boarding
Brick
Cashmere
Ceramics
Corduroy
Cork
Denim
Felt
Glass
Hessian
Lace
Leather
Linen
Marble
Patent leather
Plaster
Quilting
Rope
Rush matting
Silk
Sisal
Steel
Stone
Suede
Tweed

Take a little time to picture the textures shown in the box below left. Think about these one at a time, and you will discover that it is possible practically to *feel*, as well as see, the various textures in the mind's eye. Pick out some of them and imagine how they would look when appropriately distributed among walls, ceiling, floor and furniture. Contrast their qualities; weigh up their surfaces; juxtapose them in your mind.

Obviously, some textures are more in keeping with each other than others. Rough clearly goes with smooth, and matt with gloss – but what rough with what smooth, and what matt with what gloss, are questions of taste and situation. For example, brick walls would probably look better contrasted with linen or cotton, or the smooth white finish of shutters, than with silk, velvet or moiré. If you are very sure of yourself and your tastes, you can get away with some unconventional contrasts. Like other aspects of decoration, there are no real rules for this – only sensibilities.

To gain confidence, try to collect as many different textural samples as you can. Shop around. *Scrounge* around. Bring back samples of brick, tile, paint chips, carpet, matting, silks, velvets, other fabrics, glass, vinyl. Experiment with them and try out various contrasts.

Even when a room seems finished, the introduction of yet another contrasting texture, like adding another accent in a colour scheme, might make all the difference to the liveliness and interest of a space. As already mentioned with regard to colour, one often does not see this until some chance incident points it out – a velvet coat thrown over a cane chair, for example, or a basket or flowerpot left on a floor. Then suddenly the surface that previously had not even been considered seems just right, effectively delineating all the other colours and surfaces in the room, and one cannot imagine why it was never thought of before. But this is what interior decoration is all about, after all – the relaxed and gradual accretion not just of possessions but also of experience.

1 *Note how the cane seat on the chair, the somewhat rustic frame and the nubbly rug on the wood floor all contrast well and in an appropriate manner. Such a chair placed on, say, a velvet Wilton carpet would have looked out of place, although it would be fine on brick or tiles.*

2 *The same pattern has been used on practically every surface except the floor in this bedroom and adjoining dressing room. Another effective approach would have been to cover the chair, chaise longue and bed in a smaller-scale design with much the same colouring, or in a checked, striped or plain fabric.*

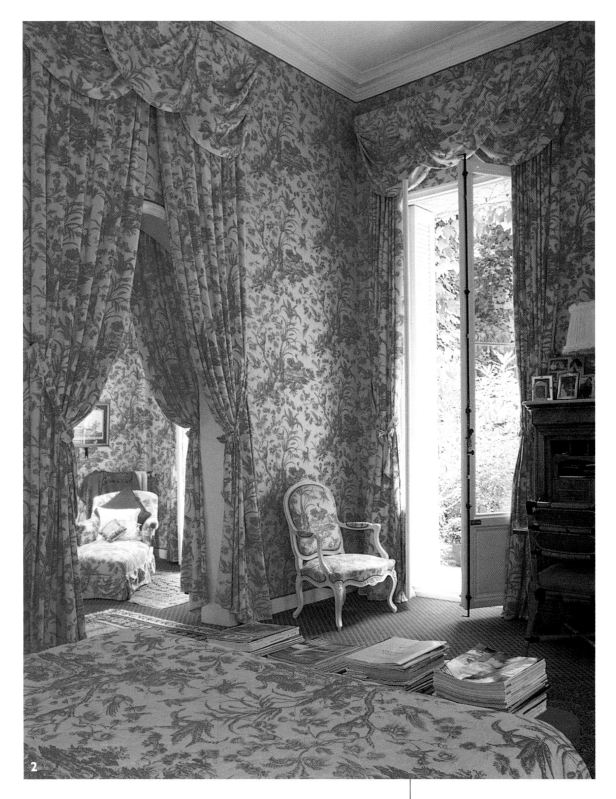

MIXING PATTERNS

Many people find it rather frightening to combine patterns, while others go overboard in mixing up scales and colours in a wholly inappropriate way. Again, it is less a question of rules and more a matter of training the eye and the sensibilities.

One way to go about it is to think of the patterns that are already being formed by your possessions. Books with their various covers and jacket designs; the way pictures and prints are hung on a wall; the arrangement of objects in a storage unit or on a table; the jagged edges of plant leaves against a plain wall; the play of light and shade; the shapes of different pieces of furniture – all these form patterns in their own right. As a result, one more fabric pattern, more or less, cannot jar as long as – and this is important – its scale, tone and proportion are right.

Large patterns that look interesting in some public place are often more suitable for just that sort of setting, unless one possesses a very sure sense of scale. Similarly, you should remember that very small patterns often merge into one colour when they are used for wall coverings or curtains.

A play of pattern, however, can be very effective, enriching the whole scheme. Properly used, it will give added depths to a room.

Here are some important points to remember when mixing patterns:

• It is best not to use more than one large-scale design in a room (or two at the most if they are similar in scale, feeling and colour). You can, however, use several different small-scale patterns with a large design. Small-scale repeats, in upholstery or soft furnishings, of a large pattern on a wall or in a window treatment can give a good sense of perspective and depth.

- The same pattern in two different colours can look good, and so can the same pattern reversed – say, green on white predominating, with white on green predominating.

- Similar patterns in the same colours can be used together to good effect, as in curtains and carpet or rugs with plain painted walls or a textured wall covering.

- Patterns with the same feeling, if not design, can also be used together effectively. Examples include paisleys in the same colouring with similarly coloured florals; ethnic fabrics or batiks with heavily patterned oriental rugs; densely patterned, slightly oriental designs with oriental or needlework rugs; mini-prints of all sorts with small geometrics; and small Liberty-type prints with revived nineteenth-century designs in the same colours.

- Do not forget the subtle effect of sheers, printed with the same design as the curtains or with an allied pattern that is either a simplified version in one colour on white (or white on white) or a toned-down version of the same colouring.

- Many companies now produce coordinating collections of papers and fabrics, using, say, one larger, predominant design in both paper and fabric. These may be grouped in various ways: with smaller-scale

geometric, fish-scale, or basket-weave patterns; with smaller-scale versions of the main design; with a single motif from the main design, used on a plain background in a fairly open manner; or with a monotone, pared-down version of the larger design. If you study these carefully, you will soon be

1 The parquet floor, black-painted cast-iron bath tub, plaster walls, steel tap, shaggy chair covering and large mirror in its gilt frame provide a variety of textural contrasts in what is actually a very simply decorated room.

2 The unadorned brick wall, large sail cloth or 'duck'-covered sofa, rough wood coffee table, smooth wood-strip floor and pair of curved iron sculptures combine rough with smooth, crisp with soft, comfort with hard edges.

3 A silky smooth wood cabinet set within a reeded frame contrasts with the black steel and glass of the desk, the tweed upholstery of the chairs, the latticework of the box on the desktop and the wide planks of the polished floor.

4 Venetian blinds give textural interest to the uncluttered wall, just as the black upholstered chair contrasts the softness of the fabric with the hard shine of the floor tiles. The scheme could hardly be more monotone, but the severe contrast in materials creates an arresting visual effect.

able to form your own groupings from different sources. They will be all the more interesting if you can mix them with an old design or two, perhaps from needlepoint or embroidered cushions or throws, antique quilts or old needlepoint rugs, in the same kind of colouring as the fabrics or paper.

Study the illustrations for examples. Collect a lot of samples of fabrics and papers, and look at them against your own furniture, walls and objects, and in different lights. See what you think works well together. Try making up various groups of your own. You will soon become confident in playing around with pattern.

Controlling Scale and Balance

The other main elements in a room's make-up – scale and balance – are often overlooked, but they are very important. Acquiring a good awareness of these aspects will allow you to choose and arrange furniture and furnishings so that the height, visual 'weight', colour, texture and pattern of each piece contributes to an overall feeling of harmony in the room.

BALANCING FURNISHINGS

If you think about balance, you automatically have to think about scale. It would look awkward, for example, to have one very large piece of furniture, like a huge sofa, in a room with a lot of small pieces and rugs; or only one tall object with a lot of low pieces. Conversely, it would look dull to have all furnishings of the same scale or the same height.

If, on the other hand, you can visually balance a large piece of furniture, like the aforementioned sofa, with a big desk, a sofa table or work table, the piece will look in context with the room as a whole. It will become one of the anchor pieces, around which the rest of the furnishings revolve.

Equally, you should balance a tall piece, like a bookcase, storage unit, armoire or bureau-bookcase, with another large piece, a big painting or print, a group of paintings or prints, or a large mirror on another wall. However, do not choose a piece of art or a mirror that is actually bigger than the chest, side table or other object beneath it or the effect will be top-heavy. Likewise, too small a painting, print or mirror on a long expanse of wall will look puny and lonely.

You could offset a tall piece of sculpture, or a pedestal or a screen in one corner of your room with a large plant or a plant standing on a column or pedestal in another. Always try to vary the height of furnishings. Have at least one or two taller pieces – such as large works of art, wall groupings or plants – in a room. And, in turn, offset large masses of furniture or art with generous rugs.

Practise these juxtapositions by moving around scaled cut-outs of furniture on floor plans drawn on graph paper (see pages 16–17). Cut out magazine pictures of rooms with

arrangements that seem particularly pleasing to you, and analyse the way they are arranged.

Colour contributes to visual weight, too, so be aware of the balance of light and dark tones in a room.

GROUPS OF ACCESSORIES

The same principle applies to groups of accessories. Keep similar objects more or less of a size; or, since that is not always possible, balance the size of one object with a stronger colour in another. Size does not matter so much with dissimilar objects where the fascination of contrast is the main objective. (For more about arrangement, see pages 208–215.)

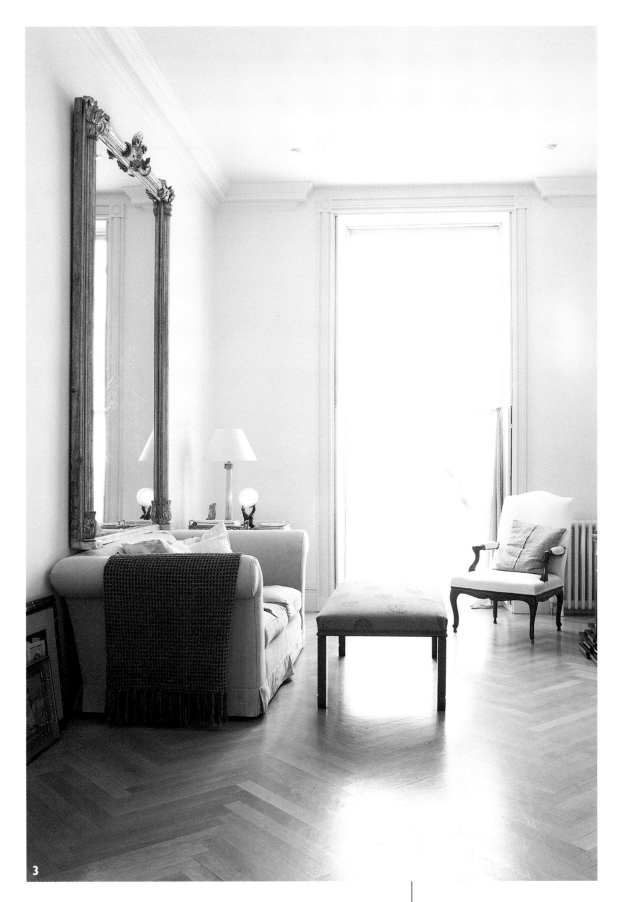

1 *A nice sense of balance is demonstrated by this vignette. The mirror over the fireplace is just that bit smaller without being too small. The flower pots are a casual contrast to the centrally placed bust, which, in turn, is a good counterpoint to the ornate carving at the top of the mirror above it and the elaborate carving in the centre of the mantelpiece below.*

2 *The crisp lines of the simple desk beneath the window are echoed by those of the Venetian blinds, while the lamp on its three steel legs complements the chair.*

3 *The very tall mirror hung over the sofa is an excellent counterpoint to the floor-to-ceiling window, while the curved legs of the* fauteuil *contrast with the straight legs of the stool.*

SIMILARITIES AND CONTRASTS

Repeat the same colour here and there in a room. The colour of a chair at one end can be repeated in a painting, a cushion or a rug at the other. Colours in a patterned ceramic table lamp can be picked up in a plain ceramic lamp somewhere else. The tones of a painting can be echoed in the plain colour of a carpet.

Look, and then look again, at your room designs, asking yourself the following questions:

- Where can the pace be varied more?
- What other shapes can be effectively juxtaposed?
- What flashes of colour will be enhanced with a little repetition here and there?
- Are there any felicitous contrasts that can be made?

By stopping to think in this way, you will ensure that you always have visual balance in mind, whatever changes you are making to a room.

part one: the basics

Once the basics of any remodelling
or decorating job have been decided
upon, you need to finalize the style.
When you are sure of your tastes
and requirements, the way you order,
arrange or transform rooms can be as
instinctive as the way you arrange
your wardrobe, no matter how well
informed you are about all the possible
styles. I have seen people manage to
create rooms that are indisputably
charming and memorable, with
almost no money and a generally
undistinguished miscellany of
possessions. This is what is meant
by a sense of style.

Style

A Sense of Style

To possess a sense of style is to possess a sense of suitability; a feeling for what is appropriate in any given situation (unless you are so sure of yourself that you can turn suitability on its head and defy the conventional). In addition, it is an understanding of the sort of arrangements, juxtapositions, colours and proportions that will all meld happily together. You also need to have a pragmatic rather than a slavish view of fashion. It is hard to ignore a prevailing look that you find sympathetic, but trying to follow every fad in home furnishings would be outrageously expensive as well as totally impractical, particularly as fashions change so fast these days.

CULTIVATING
A SENSE OF STYLE

Many people who claim to have no assured sense of style themselves can often recognize other people's natural style and instinctive good taste, amorphous though these are. Yet while acknowledging that others can put together possessions and colours in an interesting way, they persist in denying their own abilities and fail even to attempt to analyse why some combinations look better than others.

Over the years I have watched enough people develop an excellent sense of style, as well as a good eye for both the acquisition of possessions and their placement, to know that the cultivation of this skill is definitely possible. More often than not, if you really *look at* and analyse what both pleases and suits you, the development of your own sense of style follows quickly. And when you have gained confidence in your own tastes, have developed a good eye and have attained a working knowledge of the various furnishing styles, all decorative possibilities will open up to you.

CREATIVE COMPROMISE

Just as you do not have to have been born with a natural flair, equally it is not a prerequisite to have unlimited funds to indulge any whim in interior decoration. In fact, a form of short-hand – a glancing reference to a style (like using a stencilled Gothic cornice in a bedroom or a Neoclassical pediment over a bookcase) – is often more lively and amusing than the serious and scholarly placement of all the proper ingredients.

1 *This home might be called modern eclectic, with its pale colours, play on textures and interesting old pieces mixed with the modern. It looks somewhat spare, but there is a lot of charm about the room.*
2 *This is definitely country style with its battered old plastered walls, brick floors, old or distressed dressers, painted chairs, scrubbed tables and lots of old pots and earthenware.*

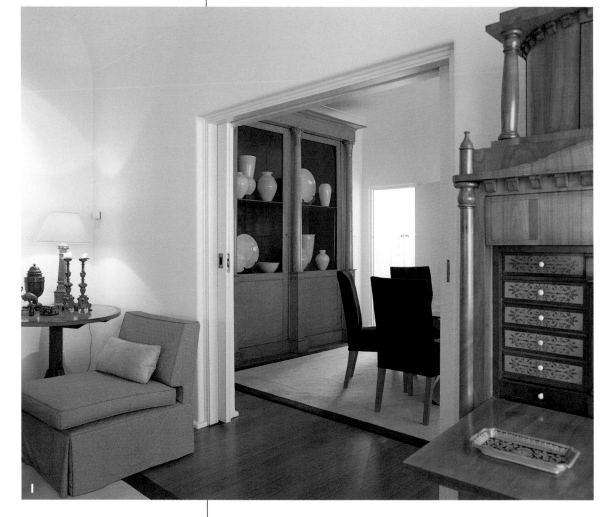

part one: the basics

The Suitability Factor

Clearly, there are certain common-sense factors to consider about any home before deciding to impose a particular style or styles. Aspects like location, climate, setting and architecture cannot be ignored.

LOCATION

Houses in the country look best furnished for comfortable rural living. Even in this context there are distinctions, since the furniture, surfaces and colours that you might use in a cottage or farmhouse would look out of place in a more formal Georgian or Regency house. Similarly, although the airy, comfortable feeling of a country home, whatever its degree of formality, has much to commend it in a city, a sophisticated urban look in the country is generally as much out of place as someone going for a walk in the fields in high-heeled shoes.

The whole point of beach houses, ski chalets and other predominantly

1 *If the kitchen on the previous page has all the main ingredients for country rustic, this room must sing out summer house. Glass walls overlooking a large stretch of water, blue-painted woodwork to match the sky, white wicker furniture, an air of luxurious relaxation – what could be more evocative of the perfect summer place?*
2 *This room is the epitome of cool: the white floor, walls, ceiling, and stone bed bases all seem to meld into one. Soft greys and ivories provide the gentlest of contrasts.*

seasonal or holiday homes is that they should be relaxed, carefree and easy to maintain. This guiding principle will dictate casual, practical, comfortable furnishings, with floor treatments and upholstery that are easily cleaned of sand, mud or snow.

CLIMATE AND WEATHER

By the same token, houses in hot climates should obviously look and feel as cool as possible (with some sort of comforting provision for the rare cooler or wetter days). Equally, homes in wetter, colder and greyer climates must, of course, look and feel warm (again, with some sort of provision for the rare hot days).

There is a lot to be said for the sensible habits of our forebears in seasonal climates: during the summer months, they used cool linen or cotton loose covers to disguise winter upholstery and often took down heavy curtains and took up rugs. Today, lack of domestic help and inadequate

part one: the basics

A SENSE OF PLACE

If a house or apartment building already has a distinctive architectural style, or if it is very much geared to its surroundings or climate (such as a home by the sea or one that is in a spectacular setting or in the tropics), it is best to be sensitive to these factors. Even if you do not actually like the building or landscape, location or climate, they are such important and fundamental aspects of the home that they cannot be ignored.

This does not mean that a period house must be decorated exactly according to its period or that a house

I *Simple modern furniture and a white-and-black scheme are kept low-key, the better to show off the intricate nineteenth-century architectural details.*

2 *The height and light in this converted barn have dictated the colours (which have been kept pale and neutral) and the furnishings (large-scale but simple). Nothing is allowed to detract from the sense of lavish spaciousness.*

3 *Entirely appropriate colours and furniture have been well chosen for this large and gallery-like space.*

storage are usually the reasons given for not making seasonal changes, but if the possibility exists for such summer and winter make-overs, it is certainly worth the effort.

ARCHITECTURE AND SETTING

Apart from the common-sense dictates suggested by location and climate, there is often some salient factor about each room in a new home

that will also help determine its treatment. It may be the view outside, or lack of it; or it may be the fact that a room is rather dark, or very light; spacious or tiny; high-ceilinged or low. A room may be beamed or elaborately detailed with cornices and mouldings; it may be panelled or have a distinctive arched or stained glass window. Perhaps it consists almost entirely of glass walls or, conversely, looks out onto a grimy brick wall.

by the shore should be furnished with fishing nets and maritime artefacts. These attempts at authenticity can all too easily look stilted and museum-like or, alternatively, banal, however much knowledge, money or zeal, or all three, are lavished on them. Instead, it simply means that you should go with the flow – be true to the feel of a place as best you can – and be attentive to proportions, architectural details and terrain without being completely cowed by these parameters.

I have seen very old homes in Europe looking marvellous with predominantly modern furniture and paintings and only one or two antique pieces; and I have also seen successful modern rooms in the United States and the Antipodes graced with old furniture and rugs alongside contemporary furnishings.

In addition, I have come across beautiful eighteenth-, nineteenth- and early twentieth-century homes complete with their original detailing, in which the carefully chosen colours and mix of furnishings make them totally and charmingly of the moment.

The factor that all these rooms have in common is that the framework, whatever it is, has been kept intact, and the proportions matched by the proportions of the furnishings. There has been no slavish imitation of the past. All the rooms are a successful synthesis of the past and the present, with a sharp eye for both comfort and balance.

THE FEATURELESS ROOM

Although suitability, spiced with imagination, is all-important when a building or room has some architectural distinction, or when climate or location dictate the approach, there are also many examples of homes that are the opposite. This particularly applies to the numerous city or suburban buildings built between the 1940s and 1980s that are almost universally anonymous, featureless and very often viewless, and where

1 Nothing detracts from the view in this comfortable room. Furniture is kept low so that the trees outside can become a major part of the decoration, making the most of the stunning location.
2 A definitely Middle Eastern feel has been created in this space with its trellised arch, different levels and piles of sumptuously coloured cushions.
3 Similarly, a precisely organized oriental-looking space has been achieved with shoji screens and the stepped pyramid of storage drawers, along with the free-standing floor light.

climate hardly seems to matter. In these homes, you can superimpose any style that your inclinations, possessions and pocket may dictate, without any guilt about lack of aesthetic sensibility.

One of the most interesting jobs that I have undertaken as a designer was the transformation, at the request of the widely travelled owners, of two adjoining featureless Manhattan apartments into something more akin to a luxurious Tunisian villa, complete with arches and fountains. As a final detail, I masked the sight of Broadway, six floors below, by stretching bright blue chiffon behind pierced shutters at most of the windows, so that one seemed to be looking out on a hot blue sky. At night the chiffon looked realistically dark. The project cost nothing like what one might assume such a transformation would cost, and the finished apartment seemed neither out of place nor kitsch, but simply the oasis of calm the owners had specified.

part one: the basics

69

Influences on Style

There are a great many general styles with generic names like country, contemporary, colonial, eclectic and so on, the most important of which are defined on pages 78–83. In addition to these broad styles, there are the styles that have become synonymous with particular periods in history. Even if you are not decorating a period house, having a clear idea of the main historical styles is undeniably useful for your decoration knowledge and skills. Interior designers have always drawn upon the styles of previous eras for inspiration, and today is no exception. The main style-periods are described on pages 70–5, but to put them in context, study the table on pages 76–7.

Running through the successive style-periods have been a handful of fundamental 'themes', or basic approaches to decorating (and, indeed, to the arts in general), that have re-emerged in different guises over the centuries, sometimes even co-existing side by side. These major influences are the Classical, the Gothic, the Baroque and the Rococo.

THE CLASSICAL

Classicism is derived from ancient Greece by way of Rome. Based on Greek and Roman forms and mathematical laws of proportion, Classical style applies not just to architecture and fine art but also to interior decoration. In the fifteenth and sixteenth centuries, the unprecedented burst of creativity and experimentation of the Renaissance marked the end of the medieval attachment to all things Gothic and a return to Classicism. Roman motifs – such as wreaths, garlands and festoons, arabesques and scrolls, vine leaves and grapes, acanthus and anthemion

(Greek honeysuckle), *putti* (cupids) and urns – became part of the vocabulary of Classical ornament from this point onwards.

Classical ideas, as interpreted by the sixteenth-century Italian architect Andrea Palladio, provided the dominant theme for the British version of Palladian architecture, introduced by the British architect Inigo Jones in the early 1600s. However, the style did not really catch on until a century after that in Britain, and around 1750 in North America.

Later in the eighteenth century, the almost obligatory 'Grand Tour' of Europe allowed the scions of the aristocracy to immerse themselves in the ruins of ancient Greece and Rome and the glories of Renaissance Italy. The Grand Tour, combined with news of the extraordinary archaeological discoveries made in Italy and Greece, particularly those at Pompeii and Herculaneum, led to the first truly international style – Neoclassicism. The Neoclassicism of the late eighteenth and early nineteenth centuries

3

70

2

1 *Chiswick House in west London is one of the great examples of early eighteenth-century Classical architecture and decoration. Built between about 1725 and 1729 by Lord Burlington with William Kent, it embodies all the qualities of noble proportions, rich but restrained decoration and the wholesale use of ancient Roman detail that are typical of the best architecture of this period. In the gallery, shown here, the decoration of the cupola, the three arches incorporating the entry way and two niches for life-size statuary combine in one space a great many of the elements of Classicism.*

2 *Note how the floor and ceiling reflect each other in this wonderfully proportioned entrance hall at Cairness House, Scotland, another superb Classical-style house. Built in 1789 and designed by the architect James Playfair, it has a noble simplicity in line, colour and ornamentation.*

3 *Detail of a cornice with typical ancient Roman architectural motifs.*

dominated architectural interiors all over Europe and in America. Cool restraint, symmetry, balance, harmony and proportion, along with Classical decorative motifs, were all features of the 'Age of Elegance'. There was another resurgence of the Classical in the mid-nineteenth century with the Renaissance Revival and other Classically inspired reincarnations. In the last third of the twentieth century, Postmodernism incorporated Classical elements and proportions into contemporary buildings and interiors.

THE GOTHIC

The Gothic style was used initially for early ecclesiastical architecture in Western Europe, from the twelfth century to the fifteenth or sixteenth, when it gradually gave way to Renaissance Classicism. A layman's

part one: the basics

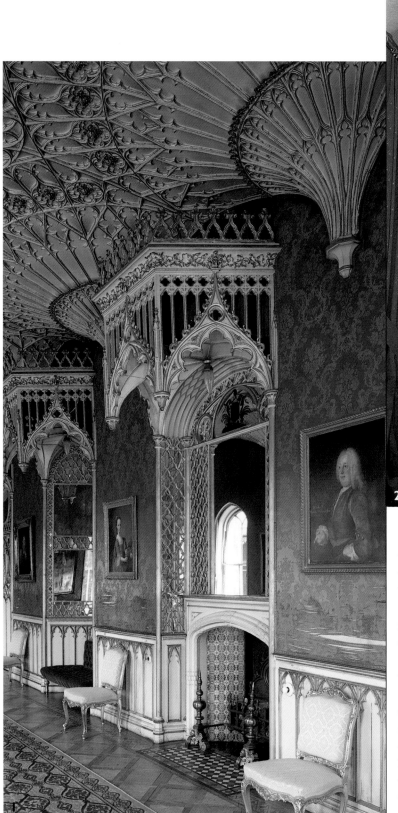

version of Gothic appeared in castles, fortresses and some early domestic and university architecture at the time.

Gothic decoration thus originated in the decoration used in medieval churches, and includes the trefoil and quatrefoil motifs, the pointed arch and pierced tracery.

In the early eighteenth century, the Gothic inspired a good deal of domestic architecture, architectural details and furniture, but in a much lighter and more graceful vein than the original. Much Gothic design of this period was spelt 'Gothick' to denote a deliberate frivolity.

The Gothic style made a strong reappearance in the late eighteenth and early nineteenth centuries, initially as a light-hearted counterpoint to the Neoclassical movement, when Gothic follies and lodges in gentlemen's parks were highly fashionable. From the 1820s to the mid-nineteenth century, the Gothic revival was a serious force again in Britain, France, Ireland, Germany, the United States, South Africa, Australia and New Zealand. The passion for all things medieval meant that it was interpreted in a much more serious way than in the previous century. The French version was known

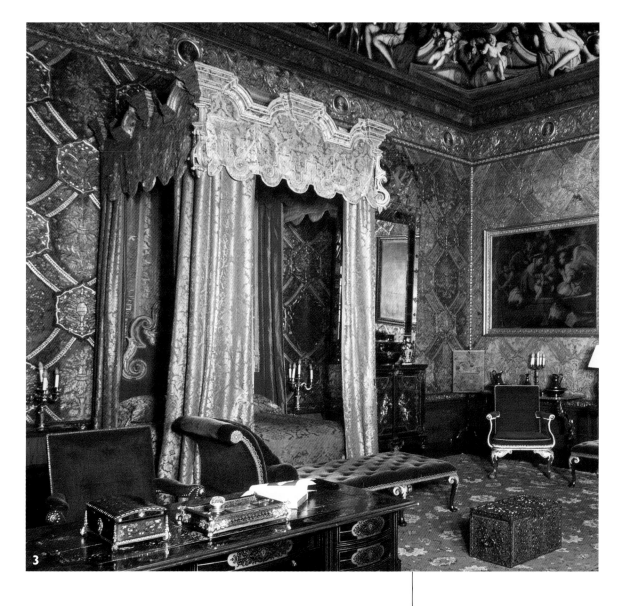

3

1 *Horace Walpole's house near London, Strawberry Hill, which he transformed into a battlemented castle in the second half of the eighteenth century, is so synonymous with over-the-top Gothick extravaganza that 'Strawberry Hill Gothick' has become part of the language. The gallery shown here has hugely flamboyant fan vaulting. Note, too, the mouldings forming the chair rail at the top of the dado and the ornate motifs on the wall covering. The whole mise en scène is as opposite to the spirit of Classicism as can be.*

2 *In a small contemporary dining room, the Gothic spirit is encapsulated in the splendid chairs.*

3 *The Baroque style spread to England via France in the second half of the seventeenth century. Chatsworth, in Derbyshire, was built between 1687 and 1707 for the 4th Earl of Devonshire and is a particularly fine example of the style, exemplified in this magnificent state bedroom.*

as Troubadour style, which became hugely popular for a few decades. Gothic revival furniture, applied architectural details, textiles and wallpaper were all produced at this time in large quantities.

In the late twentieth century, there was a mini-Gothic revival, with a wave of Gothic-style furnishings, fabrics and wallpapers.

THE BAROQUE

By the early 1600s, the Classicism of the Renaissance had evolved into the Baroque style, which emerged first in Italy and spread around Europe during the seventeenth century.

The Baroque style reached its apotheosis in France, first in the reign of Louis XIII, and then, most magnificently, in that of Louis XIV, the 'Sun

King'. It spread to Britain in the second half of the century and to America towards the end of the 1600s.

The style was splendidly ornate, theatrical, even exuberant, with heavy forms, large-scale planning and elaborate plasterwork, strapwork, metalwork, woodcarving, panelling (at that time, removable like furniture), pilasters, over-mantels and tapestries.

Grand though it was, Baroque was the first European style to treat a room as a place actually to live in, rather than just to admire in passing or to have receptions in. And it was the first time that pieces of furniture were made to go together in a room, as opposed to being part of the architecture, or otherwise monumental. Interestingly, in spite of being an

part one: the basics

offshoot of the Classical style, Baroque actually represented the reverse of Classical harmony, completely breaking the Classical rules.

Baroque remained the style of choice in Europe and America for those who could afford its extravagances, until it was finally overtaken by the Rococo or, as in Britain and the Netherlands, by Neo-Palladian Classicism. In the mid-nineteenth century there was a revival of Baroque among the multitude of other style revivals of the period.

THE ROCOCO

Rococo style first appeared in Paris in the early eighteenth century, as a reaction to the formality and opulence of the Baroque. It had its most famous expression during the Régence and the first half of the reign of Louis XV.

1 *Claydon House in Buckinghamshire is one of the few examples of the English Rococo style. But what an ebullient example it is, with its amazingly complicated plasterwork and clear pastel colours.*

2 *Claydon House is very chaste compared with this extraordinary room in the Amalienburg Pavilion at Schloss Nymphenburg, a summer palace near Munich, built by the Bavarian architect Cuvilliés in 1734–39. The Germans loved the Rococo style and went on with its elaborations long after most of Europe had moved into Neoclassical mode.*

3 *The silk wall covering in this room is an example of 'the Chinese taste', a mania for everything oriental, inspired by the merchandise imported by the East India companies. Like eighteenth-century Gothick, this was an offshoot of Rococo.*

Light and frivolous, Rococo was characterized by asymmetry in carved and painted decoration, plasterwork, panelling and furniture. Rococo motifs included seashells, ribbons and bows. Colours were a revolution for the time: clear pastels, like blues and pale greens, pale yellows and roses, were used with a great many mirrors and candelabra and sconces to dramatize the brilliance and light.

The style was enormously popular in Germany and Austria as well as in France, and, to a lesser extent, in Spain, Portugal, Italy, Russia and Poland, and across the Atlantic in North America. But it never took serious hold in Britain or in the Netherlands (apart from its offshoot, the 'Chinese Taste', or Chinoiserie, which became popular in Britain and Europe in the eighteenth century).

Eventually, the elegance of Rococo became overblown and quite outrageously extravagant, and, towards the end of the eighteenth century it gave way to Neoclassicism.

It was, however, revived in the mid-nineteenth century, when it was a favourite of the rich, of whom there were many. In France, the Rococo revival led in turn to the development of the Art Nouveau style.

part one: the basics

Year	France — Period/Monarch	France — Style	Italy — Style	Germany/Austria — Style	Belgium/Netherlands — Style	Scandinavia — Style
1500		Gothic	Renaissance	Gothic	Gothic	Gothic
1525	François I (1515–47)	Renaissance				
1550	Henri II (1547–59) François II (1559–60)			Renaissance	Renaissance	Renaissance
1575	Charles IX (1560–74) Henri III (1574–89)					
1600	Henri IV (1589–1610) Louis XIII (1610–43)		Baroque			
1625						
1650	LOUIS QUATORZE Louis XIV (1643–1715)	Baroque				Baroque
1675				Baroque	Baroque	
1700						Late Baroque
	RÉGENCE [regency of Duc d'Orléans to Louis XV, 1715–23]	Early Rococo	Late Baroque			Early Rococo
	LOUIS QUINZE Louis XV (1715–74)	Rococo				
1725			Rococo	Rococo	Rococo	Rococo
1750						
1775	LOUIS SEIZE Louis XVI (1774–93)	Neoclassical	Neoclassical			Neoclassical [Gustavian: Gustav III, 1771–92]
1800	DIRECTOIRE Directoire (1795–99)			Neoclassical	Neoclassical	
	EMPIRE Consulate (1799–1804) Napoleon I (1804–15)	Late Neoclassical [Empire]	Late Neoclassical [Empire]	Late Neoclassical [Empire]	Late Neoclassical [Empire]	Late Neoclassical [Empire]
	RESTAURATION Louis XVIII (1814–24) Charles X (1824–30)					
1825		Rococo revival / Neo-Gothic		Biedermeier	Biedermeier	Biedermeier
	LOUIS PHILIPPE Louis Philippe (1830–48) Napoleon III (President, 1848–52)			Neo-Gothic		
1850	SECOND EMPIRE Napoleon III (Emperor, 1852–70)	Eclectic	Eclectic	Louis Seize revival	Eclectic	Eclectic
1875	THIRD REPUBLIC (1870–1940)					
1900		Art Nouveau	Art Nouveau	Art Nouveau	Art Nouveau	Art Nouveau ['Jugendstil'] + Arts & Crafts
		Belle époque	['stile Liberty]	['Jugendstil']		[Larsson]
1925		Art Deco International	International	International	International	International

Year	Britain PERIOD/MONARCH	Britain STYLE		United States PERIOD	United States STYLE	Year
1500	TUDOR Henry VII (1485–1509) Henry VIII (1509–47)	Gothic				1500
1525						1525
1550	Edward VI (1547–53) Mary I (1553–58)	Renaissance				1550
1575	ELIZABETHAN Elizabeth I (1558–1603)					1575
1600	JACOBEAN James I (1603–25)			COLONIAL (1608–1720)	Renaissance ['Jacobean']	1600
1625	CAROLEAN Charles I (1625–49)	Early Baroque				1625
1650	CROMWELLIAN Commonwealth (1649–60) RESTORATION Charles II (1660–85)	Baroque				1650
1675	James II (1685–89) WILLIAM & MARY William and Mary (1689–94) William III (1694–1702)					1675
1700	QUEEN ANNE Anne (1702–14) GEORGIAN George I (1714–27)	Early Neo-Palladian ['Queen Anne']		GEORGIAN (1720–80s)	Baroque ['William & Mary'] Early Neo-Palladian ['Queen Anne']	1700
1725	George II (1727–60)	Neo-Palladian	Slight Rococo inc. Gothick and Chinoiserie			1725
1750	George III (1760–1820)	Neoclassical ['Adam style']	Neo-Gothic		Neo-Palladian / Rococo Neoclassical	1750
1775				FEDERAL (1780s–1810)		1775
1800		Greek revival				1800
	REGENCY [Regency of Prince of Wales to George III, 1811–20] George IV (1820–30)	Late Neoclassical ['Regency']	Chinoiserie	EMPIRE (1810–20s) GREEK REVIVAL (1820s–40s)	Late Neoclassical [Empire]	
1825	William IV (1830–37)				Neo-Gothic	1825
	VICTORIAN Victoria (1837–1901)	Eclectic		VICTORIAN (1837–1901)		
1850		Arts & Crafts			Eclectic	1850
1875		Art Nouveau	Aesthetic movement Queen Anne revival		Arts & Crafts ['Mission'] Colonial revival Aesthetic movement	1875
1900	EDWARDIAN Edward VII (1901–10) MODERN George V (1910–36)			MODERN (1901 onwards)	Beaux Arts / Art Nouveau	1900
1925	Edward VIII (1936) George VI (1936–52)	Art Deco International	Neo-Tudor		Art Deco International	1925

77

Vocabulary of Decorating Styles

Adam, Robert: Robert Adam (1728–92) produced, often with his lesser-known brother James, some of the most graceful and interesting furniture and interiors in the history of British decorative arts. He believed that a room's decoration and furnishings should all add up to a harmonious whole, and he perfected an approach to design that enabled him to fit his interior schemes into existing houses. Although people today think of Adam colours as soft pastels, his schemes were actually very colourful. His work deeply influenced not only other eighteenth-century architects and cabinetmakers on both sides of the Atlantic, but also students of design up to the present day. He is the epitome of late eighteenth-century taste.

Aesthetic movement: More of a late nineteenth-century philosophy than a real movement, this was inspired by the new cult of the Japanese aesthetic and by the Queen Anne revival. It prevailed only in England and America, with no counterpart in Europe. The emphasis was on maximum light, comfort and informality, with pale, quiet colours. Japanese symbols were a particular feature, as well as stylized sunflowers, lilies and peacocks.

American Colonial: See COLONIAL (AMERICAN).

American Country: A broad style not related to a particular period. Hallmarks include primitive furniture in sun-washed barn reds and dusty blues, stencilled motifs, patchwork, rag rugs, painted floorboards, floorcloths and match-board wainscoting.

American Empire: See EMPIRE (AMERICAN).

American South-west: Spanish and Native American influences on American Colonial style; sometimes called Santa Fe style. Hallmarks include adobe walls, rough-hewn furniture, Navajo rugs and other brightly coloured Native American textile designs.

Art Deco: An architectural and decorative style that flourished in Europe and America from just before the First World War up to the 1930s. It became increasingly decorative in the 1920s when it blossomed into all sorts of shapes inspired by primitive Aztec, Mayan and African art; Leon Bakst's costumes and decor for the Russian ballet, then performing to great acclaim in Paris; and archaeological discoveries in Egypt. Art Deco, a name coined much later, is short for Arts Décoratifs.

Art Nouveau: This style was fashionable on both sides of the Atlantic from 1890 to the First World War, and is known for its sinuous lines, mainly derived from vegetal forms. Victor Horta and Henry Van de Velde in Belgium,

1

Hector Guimard and Émile Gallé in France, A H Mackmurdo and C F A Voysey in England, and Louis Sullivan and Louis C Tiffany in the United States were just a few of its gifted designers. In Scotland, Charles Rennie Mackintosh and the Glasgow School developed an influential rectilinear version inspired by Celtic ornament.

Arts and Crafts movement: A nineteenth-century movement led by William Morris and C R Ashbee in Britain. The aim was to eschew mass-production methods and return to the individually crafted furnishings of the past. Though it was meant to be an egalitarian movement, its products were too expensive for the 'masses' to buy. However, Morris's papers and fabrics were copied by manufacturers like Sanderson and Liberty, who have been reproducing them ever since. In the United States, the movement centred around MISSION style, and also the PRAIRIE SCHOOL.

Baroque: Opulent, grand, ornate seventeenth-century style that evolved from RENAISSANCE CLASSICISM. It has been described as a 'piling up of decorative motifs into an unashamedly theatrical composition whether on canvas, brick or stone'. It was used with handsome results all over Britain and Europe and in Central and South America as well.

Bauhaus: Twentieth-century German school of design, an extension of the Weimar School of Arts and Crafts. Founded in 1919 by Walter Gropius, it was the most powerful single influence in the development – and acceptance – of modern design. In 1925, the Bauhaus School moved from Weimar to Dessau, and the new office Gropius designed became a model for the contemporary 'dateless' look that was the epitome of the INTERNATIONAL STYLE for decades after. Most of the school's principals moved to the United States at the onset of Nazi rule.

Beaux Arts: Late nineteenth-/early twentieth-century American equivalent of the RENAISSANCE REVIVAL style popular in Europe and Britain at much the same time. It was named after the École des Beaux Arts in Paris, where many of its architectural exponents had trained. With the rapid growth of wealth in the United States, a great many new mansions were built based on French *châteaux*, Italian *palazzi* and TUDOR, ELIZABETHAN and JACOBEAN manor houses. Beaux Arts architects combined modern technology and its creature comforts with historically derived details, such as acanthus leaves twisting around electric light switch plates, and dolphin feet on bathtubs. Colours and details were rich and exotic, with lavish plasterwork, beautiful joinery, panelling and gilding, as well as much Japanese influence.

Belle Epoque: French term for the opulent and glamorously comfortable period at the turn of the nineteenth century and the beginning of the twentieth, when, for the rich, all seemed 'sweetness and light' before the onset of the First World War.

Biedermeier: An Austrian and German (and contemporaneously Scandinavian) decorative style popular from the 1820s to the 1840s, often known as 'the poor man's EMPIRE'. Its simple graceful furniture, mostly in golden-hued wood with ebony or black-stained ornamentation, is very popular today.

'Chinese taste': See CHINOISERIE.

Chinoiserie: European imitations of oriental decoration, furniture and decorative objects. The 'Chinese taste', for Chinese silks, porcelains, lacquerwork, hand-painted wallpapers and other items, as well as items from Japan and India, swept Europe and the United States in the eighteenth century after trade had begun with China. The demand was so high that European companies started making pseudo-oriental imitations, or chinoiseries.

Classical: Style based on the disciplined lines, mathematical laws of proportion and ornamentation of ancient Greek and Roman art and architecture, revived during the Italian Renaissance. Various forms of Classicism have woven in and out of the centuries ever since. It is characterized by cool elegance and restraint, symmetry and balance, geometrical forms, clean lines, and Classical architectural detail (columns, pilasters, etc) and motifs, like laurel wreaths, acanthus leaves and anthemion (Greek honeysuckle). See also NEOCLASSICAL.

Classical orders: The five styles of CLASSICAL architecture – Doric, Ionic, Corinthian, Tuscan and Composite, which appeared in that order. They are based on the proportions and decoration of different styles of column, but in Classical architecture, even the proportions of the different sections of a wall could be based on those of a column. Sometimes the cycle of all design is compared to the sequence of Doric (simple, spare lines), followed by Ionic (more ornamental) and then by Corinthian (highly ornamental), and in many ways the flow of design styles does follow that order over and over again.

Colonial: Although generally thought of as an American style – see COLONIAL (AMERICAN) – Colonial also evokes the eighteenth- and nineteenth-century colonial experience in stiflingly hot climates, with verandas, white-painted weatherboarding, clapboard, handsome porticoes and pillars, shutters, mosquito nets, slatted furniture, rattan, muslin and bare floorboards.

Colonial (American): This covers the early 1600s (when the early settlers had to make do with furniture that was primitive or imported) and the late eighteenth century when the Federal government was established.

Colonial revival: Highly popular 1880s (also 1930s) American style, mixing the painted wood panelling, stencilling, and so on, of AMERICAN COUNTRY, with the fluted pilasters, Windsor chairs, etc, of early FEDERAL style.

Country style: See AMERICAN COUNTRY, ENGLISH COUNTRY and FRENCH COUNTRY.

Contemporary: In interior design this means 'of today', with current furnishings, colours and mixtures.

Cromwellian: The period of the Commonwealth in England (1649–60), when Oliver Cromwell was Lord Protector of England, prior to the

2

RESTORATION of the monarchy. It was a rather stagnant time for architecture, decoration and furniture.

De Stijl: The name for a group of avant-garde Dutch designers in the 1920s who worked only in right angles and primary colours. Members of the group included the painter Piet Mondrian and the furniture designer Gerrit Rietveld.

Rietveld's architectural masterpiece was the Schroder House in Utrecht. With its clean-cut surfaces and metal-framed windows in continuous strips running up to a ceiling devoid of mouldings, this was one of the model interiors for the INTERNATIONAL STYLE.

Directoire: French style, from the last five years of the eighteenth century, between the assassination of Louis XVI during the French Revolution, and the *coup d'état* of Napoleon Bonaparte. This was really a simplified version of the last part of the LOUIS SEIZE style. The designs were elegant and simple, though the

3

1 *William Morris's bed at his house Kelmscott Manor, in Gloucestershire, England. Morris spearheaded the Arts and Crafts movement.*
2 *Design by Charles Rennie Mackintosh at the Glasgow School of Art. Mackintosh was a great exponent of the British version of Art Nouveau and was an international influence.*
3 *An Art Nouveau stair rail by the Belgian Art Nouveau designer Victor Horta.*

materials were of inferior quality to previous decades.

Eclectic: A combination of any number of styles and periods which, for this reason, is generally more idiosyncratic and interesting than any one style. The nineteenth century was a period of rampant eclecticism, when a number of style revivals co-existed.

Edwardian: The period between the 1890s and the First World War. Design was much lighter and airier than the Victorian decoration that had gone before. The period encompassed the AESTHETIC MOVEMENT, ARTS AND CRAFTS MOVEMENT, ART NOUVEAU and the QUEEN ANNE REVIVAL.

Elizabethan: Style during the reign of Elizabeth I of England in the second half of the sixteenth century. The period was one of great British prosperity so there was an increased demand for more luxurious buildings and furniture. The style was largely based on the RENAISSANCE as translated by the French and Flemish, so was actually quite idiosyncratic, with much carving and inlay. CLASSICAL architectural orders were used, though rarely in the proper proportions. Small wood panels were combined with pilasters and columns. In low-ceilinged rooms, the panelling generally rose from the skirting to a primitive cornice. In grander homes, an oak dado was surmounted by a moulding, then panelling and finally an entablature. Flooring downstairs was most often flagstones or slates, and upstairs it was random-width oak planks.

Empire (American): The slightly more subdued American version of the French EMPIRE and English REGENCY styles appeared in the early part of the nineteenth century. Inspired by Greek, Roman and Egyptian sources, the style encompassed many NEOCLASSICAL motifs together with lions'-paw feet, sphinxes and Egyptian motifs, as well as the American bald eagle. Light cream or white woodwork was generally offset by red, green, blue or yellow walls, or by European hand-blocked wallpapers with all-over patterns or scenic views. Either

part one: the basics

way, these backgrounds provided good foils for the mahogany furniture and the gilt mirror frames and details.

Empire (French): The Empire style was a French style of the early nineteenth century. Named for France's First Empire, it includes the Consulate (1799–1804) as well as the reign of Napoleon I (1804–15). Sometimes the reigns of Louis XVIII (1814–24) and Charles X (1824–30) – France's Restauration period – are also included. Motifs were strongly influenced by the discoveries of the ruins of Herculaneum and Pompeii, and Napoleon's Egyptian Campaigns, hence the plethora of ancient Greek, Roman and Egyptian motifs. Colours included Empire green, Empire ruby, lemon yellow, azure blue, amethyst and pearl grey, all mixed with gold and white.

English Country: A broad, general style for which 'benign neglect' and 'faded elegance' are good descriptions. It is characterized by comfort, mellow colours and slightly faded chintzes, rugs and needlework cushions.

Etruscan: A decorative style based on Roman antiquity and Etruscan ornaments. ROBERT ADAM used many Etruscan motifs and ideas in his houses and, in turn, influenced the French, who called it le style étrusque and used it greatly in the late eighteenth century.

Federal: The term used to describe American architecture and design from the 1780s until the early nineteenth century and based on Neoclassicism. Highly prized in the United States, the style drew upon the designs of Sheraton and Hepplewhite, the early REGENCY in Britain and the early EMPIRE in France. It used most of the familiar NEOCLASSICAL motifs plus the American bald eagle as a symbol of the new federal government. Furniture was mainly mahogany or painted wood, and rooms reflected the abundance of new fabrics and French wallpapers in the country.

French Country: Also known as Provençal or French Provincial, this style is characterized by Provençal print fabrics; sunny colour schemes of bright yellows, blues, pinks and reds; white-washed or colourwashed walls in soft tones of ochre, honey, rose, apricot and russet; terracotta-tiled floors; and large, solid, unfussy furniture in pine or chestnut, consisting of rustic, simplified versions of both LOUIS QUINZE and LOUIS SEIZE designs.

Georgian: A term applied to British architecture and design during the reigns of George I, II, III, and IV – ie, from 1714 to 1830 – a long period which went virtually from the PALLADIAN REVIVAL to the REGENCY. Sometimes called the 'age of elegance', it was the golden age of British design in every field.

Gothic: The predominant style of ecclesiastical architecture in Europe during the Middle Ages, and one of the great influences on design throughout the last millennium. The Gothic was much in favour in the eighteenth century as an antidote to rigorous CLASSICISM (when it was often spelt 'Gothick'). It was enormously popular again in the nineteenth century, when it was called Neo-Gothic or the Gothic revival and was part of a reverence by the ARTS AND CRAFTS movement for all things medieval.

This revival interpreted it more seriously. Gothic decoration includes pointed arches, tracery, ogees, and medieval motifs such as the trefoil and quatrefoil.

Grand Tour: An almost obligatory part of the education for rich young men, particularly the British, who became known in Italy as milordi. They flocked to Italy, Greece and, to a lesser extent, France, to steep themselves in classical antiquity. After two or three years of travelling, they returned laden with antiquities, furniture, sculptures, paintings and ideas on architecture, which greatly influenced the public taste.

Greek revival: An architectural movement that developed within the NEOCLASSICAL style stressing Greek rather than Roman and RENAISSANCE styles. It was at its height in Britain in the 1790s; and, in the 1820s–40s, it became equally popular in the United States, where it influenced many houses built at the time as well as a good deal of furniture. It was also popular in Europe, particularly Germany. Staircases became much lighter than previously, with splendid curves and slender stair rails. Painted, papered and fabric-covered walls replaced wood panelling and were accompanied by handsome plaster cornices and beautiful mantelpieces.

Gustavian: A charming late eighteenth-century Swedish period-style, named after Gustav III who reigned from 1771 to 1792 and made the Swedish court a northern Versailles. The rooms were full of light from large windows, chandeliers and mirrors. Walls, which were often hung with canvas, were painted with panels, swags, columns or flowers. The style is typified by painted furniture; simplified Neoclassical designs; symmetry and understated elegance; cool colours such as blue-grey, straw yellow, muted pink and pearl grey; checked fabrics; and distinctive tiled stoves.

High-tech: Also spelt hi-tech, this 1970s style was based on industrial components with a dash of MINIMALISM.

International style: Also known as Modernism, this was started by the BAUHAUS in the early 1920s. It advocated sleek lines, simplicity, natural textures and pale, neutral colours. Gropius, Le Corbusier and Mies van der Rohe were founder members of a style that has profoundly influenced architects and designers up to the present day.

Jacobean: The style-period during the reign of the British King James I during the first quarter of the seventeenth century. (Sometimes it is extended to include also the Carolean period – the reign of Charles I, during the second quarter of the century.) Jacobean was essentially a more elaborate version of ELIZABETHAN style, but new ideas and proportions gleaned from the Palladian CLASSICISM of the Italian RENAISSANCE were better understood and were interpreted more accurately.

Louis Quatorze: During the long reign of the 'Sun King', Louis XIV (1643–1715), France reached extraordinary heights of aesthetic splendour. With the magnificent Palace of Versailles as the seat of the French court, the opulent grandeur of BAROQUE style was allowed full rein. From that time till the first quarter of the nineteenth century, France was the leader of European taste. Bottle green or crimson velvet, tawny serge and damask wall hangings; embossed leather, sometimes decorated with foil, silvered or gilded; tapestries; carved and gilded panelling (*boiserie*); marble or parquetry floors with Savonnerie carpets; gilt-bronze chandeliers, wall brackets, clocks and other objects all typified the grandiose interiors of France in the *siècle d'or* ('golden century').

Louis Quinze: The French version of ROCOCO, which reached its height during the reign of Louis XV (1715–74). Colours were pale pastels with cream and white. Mirrors were used lavishly. They were set over console tables; were recessed into carved and gilded panelling (*boiserie*) opposite tall over-mantel mirrors; and were used to disguise fireplaces in summer, as well as on ceilings and sometimes on sliding window shutters; occasionally entire walls were lined with them. Add to this the elaborately framed hanging mirrors, the hundreds of candles set into crystal candelabra and the *girandoles* (candlesticks set into mirrors) and you get a picture of the dazzle.

Louis Seize: The NEOCLASSICAL style that swept through Europe from the 1750s was known in France as *'le goût grec'*. However, it is also known simply as Louis Seize, after the reigning monarch Louis XVI (1774–93), who presided over

the full resurgence of Classicism in France. Neoclassical motifs like caryatids, acanthus and laurel wreaths appeared on furniture. Sky-blue cloud-painted ceilings and colours like terracotta and purple were added to the predominant gold and white, as Etruscan and Egyptian details began to be added to the Classical repertoire.

Mannerism: The transition between the RENAISSANCE and BAROQUE movements, in which designs included strangely attenuated human figures and 'grotesque' ornament in the form of griffins, birds and insects set within cartouches connected by strapwork designs. The term 'grotesque' was derived from ancient Roman decoration excavated during the Renaissance, and had its roots in the word grotto, or cave, rather than the current meaning. It was a deliberate reaction to the discipline of CLASSICISM and was particularly popular in northern Europe in the sixteenth and seventeenth centuries.

Minimalism: A 1970s, 1990s and current movement which follows Mies van der Rohe's dictum that 'less is more'. All ornamentation is eschewed along with clutter and most colour. At its best it is admirably clean-lined.

Mission: An 1890s/early 1900s American offshoot of the ARTS AND CRAFTS movement. Its exponents, particularly the Roycroft community and Gustav Stickley, believed they had a mission to promulgate utility of design. The name is also linked with the simple furniture of the early Spanish missions in California and New Mexico. The style is said to have begun when members of the congregation of a Franciscan Mission church in San Francisco made their own chairs to replace decrepit pews.

Modernism: See INTERNATIONAL STYLE.

Neoclassical: The first real international style and a major design force from 1760 to 1830. Originally a reaction against the frivolity and excesses of the ROCOCO, it was the design equivalent of the Age of Reason. The style was influenced by the major archaeological

discoveries of ancient Greece, and of ancient Rome at Herculaneum and Pompeii in 1738 and 1748, as well as the Egyptian Campaigns. Motifs included acanthus leaves and lyres from Greece, lions' heads and paws, laurel wreaths from Rome and crossed spears, swans' necks, sphinxes and palmettos from ancient Egypt.

Neo-Gothic: See GOTHIC.

Orders: See CLASSICAL ORDERS.

Palladian and Neo-Palladian: Architectural style derived from the designs of Andrea Palladio, the great RENAISSANCE architect who based his pure, exquisitely proportioned buildings on the precepts of ancient CLASSICAL architecture. His designs were first introduced to Britain by Inigo Jones in the seventeenth century, and revived in the early eighteenth century. Interestingly, although Neo-Palladian (or Palladian revival) architecture was severely geometric, the furniture was rather BAROQUE in feeling. This is mainly because William Kent, the great eighteenth-century promulgator of Palladio's work, had no real model for ancient Classical furnishings, and so

1 A 1920s building by the Swiss-born French architect and furniture designer Le Corbusier, who was a leading influence on the International style.

2 A Swedish bergère with the grey-painted frame typical of the very popular Gustavian style.

2

part one: the basics

adapted the Baroque furniture he had seen in Palladian villas in northern Italy.

Prairie School: Designs by the American master architects Frank Lloyd Wright and Louis Sullivan, and a group of other architects and designers centred around Chicago from the late 1880s to the early 1900s. Its various influences were the low, rugged, rambling ranch houses of the prairie, hence its name; the ARTS AND CRAFTS MOVEMENT from Britain; and the movement's American offshoot, MISSION.

Provençal: See FRENCH COUNTRY.

Queen Anne: This gently simplified British adaptation of the BAROQUE was named for Queen Anne, who reigned from 1702 to 1714. Nothing much changed in room decoration from the WILLIAM AND MARY period preceding it, but furniture became fluid and beautiful, based on simple elegance, subtle curves and understatement. The vogue grew for CHINOISERIE and for 'chinaware', which often covered every available shelf as well as the walls. Wallpapers had a huge success with the middle classes, while the aristocracy were hanging Chinese silks. The style continued for several years after the monarch's death, till it gave way to the PALLADIAN REVIVAL style.

Queen Anne (American): In America the QUEEN ANNE style began to take hold just as it was waning in Britain (ie, around 1720), and was influential until the middle of the eighteenth century.

Queen Anne revival: The so-called Queen Anne revival at the end of the nineteenth century in Britain had very little to do with the early eighteenth-century QUEEN ANNE style, and was much more a mixture of NEOCLASSICAL designs, with the odd nod to ROCOCO. It was led by the English country-house architect Richard Norman Shaw, who tried to reproduce this lightness of touch in revolt against Victorian heaviness.

Régence: Early eighteenth-century French style of richly gilded interiors during the transitional period between the magnificent BAROQUE of LOUIS QUATORZE and the full-blown ROCOCO of

LOUIS QUINZE. It roughly coincided with the period when Philippe d'Orléans was regent to the young Louis XV.

Regency: The late NEOCLASSICAL British style named after the Prince Regent, who was renowned for his expensive tastes. It was actually in favour during the first four decades of the nineteenth century and used Greek, Roman, Egyptian, French, Chinese and Hindu motifs. One characteristic motif was the eagle, which appeared, for example, in gilded pelmet

boxes, with the eagles supporting the curtains in their beaks. Also absorbed into the visual language of the style were pyramids, sphinxes, winged lions and crossed-spear motifs, plus striped tenting and chairs with sabre legs, all inspired by the military campaigns of the time against Napoleon, particularly in Egypt. Walls were often painted in deep colours like terracotta, maroon or yellow. As well as tented walls and ceilings, clouded ceilings were fashionable.

Curtain treatments were elaborate and multi-layered, with outer curtains, under-curtains, muslin curtains and sunblinds, either on poles or with deep valances, and with complex trimmings.

Renaissance: One of the great water-sheds of design started in Italy in the great *quattrocento*, the Italian equivalent to the glorious Greek fifth century BC. The Renaissance, meaning rebirth, was the first revival of the CLASSICAL style. It was most prevalent in the late

fourteenth and fifteenth centuries in Italy, where the northern Gothic style had never really taken root, but it lingered until the seventeenth century. It spread to France in the first half of the sixteenth century and then to Spain, the Netherlands and Germany. In England, a somewhat remote version resulted in the TUDOR style in the late sixteenth and early seventeenth centuries.

Renaissance revival: Also known as Neo-Renaissance, this was a much

favoured style on both sides of the Atlantic in the latter part of the nine-teenth century. Its heavy forms and elaborate decoration were actually taken from both the RENAISSANCE and the BAROQUE, and marked a return of interest in the NEOCLASSICAL style.

Restoration: The period after Charles II was restored to the British throne in 1660 following the CROMWELLIAN period. Restoration style was the first real English BAROQUE, impregnated with a sense of luxury and sumptuousness brought back by Charles from his sojourn at the grand court of Louis XIV. He imported Dutch, Flemish, Spanish and French craftsmen, but the most famous craftsman of the period was the woodcarver Grinling Gibbons. The taste for walnut started at this time, along with that for gilded gesso, silver decoration and marquetry. Panelling inspired by the *boiserie* at Versailles ran from the dado to the ceiling, capped by a sophisticated cornice, with smaller, rectangular panelling set under the chair rail. Made from oak or walnut, it was left in its natural state and waxed, or was sometimes marbled. Tapestries were often hung within the larger panels. Softwoods were frequently grained to resemble the more expensive walnut or oak. Mouldings and carvings were often gilded. If panelling was not used, walls were plastered and covered with damask or velvet. Cheaper alternatives were the new wallpapers. Oriental rugs began to be used on the parquet floors, rather than on tables. Adding to the richness were candle sconces in silver, brass and iron, and the first crystal chandeliers.

Rococo: This movement originated in France around 1700. The style was particularly identified with the reign of Louis XV and spread all over Europe during the early eighteenth century, particularly to Germany, Austria, Spain, Scandinavia and the Netherlands. It never reached quite the same heights of popularity in Britain and America, although there were many Rococo pattern books in circulation. A reaction to the formal heaviness of the BAROQUE, it was a light-hearted, frivolous style. Its decoration relied on shells and flowers, its forms were curved, its furniture more comfortable, its colours pastel. Candles were reflected a hundred times by mirrors; windows were enlarged; the forms and motifs of CHINOISERIE were embraced, as well as anything to do with monkeys, often dressed up in human clothes.

Rococo revival: Also known as Neo-Rococo, this curvilinear, rather florid nineteenth-century style started in Britain, where French taste was once again vastly admired, in spite of the Napoleonic Wars. It was popular too in France, where it was known as *le style Pompadour*, during the reign of Louis-Philippe (1830–48). It reached Germany during the second half of the century and from there spread to the United States.

Santa Fe: See AMERICAN SOUTH-WEST.

Shaker: A style loosely based on the simple, functional interiors of America's Shaker sect, founded in 1774 but at their most populous in the first half of the nineteenth century. They are best known for their beautifully crafted, clean-lined wood furniture, much of it built-in, their stacking oval boxes with dovetail joints and their habit of hanging chairs, brooms, mirrors, baskets, etc, on peg rails around the room, to keep the floors clear. They held that 'beauty rests on utility' – a philosophy that was, in many ways, a precursor to the late nineteenth- and early twentieth-century doctrine of functionalism, and the American architect Louis Sullivan's famous tenet, 'form follows function'.

Troubadour: French, nineteenth-century version of the NEO-GOTHIC style, much influenced by the cult of medievalism. Gothic decoration was applied to furniture, tapestries and small objects.

Tudor: Roughly the first half of the sixteenth century, this style-period covers the reign of the English Tudor monarchs, apart from the ELIZABETHAN period of Elizabeth I. Gothic forms still predominated at the beginning of the

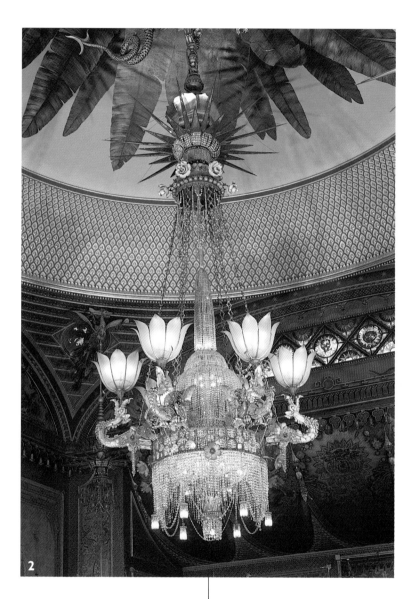

period but were being slowly diffused by the gradual introduction of ideas from the Renaissance. Pargetting (decorative plasterwork), very often richly coloured, covered the ceilings with Tudor roses, scrolls, cartouches and fleurs-de-lis. Walls were generally panelled, and the field (centre) of the panel was usually carved with a linenfold design.

Victorian: The umbrella title given to the period of Queen Victoria's reign in Britain from 1837 to 1901. In fact, the

name was given to most nineteenth-century design all over the world during that time. It included an eclectic mixture of nostalgic revivalist styles, like Neo-Baroque, Neo-Renaissance, Neo-Rococo and so on, as well as the avant-garde reactions to this selectivity, like the ARTS AND CRAFTS MOVEMENT, THE AESTHETIC MOVEMENT and ART NOUVEAU.

Vienna Secession: In Germany and Austria, at the beginning of the twentieth century, the newly established

1 *William Palmer House in Michigan, USA, designed in the early twentieth century by the great American architect Frank Lloyd Wright, one of the 'Prairie School' of architects.*

2 *The gasolier hanging down from the great dome in the Banqueting Hall of the Royal Pavilion, Brighton, England, includes a Chinoiserie dragon perching on the chain. The Royal Pavilion was designed for the Prince Regent by John Nash during the Regency period.*

Vienna Secession group began designing deliberately stark buildings with integrated interiors. Walls were plain plaster, devoid of cornices and mouldings. These were the precursors to standardized mass housing.

William and Mary: This BAROQUE style, practised in the late seventeenth century in Britain then in America, was named after the joint reign in Britain of the Dutch William III (1689–1702) and his English wife, Mary II (1689–94). It was a more toned-down style than the exuberant Restoration period that preceded it, and a precursor of the splendid early eighteenth-century QUEEN ANNE style. William brought with him a whole team of Dutch craftsmen, as well as promulgating his own taste for the blue-and-white porcelain being shipped from China by the Dutch East India Company. This was also the time when many Huguenot craftsmen, among them the renowned cabinetmaker Daniel Marot, were forced to flee France for Britain by Louis XIV's revocation of the Edict of Nantes. This injected a whole new vigour into British craftsmanship.

part one: the basics

PART TWO

THE SPECIFICS

The walls and ceiling are the largest part of the framework of a room, and, although not necessarily as expensive to cover as floors and windows, the ways in which you choose to treat them can either make or break the overall effect of the room. Historically, walls have always merited decorative interest and attention, and ceilings were almost always treated rather elaborately right up to the 1920s. Sadly, from then on, most of them reverted to a boring blankness. Yet, for both ceilings and walls, there is a great deal that can be done which can alter the whole atmosphere of a room.

Walls and Ceilings

Decorative Options

It is one thing to decide between paint, plain plaster, paper, fabric, mirror or panelling for the walls and ceiling of a room – it is quite another to know the extent of all those options. Most people need an injection of ideas for what to do with such wide expanses, as well as advice on how to make the most of the plethora of techniques used today.

SPATIAL EFFECTS

As already mentioned in connection with colour (see page 47), what you choose to do to the walls and ceiling can make a significant difference not just to a room's character, mood and style but also to its seeming proportions and size. In fact, the clever use of pattern, texture and architectural details, as well as colour, can make it look smaller or longer, wider or narrower, cooler or warmer, lighter or darker and disguise any eyesores.

Of course, the *actual* space can also be altered, through structural changes such as adding walls or taking them away, which, unless they are load-bearing, is comparatively easy. By the same token, ceilings can be lowered physically, either to make proportions better or to form a deep-enough recess to install good lighting, especially for art and objects. Sometimes, too, ceilings can even be raised without too much expense, as long as there is enough space below the room above.

I *The elegant double doors and well-proportioned shelves in this room are actually cunningly executed* trompe l'oeil. *It is stunningly realistic.*
2 *A shoji screen has been used as a room divider between this kitchen and living space, letting light through and creating an attractive division where before there might have been an uninteresting wall.*

3 *A very grand trompe l'oeil curtain and tented ceiling are painted over and above the wide blue and white stripes in a tiled dressing-lobby area off a bathroom. The illusion is all the stronger for the propped processional lantern and the exotic gilded archway.*

part two: the specifics

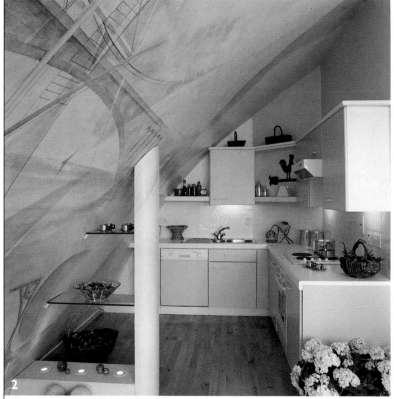

3 An elaborately painted and plastered ceiling and painted wall panels give these two rooms a feeling of great grandeur even though the furniture and curtains are comparatively simple. The fireplace and the various bronzes are balancing features.

DECORATIVE CEILINGS

Decorative ceilings are a great source of pleasure in old houses and apartment buildings and are a source of wonder in some of the stately homes, châteaux and *palazzi* open to the public. Ceilings have been a blank canvas, so to speak, for beams, mouldings, *trompe l'oeil* effects, pictorial scenes, designs and paint finishes for centuries. The eighteenth-century architect and designer Robert Adam used designs on the ceiling that were taken from a room's woven carpets.

Yet ever since the late 1920s and early '30s, ceilings have been more or less ignored. We have got into the habit of creating a smooth surface, erasing lumps and bumps, cracks and stains as much as possible and then simply painting them, most often in white.

1 A canopy of billowing striped sheer fabric is threaded gently over the tops of beams in this bedroom, both to 'lower' the double-height ceiling and to soften and lighten the spare four-poster bed and simple side tables. The white floor, ceiling and walls make the lines of the furniture and the design of the bedspread stand out in sharp relief.

2 The sharply sloping ceiling in an attic kitchen has been painted to look like stretched and slightly wrinkled fabric, which gives the illusion of somewhat more space than there is. The glass shelf structure on the left of the room looks as if it is piercing right through the faux material.

part two: the specifics

1

If ceilings are a reasonable height:

- Edge the top of the cornice, if there is one, with strips of brass or with lengths of gilt picture frame moulding fixed end-to-end.
- Paint the top stringing of a cornice (the part that edges out onto the ceiling) in a contrast colour, or cover it with gold or silver leaf.
- Add mouldings, such as a cornice or a ceiling rose, if you do not have them already. The most beautiful, and most expensive, are plaster mouldings. But if the ceiling is fairly high, you could use fibreglass or polypropylene mouldings, which are less expensive, easy to fix and difficult to tell from the real thing at a distance.

If ceilings are too high:

- Install a picture rail about 45cm (18in) below the ceiling, and paint the wall above it in the ceiling colour, to bring the eye down.
- Paint the ceiling a darker shade than the walls.
- Lower the ceiling and take the opportunity to install some recessed lighting, which will draw attention to what is on the walls.
- Add a chair rail and dado to break up the height of the walls. (For painted or papered dados, see page 107.)

If ceilings are too low:

- Vertically striped paper or painted stripes lead the eye up to give the illusion of more height.
- Install curtain pelmets just below the ceiling (rather than just above the tops of the windows) to make the windows appear taller, and so in turn exaggerate the ceiling height.
- Make tall, narrow panels for the walls using moulding, paint or paper, again to draw the eye upwards.
- Use a shimmer paint on the ceiling.
- Install cool fluorescent tubes and stretch voile or double-thickness cheesecloth just below, to light up the ceiling and make it appear to float.

2

In a well-proportioned modern room, I would agree with the dictum that 'less is more'. But it is the dull, unadorned whites and creams with no integral interest that we should do something to enliven. Occasionally one sees a cloud-painted ceiling, a mural, some tongue-and-groove panelling or even a ceiling simply painted or tinted darker than the walls, but all these examples are rare. Yet uninteresting rooms can be made to look altogether more distinguished by giving the ceiling a special treatment. Possibilities include applying mouldings or cornices, giving them a specialist paint treatment, using fabric to create a tented effect or pasting up a striking ceiling paper.

In the box on the right are some recommendations for rooms of different heights, but obviously the choices

1 This exceptionally high-ceilinged room also has extremely tall windows, so the deep squares formed by the beams draw your attention to the ceiling as well as helping the proportions of the room. The ceiling is further enhanced by the branch used as a fanciful chandelier.

you make will have to be governed by common sense, practicality, suitability and, of course, cost.

All the same, there are so many new materials and new methods, and updated revivals of old techniques, that it is helpful to know something about the range of possibilities.

2 Dark vertically striped paper makes a somewhat low-ceilinged room seem much taller – an illusion that is helped by the tall, skinny floor lamp and the large urns.

3 The kitchen ceiling is made to seem lower through the use of dark paint. The low-hanging light fitting and gleaming floor also help to detract from the height.

4 Painted trim in this airy space is cleverly placed on the tongue-and-groove panelling to give the illusion of a tray ceiling. The same trim used as coving as well as around corners, window frames and the French doors makes the space seem very crisp and clean. Note the painted blue-and-white floor and how the blue is repeated in the sofa upholstery and the bench outside.

3

4

part two: the specifics

A Guide to Paint

Paint is a wonderfully versatile medium. Not only is there a huge range of colours available today, but virtually any shade can be mixed, whether by trial and error at home or by computer in a paint shop. It comes in a variety of textures and finishes, and in a choice of covering and protective qualities. Moreover, it can be used not just in the conventional way but also to simulate more precious surfaces.

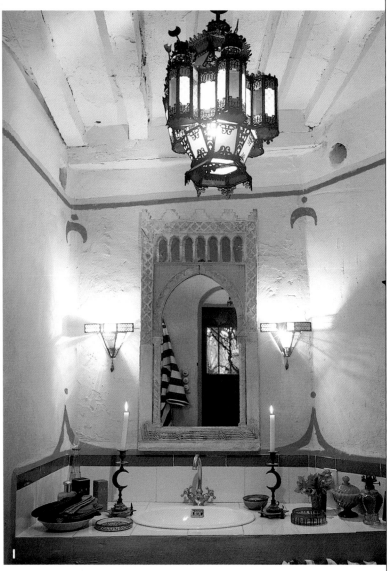

PAINT VARIETIES

Paint basically consists of a pigment dispersed in some sort of binder, along with a solvent which makes the paint more workable and which evaporates when the paint dries. Some paints also contain resins or silicas to provide particular characteristics, such as quick-drying or anti-mildew qualities, textural effects or special finishes that at one time could only be achieved by skilled decorative painters. For example, ranges are now available that emulate fabric, suede, leather, 'wet looks', verdigris and antique patinas.

Most paints are either water-based or oil-based. Both types come in several different finishes, which grade from dull to shiny in increments known variously as matt or flat, eggshell, satin, silk, semi-gloss and high gloss. Oil-based paints are going out of favour because of their white-spirit content. Water-based paints are combinations of resins (usually vinyl or acrylic) in water suspensions. Today, 'high-tech' acrylics and vinyl silks, used in conjunction with acrylic primers or undercoats and with acrylic varnishes, are giving much the same professional finishes as those that used to be achieved with oil-based paints.

The main advantages of water-based paints over the oil-based variety are that water-based paints dry more quickly, leave no smell and can be washed off hands and out of clothes. They used to be less hard-wearing, less easy to wipe down and less attractive. However, all these disadvantages have been dispatched with the advent of the new colourwashes and varnishes. These can be applied afterwards (and even on top of existing emulsion walls or vinyl

silk woodwork), to give interesting translucent depths as well as durability to even the flattest of surfaces.

Non-drip paints

Both water- and oil-based paints are available in non-drip versions which do not need thinning or stirring, so that they can be applied immediately from tin to wall or ceiling. Trays of 'solid' emulsion, complete with a roller, are virtually drip-proof and so are especially useful for ceilings.

Acrylic paints

Acrylics cover well and dry quickly, with less smell than oil-based paints.

Epoxy enamels

These have a hard gloss finish which resists dirt and abrasion and can be used on ceramic tiles (as well as on masonry, metal, fibreglass and porcelain). They are therefore ideal for painting over tiled walls in a kitchen or bathroom that is not to your taste. However, they do need careful handling and a long drying time, so follow the instructions on the tin carefully.

Textured enamels

As they dry, textured enamels separate to give a 'crazed' finish, so they are useful for painting wood panelling (as well as wood furniture and lamp bases), although a more subtle antique effect can be achieved in other ways (see page 101).

Distemper or whitewash

There has been an impressive revival of this primitive old paint, which consists of a chalk, known as whiting, dissolved in water and animal glue, with pigments added. It has long been used inside old houses because it lets the walls 'breathe', allowing moisture from damp walls to pass through it. But the reason for its recent revival is its soft, subtle colour ranges and lovely powdery appearance (yet, if made with a good-quality rabbit-skin glue, it is not a powder that readily sheds). Moreover, only one coat is needed.

with the colour, brush it on with a large, wide brush in regular vertical stripes, brushing one way only and as evenly as possible.

One disadvantage is that, although you can go on applying one coat over another, you will have to strip it all off if you want to use conventional (ie. synthetic) paint at any time. Another drawback is that it is not washable

2

Remember, though, that it will dry much lighter than it looks, so when you are tinting it, let a sample dry first to determine whether you need more pigment. (If you are in a hurry, you can speed up the process by drying it with a hair dryer.) When you are satisfied

and cannot be varnished. However, some versions contain a little linseed oil to help counteract this. Alternatively, casein paint – which the American settlers knew as milk paint – looks similar to distemper but is more water-resistant and durable.

PAINT ALCHEMY

Many transformations can be produced through simple tricks with paint:

- Delineate a dull space with bands of colour, by painting skirting boards and/or mouldings in a shade that contrasts with light-coloured walls. Repeat the skirting-board shade in the border of a rug or carpet.

- Paint two or three bands of subtle colour in different widths on the walls, starting from just above the skirting board.

- Form a false cornice by painting one or two 5–7.5cm (2–3in) stripes immediately under the ceiling.

- For an interesting panelled look, stick rectangles of contrasting tape on plain painted walls, spacing them evenly.

- Disguise so-called eyesores – a confusion of unboxed pipes, off-centre doors or windows or too many breaks in ceiling levels, for example up a tall staircase – by painting the area in a dark colour so that everything melds together. Crispness can be regained with a pale floor covering.

- On the principle 'if you cannot hide it, brazen it out', make a confusion of pipes look sculptural and interesting by picking them out in contrast paint.

1 A fanciful Middle Eastern feeling has been given to this bathroom by the painted motifs and borders on the walls as well as the exotic coloured glass lights and the painted plaster-framed mirror. The sickle-moon, candlesticks and ceramics on the granite basin surround add to the Islamic influences.
2 Deeper yellow squares and rectangles make a most interesting abstract design, as well as confusing the angles on this wall.

part two: the specifics

TINTING AND APPLYING A GLAZE

When you tint a glaze, start with a small amount of tinting medium and slowly build up the amount of colour until you get the shade you want.

- Squeeze a blob of artist's oil paint or stainer into an old saucepan and stir in several tablespoons of turpentine or white spirit. Mix thoroughly until smooth. Test this mixture on a small area of wall prepared with your base coat.

- If you want to add more colour or change the tone slightly, mix a bit more tint with some turpentine or white spirit in another old pan. Add this to the glaze and test again. Continue until you get the exact shade you want, but never add the artist's oil colour or the stainer straight from the tube, as it will not readily homogenize.

- Be sure the base coat is completely dry and then apply the glaze evenly and confidently using a sponge or rag and working in vertical strips. Keep it at the same consistency, and work quickly to avoid drips and clumps. Once the glaze is applied, it will dry fast.

- When the glazed finish has dried for 24 hours, you may want to varnish it. This will not only protect the glaze but will also tend to darken the finish slightly, giving it a mellow look. It is available in flat, semi-gloss and gloss versions. Apply it with a roller, and brush it out with a large brush to get rid of any bubbles.

COLOURWASHES

A colourwash is applied with a sponge or a decorator's brush over a base coat of matt emulsion – even over existing emulsion on walls or woodwork – to give an attractive transparent finish of much greater subtlety than just plain paint. Colourwashes are available commercially, or you can make your own using a dye known as a universal stainer. Or, you can simply mix small amounts of artist's gouache or acrylic colour with water, and add the mixture, a little at a time, to soft-white emulsion that has been diluted with water in a proportion of at least three parts water to one part paint.

TRADITIONAL PAINT TREATMENTS

In previous centuries, paint colours had to be mixed individually, rather like an artist mixing tones on his palette. The inferior grinding of pigments often gave an uneven, textured quality to walls.

Early decorators practised many special paint effects on walls, as well as on woodwork and furniture. At first, the techniques were used to simulate more expensive materials such as rare hardwoods or marble, and were truly *faux* ('false') finishes, but soon they were also being used simply for their decorative effect.

Today these same techniques are enjoying renewed popularity, and they still fall into the category of either a decorative finish (such as dragging, stippling, stencilling and so on) or a *faux* finish (which imitates other materials like marble, tortoiseshell, lapis lazuli, various woods, malachite and ivory). Whether you want to experiment yourself or just commission various finishes, it is useful to know something about the main techniques.

GLAZES

Most special paint effects rely on glazes, which either are applied over a dry, opaque base coat in order to give a translucent effect or are distressed in some way to achieve a particular effect like dragging, ragging or stippling.

A glaze is a transparent film, usually tinted, and it adds richness and depth to any wall treatment. If a glaze is tinted with a hue from the same colour family as the base coat, the resulting shade will be a delicately deepened tone. On the other hand, if the glaze and the base coat are from different colour families, the resulting colour will be an entirely new one, with the additional richness of translucence.

Any glazing technique will look better with colours that are similar in intensity, or with a darker colour over a

lighter one. A Sienna brown glaze over deep green, for example, produces a lovely terracotta; dark grey over Pompeian red looks like Moroccan leather; and dark green over medium green makes walls a subtle jade.

Glazing liquids, often called scumble glazes, are available at good paint shops. Traditionally, they were oil-based, but now water-based acrylic glazes are also available. You will need a smaller amount of glaze than you would of paint because you will be applying a thinner coat. It looks like canned cream of chicken soup to begin with, but if it seems too thick, it can be thinned down gently with white spirit.

1 *Trompe l'oeil* panels in sand and pale papaya counteract the elaborate white-painted plaster-work above them, as well as making an interesting background for the collection of ceramics on the chest.

2 *A tracery of twiggy trees painted onto the yellow walls in this hall adds a softness in contrast to the diamond-shaped floor tiles. The door has been dragged with the same cheerful yellow shade.*

3 *Deliberately uneven-textured walls in this old bedroom have been stencilled with white fleurs-de-lis which look good with the small but quite elaborate bedhead.*

part two: the specifics

1 *Mint green loosely ragged over blue-grey (used on its own for the room next door) creates an unusual effect.*

2 *A painted dado, chair rail and borders in 1930s colours look as ancient and worn as an Etruscan fresco, making an unusual background for the classic 1920s leather chair.*

3 *Printed leaf shapes (made by dipping real leaves in paint and patiently reapplying them to the wall) are strewn as thickly in this cloakroom as on an autumn path. Note how the mirrors have been painted in the same tones as the leaves, which look particularly mellow against the yellow walls and the various brass fittings.*

4 *Stippled apricot walls are paired with a dragged umber-tinted cream doorway in this vignette. Yellow stippled onto a red background makes a far truer apricot than any conventional or even specially mixed paint colour.*

ADDITIVE AND SUBTRACTIVE TECHNIQUES

Most decorative finishes can be classified as either additive or subtractive. With additive techniques, a glaze or wash is applied in a broken film over a dry base coat using a sponge or a rag (the texture affects the finish). Additive techniques are the simplest since the drying time of the glaze or wash is not critical and you can work on your own. It is best to work in vertical strips. Once the first glaze is dry, you can always add a further one on top or a second coat in a different shade.

With subtractive techniques, a glaze is rolled or brushed onto a dry base coat (usually an oil-based semi-gloss in soft white or cream) and then distressed with a sponge, a wad of tissue paper or of hessian, a soft rag, a stippling brush, a comb or another tool of your choice.

Subtractive methods are a great deal easier if done by two people: one to apply the glaze and the other to distress it, since you have to work quickly before the glaze dries.

The effects you get with techniques like ragging, rag-rolling, sponging and shading depend upon whether they are done with a colourwash or a glaze, and they can be done using either additive or subtractive methods. Stippling, dragging and combing are best done with glaze in subtractive mode.

DRAGGING

Dragging is achieved by applying a glaze of transparent colour over a chosen base coat (semi-gloss so that the glaze doesn't sink into the surface) and then dragging a dry, wide brush through it before it dries. The glaze is generally a darker shade than the undercoat, and the resulting softly textured look of fine, irregular vertical striations gives a distinguished look to a wall or woodwork.

STIPPLING

Stippling is a little less difficult than dragging but just as decorative. It is often used in conjunction with dragging – for example, dragged mouldings and a stippled ground on panelled walls. It can look as soft as chamois leather, or as pitted as an orange peel, for stippled walls are dappled with flecks of colour without emphatic definition, allowing the base colour to become very much a part of the whole.

As with dragging, the tinted glaze is applied to the chosen semi-gloss base coat, and then removed with a professional stippling brush (available from specialist paint stores) or with a scrubbing brush. You can also use a large sponge for a more muted look.

RAGGING

Ragging is a more free-flowing and irregular version of stippling, which is therefore easier to do alone. It is good in a small space because the somewhat cloudy effect creates an illusion of airiness and softness. Ragging is done with a bunched-up rag or piece of cheesecloth, hessian or tissue paper. The coarser or crisper the material, the coarser or crisper the result.

Try rolling pastels over a creamy-white base coat. Alternatively, for an

part two: the specifics

extremely subtle look, use a tinted white over white, or an umber-tinted cream over cream.

LACQUERING

This ancient craft originated in the Far East. If done properly, the process is very time-consuming, since up to 40 coats of lacquer are applied, each of which is buffed and burnished with a pad of wire wool before the next coat can be applied. But the effect is as deeply rich as it is rewarding, and the surface is extremely hard-wearing. Happily, there are a number of

facsimile techniques which are less time-consuming, although they still require a good deal of patience.

If you are lacquering walls (as opposed to a piece of furniture, which is where it is more often used), you have to start with an absolutely smooth surface. The simplest method is to apply a couple of coats of thinned-down eggshell or high-gloss varnish over two or three coats of oil-based flat or semi-gloss paint, depending on how shiny you want your surface. A more complex method is to apply a series of tinted glazes over a base coat.

The whole is then varnished for protection and increased depth. This creates an extremely pretty deep gleam rather than a high gloss. Remember that, when you are applying varnish to any surface, the room must be totally free of dust.

ANTIQUING

Another very effective technique is antiquing. This artificially ages a surface, even one of the decorative surfaces described above, by applying either a 'dirty' wash or a glaze tinted with a small amount of raw umber, burnt umber or burnt sienna, which makes the surface appear softer and deeper and gently aged. You can either mix up your own or use a commercial 'ageing' liquid. Similarly, woodwork can be helped along to a distinguished old age by applying a light umber-tinted wash or glaze.

CRACKLE-GLAZE AND CRAQUELURE

These products are applied to painted surfaces to reproduce the network of fine cobwebbing that often appears in old painted and varnished surfaces. They are used to give modern materials – such as MDF (medium-density fibreboard), resin-manufactured objects and modern unit furniture – the verisimilitude of graceful ageing. Both products are available commercially. (An alternative method, which produces a realistic aged appearance, is to paint a surface with an acrylic or red oxide metal primer, and contrast it with matt emulsion colours, followed by polyurethane varnish, perhaps topped off with an antiquing glaze.)

GRISAILLE

This technique utilizes shading and highlighting to trick the eye into supposing that a surface is raised or indented. It was usually executed in greys, black and white, but it can also look effective in different shades of terracotta, or in umber and cream. It is effective for suggesting architectural details like panels, architraves and mouldings, but it also looks extremely good (if the application is skilful) in classical images like urns, caryatids, pilasters, columns and *putti* (cherubs).

STENCILLING

The ancient art of stencilling originated in China before 3000 BC and was apparently used in Europe from the sixth century AD. It continued to grow as a popular form of decoration up until the eighteenth century, and was popular once again in the nineteenth century. It was favoured by the early settlers in America, where it was used instead of more expensive wallpapers (and was also used on floors, furniture, bed linen and window hangings). Now many popular wallpapers emulate stencilling – *plus ça change*.

In any event, it is a useful and decorative art to practise and is fairly easy. Just remember that stencils look a good deal better in soft, slightly uneven colours that do not look too newly applied. Instant ageing can be applied here, either by rubbing it with fine wire wool or by painting over the design with a thin wash of off-white emulsion or an umber-tinted glaze or varnish.

PLAIN PLASTER

Plaster, which used to be the main ingredient of an interior wall, should not be forgotten. Old-fashioned plaster walls were made by trowelling layers of a mixture of lime and wet sand onto a wire mesh, which meant walls could be curved and variously shaped, if so desired. After six months or so of waiting for the plaster to dry out, it was generally painted or papered, although its natural creamy pink colour is a nice finish in itself, particularly if sealed or wax-polished. Today, comparatively few walls are made like this, but you can apply a skim coat of plaster to chipboard, MDF (medium-density fibreboard) or plasterboard.

Plaster can be left natural, or it can be textured with marble or metallic powder for a sparkle, or, more roughly, with straw, wood chips or sawdust. The purest finish of all is obtained by burnishing with kaolin (available from builders' merchants), which is used to whiten porcelain. Rubbed onto plaster, it makes it a gleaming pure white.

part two: the specifics

Vocabulary of Paint Terms

Old black-and-white framed photographs contrast well with a patchy, threadbare wall in an Indian palace. This look can be emulated by distressing or antiquing a wall but here it is entirely genuine.

Acrylic colours: Quick-drying artist's colours, which are excellent for STENCILLING. The PIGMENTS are mixed in a water-soluble polyacrylic base, resulting in clear, matt colours. Can be used diluted with water for a transparent effect or undiluted for an opaque effect.

Acrylic varnish: See VARNISH.

Antiquing: Artificially ageing paint, usually by rubbing over the new paint surface with a 'dirtying' GLAZE or a COLOURWASH of raw umber, burnt umber or burnt sienna. (On furniture, the surface may then be wiped over with a cloth, leaving the darker colour in the crevices.) Antiquing also applies to rubbing off new paint with wire wool to give a patchy, threadbare look.

Badger softener: Finest badger-hair brush to blend and soften a COLOURWASH or a GLAZE that has been applied with a different brush, a sponge or a rag and is not yet dry. A DUSTING BRUSH is a less expensive substitute.

Bagging: Creating a textured finish by wrapping a rolled-up cloth in a plastic bag, and then working over a newly applied oil-glazed surface either in a particular pattern or at random. Never do more than 2 square metres (2 square yards) at a time, or the GLAZE will dry before it has been textured.

Base coat: Applied before topcoats of paint or glaze to give a good surface and coverage. If you are painting over a dark colour with a light one, you may need two coats of base coat and one topcoat. (It is a good idea to thin the first coat with a little water.) If you are painting a dark topcoat over a light base coat, tint the base coat with a little of the topcoat or buy an appropriately tinted standard base coat. A PRIMER is usually used on a new surface like wood or plaster before applying a base coat.

Blackboard paint: Used for creating a blackboard on a surface, such as on a portion of wall in a child's room or on a large piece of primed and undercoated board fixed to a wall.

Broken colour: Two or more coats of different-coloured paint, in which the top layer(s) have been partially removed to reveal the colour beneath.

Brushes: Many different specialized brushes are used in painting, depending on the method used. These include a BADGER SOFTENER, DECORATOR'S BRUSH, DRAGGER, DUSTING BRUSH, FITCH, FLOGGER, MOTTLER, OVER-GRAINER, STENCILLING BRUSH, STIPPLING BRUSH and SWORDLINER.)

Buttermilk paint: See MILK PAINT.

Button polish: See SHELLAC.

Casein paint: A paint made from pigments in a casein (milk-curd) medium. It is opaque and powdery (though less powdery than DISTEMPER). Use it thinned with two parts water for a COLOURWASH, or with white casein for cream and pastel shades. Tough, water-resistant and inexpensive, but not widely available.

Cissing: The reverse of SPATTERING, this is achieved by applying a GLAZE or COLOUR-WASH to a dry base coat, and then, while the glaze or colourwash is still wet, spattering on white spirit or turpentine (for oil-based paint) or water (for water-based paint).

Colourwash: A delicate, transparent wash of colour. It was traditionally achieved with watered-down, tinted DISTEMPER but today is generally done using a proprietary product or an EMULSION, GOUACHE or ACRYLIC paint diluted with water.

Combing: Broken finish, or a pattern such as basket-weave, achieved by dragging a coarse comb of specially cut stiff cardboard or plastic, or of wood or steel, through a wet GLAZE.

Crackle-glaze: Obtainable from specialist paint shops to imitate the effect of old, peeling paint. Crackle-glaze is applied between two different-coloured coats of water-based paint, producing a network of cracks in the top layer of paint through which the underneath layer is visible.

Craquelure: A method in which two VARNISHES that dry at different rates are applied to a painted surface to imitate the crazing that develops in layers of old varnish. It produces finer crazing than CRACKLE-GLAZE but is expensive.

Decorator's brush: A thickly bristled brush ranging from 12mm (½in) to 15cm (6in) in width and used for painting walls and other large, flat surfaces.

Distemper: Powdery paint which can be mixed to make extremely pretty pastel colours and COLOURWASHES. Also known as whitewash, it is made from animal glue, whiting (finely ground chalk), pigments and water.

Distressing: Making surfaces look older and time-worn through techniques such as BROKEN COLOUR.

Dragger: A long-bristled brush used for dragging.

Dragging: The process of dragging a dry brush such as a DRAGGER or FLOGGER through a wet GLAZE or COLOURWASH to produce an irregular, fine-lined effect.

Dusting brush: Used for small-scale stippling work, such as on a skirting board, but can also be used for softening and blending instead of a BADGER SOFTENER, or for dragging instead of a DRAGGER. The soft, medium-length bristles should be very carefully cleaned and never immersed in solvent or the bristles will drop out.

Emulsion: Water-based paint consisting of pigment bound in a synthetic resin. It is available in matt or flat, silk, satin or sheen, and gloss finishes. Soluble in water, it is quick-drying and does not necessarily need an undercoat. Matt and vinyl silk emulsions are available; the vinyl silk is more durable and is wipable.

Enamel: Oil-based paint which is so dense that only one coat is needed; most often used for small areas of wood or metalwork.

Epoxy enamel: A tough oil-based ENAMEL paint with a hard finish that resists dirt, grease and scratches. Ideal for painting over ceramic tiles as well as over porcelain, fibreglass, masonry and metal.

Fitch: A small, rather stiff-bristled brush used for small-scale work, such as detailed STIPPLING work and SPATTERING. Available in fan, angled, oval and flat shapes.

Flogger: A long-bristled brush used for DRAGGING and GRAINING, as it picks up the GLAZE easily when pulled across the surface. The brush is used with a slapping technique.

Gilding: Adding a gold finish. Traditional gilding uses gold leaf, or some other metal leaf, which is fixed to a surface with GOLD SIZE. A gilt effect can be reproduced using bronze, silver or aluminium powders.

Glaze: Traditionally a transparent oil-based finish also known as scumble, but a water-based, acrylic glaze can now be obtained which is much faster-drying. A tinted glaze has to be applied before any sort of broken finish can be produced.

Glue size: See SIZE.

Gold size: A rapid-drying oil VARNISH, usually used as an adhesive in traditional GILDING and as a medium for some quick-drying paints.

Gouache: Beautiful concentrated colours in a water base which give an especially clear, fresh, matt finish. They can be used neat to decorate panelling (or furniture) or can be used to tint water-based colours or COLOURWASHES.

Graining: A highly specialized art reproducing every sort of wood grain using paint in a most realistic manner.

Japanning: Old term for LACQUERING, dating back to late seventeenth- and early eighteenth-century imitations of imported lacquerwork from the Far East.

Lacquering: A technique involving the patient application of many coats of VARNISH, one upon another, sanded down each time when dry before another coat is applied, to create a smooth, lustrous finish. The original lacquering technique, which was developed in the Far East, involved applying many layers of a lacquer made from the sap of the lac tree. Lacquering is used for furniture, but a lacquer effect on walls can be produced by applying eggshell or high-gloss varnish over paint (with a roller to avoid brush strokes) or by using a tinted GLAZE.

Limewash: A version of DISTEMPER that uses slaked lime instead of whiting in its composition. It has a caustic action and so can irritate the skin.

Liming: The process of 'whitening' wood, particularly oak. Excellent for new panelling and for elderly, as opposed to

old, oak furniture. Use the new liming paste which incorporates an inert white pigment and no caustic lime.

Lining brush: A thin brush used to make narrow decorative lines. Artist's sable brushes work very well, or a SWORDLINER can be used.

Marbling: The technique of producing *faux* marble. This can either copy a particular type of marble as closely as possible or give the general effect of marble. The latter approach is sometimes known as marbleizing.

Milk paint: A simple CASEIN PAINT, in which powder colours are mixed with buttermilk or skimmed milk. It was widely used in Colonial America and produces lovely, clear colours and a smooth, flat finish. Protect with matt VARNISH.

Mottler: A brush used to mottle, highlight or distress GLAZES when GRAINING.

Oil paint: This comes in three finishes: gloss, semi-gloss or eggshell, and matt or flat. It is soluble in white spirit or turpentine and takes much longer to dry than water-based varieties.

Over-grainer: Very small brush with clumps of soft hairs like individual long-pointed artist's brushes. It is used to add fine details or a darker grain to a GRAINED surface – in other words, to delicately *add* colour, rather than take it off as most paint-finish brushes do.

Pigment: The colouring element of paints. It is available in many forms, including powder; compressed cakes or blocks; artist's oil, GOUACHE or ACRYLIC colours; and universal STAINERS. In general, like should be mixed with like – SOLVENT-thinned pigment with solvent-thinned paint, and water-thinned powders with water-thinned paint – but universal stainers can be mixed with either oil- or water-based paints.

Polyurethane varnish: See VARNISH.

Priming: A primer is generally used on new surfaces (wood or plaster) to seal it before applying an UNDERCOAT and then the final finishes.

Ragging: Using rags to achieve a particular painted finish. The exact finish depends upon the type of fabric used.

Rag-rolling: Using a rolled rag to get the desired effect when RAGGING.

Rottenstone: Fine, grey abrasive powder, bought from specialist paint shops. It is mixed with lemon oil, baby oil or sunflower oil to form a paste, which can be used to give the final polish to a wall that has been varnished.

Scumble: See GLAZE.

Shellac: A quick-drying spirit-based VARNISH, available in 'transparent' form (actually, a yellowy-brown), orange or white (which is almost clear) and a form called 'knotting'. The knotting variety is used to seal knots on new wood surfaces. Orange shellac, also known as button polish, can be used to go over metal leaf to simulate gold.

Size: Also known as glue size, this serves as a medium to bind paint. In addition, it can be used as a sealant, instead of PRIMER, to prevent fresh plaster (and also unpainted wood) from absorbing too much paint when being painted, or too much paste when being wallpapered. Plastic-based sizes such as PVA (polyvinyl acrylic) are used with synthetic paints like EMULSION, and animal sizes with natural paints such as DISTEMPER and CASEIN PAINTS. The best quality is made from rabbit skin.

Solvents: Used to dilute paint, GLAZE or VARNISH and to clean brushes. WHITE SPIRIT and TURPENTINE are both solvents for oil-based products, and water is the solvent for water-based products.

Spattering: A simple, BROKEN-COLOUR technique that consists of spattering a dry surface with dots of colour. It is an additive technique.

Sponging: This technique can either be additive (by sponging colour onto a previously painted surface) or subtractive (by dabbing GLAZE off for a distressed effect). Either way, it is one of the easiest finishes to achieve.

Stainers: Synthetic dyes, which are obtainable in good artist's suppliers and paint shops. They can be used for tinting paints and GLAZES. Universal stainers can be used for either oil-based or water-based paints.

Stencilling: The application, usually repeated, of paint through cut-out shapes in a stencil, using a STENCILLING BRUSH or sponge. A stencil that will be used on walls should be cut from oiled manila card or acetate to make it long-lasting.

Stencilling brush: A short, plump brush with shorn-off hog's-hair bristles, which looks rather like a shaving brush. It gives a more interesting effect with a crisper edge than an ordinary brush.

Stippling: A good, soft finish for a large area. The effect is produced by gently dabbing a STIPPLING BRUSH against a wet GLAZE or coat of paint.

Stippling brush: A rectangular brush with long and short detachable handles. The long one is used for STIPPLING walls, the short for close work. It lifts off fine flecks of paint to produce the typical stippled and freckled effect very well indeed. Cheaper alternatives are a man's old hairbrush or an old clothes brush.

Swordliner: A type of LINING BRUSH used for making fine, thin lines, particularly in MARBLING. Its bristles taper to a point.

Trompe l'oeil: Literally, to trick or deceive the eye by painting illusionist effects, particularly using shading and highlighting, and perspective.

Turpentine: A SOLVENT used for cleaning brushes as well as for thinning artist's oil paints.

Undercoat: Standard paint to apply as a thin, dry coat before main coats of paint for a better finish.

Universal stainers: See STAINERS.

Varnish: Final transparent layer to harden and protect a decorative finish. Varnishes come in matt or flat, semi-gloss and gloss finishes. The quick-drying acrylic varnishes, which are water-based, are superseding polyurethane and oil-based varnishes.

Verdigris: The blue-green shade that copper and bronze turn with age. It can be replicated in paint on any surface.

Wash: See COLOURWASH.

White spirit: A SOLVENT used to dilute oil-based GLAZE or paint and to soften old EMULSION finishes.

Whitewash: See DISTEMPER.

part two: the specifics

Wallpapers

Wallpapers, from cheerful stripes to the most opulent scenic papers, are quick to set a mood. They cheer up a dull room, change the feeling, style and apparent proportions, and give a proper unity. They are also extremely useful for disguising flawed or uneven walls. An enormous choice of patterned, textured and plain, or almost plain, papers is available today, from the inexpensive machine-made variety to expensive hand prints. In addition, there are separate borders (which can be used on plain walls or on top of paper); borders that match or coordinate with papers; friezes; and papers in different scales of the same design to be used together.

In fact, the difficulty is more one of narrowing down the choice than of finding a paper that is suitable within a price range.

LINING PAPER

If your ceiling or walls are really uneven, lining paper will help achieve a good finish. The heavier the lining, the better it will hide defects. On walls it should be hung horizontally and stuck precisely edge-to-edge so that no bulge will show through when the actual wallpaper is put on.

VINYL WALLPAPERS

Vinyl wallpapers are waterproof and tougher than so-called washable papers, because they are made from polyvinyl chloride with a backing, rather than being just a paper with a plastic coating. They can be scrubbed (with slight, not heavy, pressure) as opposed to the gentle washing which is all that washable papers can withstand. Vinyl papers are, therefore, a good choice for bathrooms, kitchens and children's rooms, as well as halls and passageways or anywhere that walls are likely to be touched a lot.

However, they must be stuck on with a fungicidal adhesive, otherwise a disagreeable mould can form beneath.

TEXTURED PAPERS

These heavy wallpapers with their embossed patterns are particularly useful for covering irregular surfaces. Designed to be painted over, they are most often used for dados in hallways because of their durability. The best-known examples are Lincrusta and Anaglypta. The other principal type of textured paper is flock wallpaper, with a relief pattern that imitates cut velvet. Textured papers go in and out of fashion; they were very popular in the eighteenth century, at the end of the nineteenth century and from the 1930s to the late 1950s, and are now often seen again.

Some coloured and neutral hessians, grass-cloths, silks, linens, felts and foils can be bought with a paper backing, enabling them to be hung like ordinary wallpaper. In fact, many firm materials that are suitable for covering a wall can have a backing superimposed, so that you can achieve the luxury of a fabric-lined room without the trouble of battening or upholstering the walls.

FACTORS TO CONSIDER

Before finally settling on a paper, spend time thinking about the effect you want to create. Pin up a length of paper on the wall. Try it out with window treatments and upholstery fabrics, both existing and possible, before you make a final choice. Look at patterned papers carefully. It might not be apparent in a small sample that a floral design is actually in stripes, or ogees, or on a diagonal, but they often are. So get samples showing repeats, and always familiarize yourself with the overall effect of a design before finally choosing.

When measuring up a room for wallpaper, bear in mind the size of the repeat in the design (this is almost always stated on the paper). Lengths of paper must, of course, be matched together perfectly.

1 *In an undistinguished room, an all-over patterned paper, used literally all over walls and ceiling, can inject instant character. The fabrics on the daybed and at the window tone in well, as does the painted chest cum coffee table.*
2 *A textured camel-coloured grass-cloth wall covering makes a good-looking background for the dark furniture and the striped rug and bed valance in this bedroom.*

3 *'Print room' paper on a creamy-yellow background recreates the feeling of an eighteenth-century print room, when engravings were stuck straight onto the walls and given exotic paper 'frames'.*

part two: the specifics

WALLPAPER BORDERS

Borders come in various depths and in every conceivable design, from florals, fanciful ribbons and swags, and children's motifs to china dogs, gardening and sporting themes; and from serious, seemingly three-dimensional copies of architectural mouldings to narrow solid-colour strips. No more than 5cm (2in) deep, the latter are useful for subtly delineating the perimeter and detailing of a room. Indeed, the chief roles of a border are either to define or to break up a given space, and either to take the place of missing architectural details or, if these exist, to define them further.

Borders at the tops of walls

The most common way to use a border is to buy one that coordinates with or matches your chosen paper, and run it around the top of the wall, just below the ceiling or just below the cornice if there is one.

Personally, I do not see the point of running a very deep border under an existing moulding because I think it makes walls look top-heavy (unless a ceiling is inordinately high, in which case it will help to lower it visually).

If there are existing, fairly elaborate mouldings, you might like to consider using one of the slim, solid-coloured borders, rather than a border

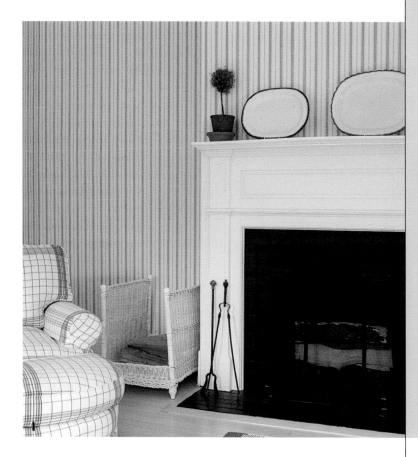

CHOOSING WALLPAPER PATTERNS

The kind of pattern you choose depends entirely on personal taste and the proportions of the room. There are, however, certain guidelines that make the task of choosing patterns easier.

- In a living room, it is preferable to use a simple design or fairly plain paper (such as a paper made to look like a decorative paint effect). Strong or definite patterns can be distracting and do not make good backgrounds for paintings and prints. A border or frieze is a good way to finish the paper off here.
- Dark papers generally make a room seem smaller.
- Vertical stripes will make a room seem taller.
- Horizontal stripes will seem to broaden out a space.
- Mini-prints, small geometrics, stripes, *faux* panels, linear prints, small florals or gentle modern abstracts can be successfully used in bedrooms.
- Small prints are a good choice for small bedrooms.
- More open patterns look best in larger spaces.
- Scenic and geometric designs, florals, large abstracts, papers with borders or trellis papers can be used to good effect in halls and corridors and on staircases. (Bear in mind that whatever you choose for the hallway in a house generally has to go up the stairs as well.)

that has been made to go with the paper. If the wallpaper is a stripe or *faux* finish or is fairly plain, this border could be in a tone that is deeper than the paper or contrasts with it. Or, if the paper is patterned, the border could be in a colour that appears in the paper. This will help define the demarcation point and draw attention to the moulding without competing with it for attention.

More border ideas

Of course, a border does not have to be used just with wallpaper. Any border that seems appropriate can be used on plain painted walls, either to take the place of an architectural moulding or simply to add a little pizzazz.

Borders can be run along the tops of skirting boards, around windows or doors, or even vertically down the corners of rooms. They also look highly effective when defining the angles of the sloping walls in an odd-shaped attic room.

Use a border to make a false chair rail, and then paste a contrasting or coordinating paper below it, to create a false dado. Or do the same on a plain painted wall, with either wallpaper or a different paint finish below. When you meet a doorway, either stop the border at one side and resume it on the other, or run it around the door as well. Another idea is to paste a narrow border both above and below an actual chair rail.

Making your own borders

Although it is a fiddly operation, it is often worthwhile cutting up wide borders and friezes to use in different ways around a room or in adjoining rooms or hallways. For example, if a border or frieze is many-edged, like an oriental rug, you can cut off some to form a narrow border to run around doors or windows. Or use them to form panels on a fairly plain background such as painted walls, leaving enough edge to frame the main border, which will go under the ceiling as usual.

Alternatively, buy extra border so that you can leave the main border alone and use the surplus to provide coordinating edges to define doors, skirting boards or the corners of a room, or to run around a corridor or bathroom off a bedroom.

Another way to create your own borders is to cut strips from any wallpaper that has the right linear design (such as side-by-side or vertical repeats or stripes). Or you can stick on ribbon, such as petersham, braid, cord or thick wool.

1 A simple striped paper is hard to beat for instant elegance. This one, teamed with checked cotton upholstery in a similar shade of blue, makes a good background for the bordered creamware platters arranged on the mantelshelf.
2 A mini-patterned 'little nothing' paper, again used on walls and ceiling, provides an effectively neutral background for a decorative bed and a print collection.
3 The deep swagged border pasted over black marbled paper in a high-ceilinged hall, already complete with cornice, helps to reduce the apparent height of the space, thus giving the illusion of much better proportions than actually exist.

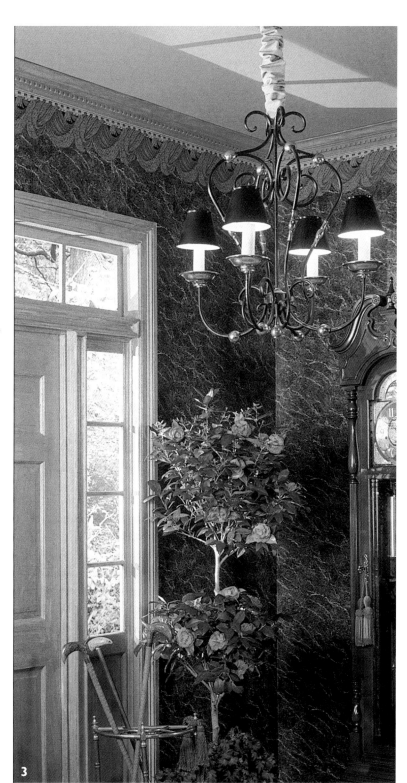

part two: the specifics

MAKING A LITTLE PAPER GO A LONG WAY

If your taste runs to very expensive wallpaper, you can get much of the effect at much less of the cost by the following ploys:

- Use it below a chair rail only. If you do not have a chair rail, create one (at chair-top height) with an appropriate moulding or a wallpaper border.
- Buy only one or two rolls, depending upon the size of the room, and cut the paper into panels (first working out the size of the panels on a plan of the walls drawn to scale on graph paper and then drawing them on the wall). Paste the paper within the drawn frames, and frame the panels with narrow wooden moulding, picture frame moulding or strips of paper border.
- Use one roll of paper like a very large painting on an empty wall, framing it with moulding or a paper border.

WALLPAPER FRIEZES

If a border is deep enough, it can justifiably be called a frieze. Some will even fill the entire space between picture rail and ceiling in a very high-ceilinged room, which will usually help to lower the height. If a high-ceilinged room has no mouldings, you can create the appearance of a picture rail by using a slim moulding in a coordinating or matching colour and then pasting a frieze above. You can also buy embossed friezes in materials like Lincrusta, which tend to emulate old

and ornamental plaster cornices, and are also generally deep enough to fill the gap between a picture rail and the ceiling. They need to be painted, and this can be done to imitate old plaster by 'antiquing' the paint (see page 101).

ILLUSIONIST DETAILS

Apart from all the conventional and unconventional ranges of papers and borders, you can choose from ranges of cut-out paper architectural details, scenic papers and wall panelling, to create your own architectural fantasies, interior follies and *trompe l'oeil* illusions. It is possible to buy elaborate paper swags and rosettes; columns (Doric, Ionic, Corinthian or Tuscan), pilasters, cornices and broken pediments; balustrades and balusters; arches and arched alcoves; urns, classical busts and statues; and scenic and sky papers.

Or you can use tongue-in-cheek 'panelled', 'book-lined' or 'print room' papers, which are especially fun in cloakrooms, small halls and corridors, dressing rooms and walk-in wardrobes. 'Railroading' (hanging rolls horizontally) panelled paper can create a very realistic-looking dado.

1 Narrow, plain-coloured borders can be used to create all kinds of perimeters and illusions, from delineating doors, windows and mouldings to making faux panelling and other shapes. Here, three colours to match the bed curtains have been pasted close together to outline a teenager's sleeping alcove.

2 *A cherubim grisaille border on grey craquelure-effect paper has been delineated with a plain blue band to match the grey and blue Classical-motif blinds.*

3 *'Bookshelf' or 'library' paper cut into a panel has been framed with a wood surround to make a tongue-in-cheek book collection.*

part two: the specifics

UNUSUAL PAPER WALL COVERINGS

It is, of course, quite possible to cover the walls with other sorts of paper. Although by no means meant for the purpose, they can look extraordinarily effective, given the will, the time and, in some cases, the skill.

Tissue paper

Once, in Spain, I saw a beautiful, ethereal room unlike anything I had seen before. The walls turned out to be covered in layers of pastel-coloured tissue paper, stuck over each other like *découpage* and given a top layer of plain white tissue and several coats of eggshell varnish. The pale blues and roses, yellows and greens gleamed softly through the white, making the walls look opalescent. This is a charming and inexpensive idea for a bedroom, combined with, say, a bed dressed chastely in white linens and a pale wood floor bleached, stained or painted white or grey.

Craft or wrapping paper and newspaper

Rolls of caramel-coloured, green or blue craft paper, or rolls of biscuit or caramel-coloured parcel wrapping paper, used matt side out, also make handsome rooms. The texture of the paper is attractive and the cost is small. However, although wider at 90cm (36in) than most wallpaper, it is somewhat thinner. Therefore, the wall will first need to be either painted in pale emulsion or hung with lining paper, because a bright paint colour or a patterned wallpaper would show through. Another drawback is that you have to buy whole rolls of paper. A minimum quantity is a 75m (245 foot)

roll, which is more than enough for several average rooms. You can give away, or sell, the extra, use it for a lifetime's supply of parcels or cut it up for children's paintings.

You will need to cut out 'drops' from ceiling to floor on as big a table as you can find, bearing in mind the paper's increased width. Paste the back of a sheet with wallpaper paste, handling it carefully, and position and smooth it out well with a clean, dry cloth. It is probably better to overlap the sheets slightly rather than to join them edge-to-edge.

Another interesting effect can be obtained by similarly pasting up sheets of newspaper.

1 *Differently coloured squares of paper have been pasted onto much larger, contrasting areas of colour to turn these walls into an interesting abstract.*
2 *Sheets of newspaper on the walls of this bathroom have been protected by a couple of coats of polyurethane varnish, both to protect and harden the surface and to give it a feeling of age.*
3 *Plain blue walls in another bathroom have an unusual and striking border of silver-leaf squares. Marble floor tiles have been used to create a dado, but a similar effect could be created using squares of marbleized paper over chipboard.*

Alternative Wall Coverings

When deciding on wall treatments for main rooms and bedrooms, nearly everyone thinks first of some kind of paint or wallpaper treatment, but there are myriad alternative wall coverings that can look splendid, including fabric, mirror and tiles.

FABRIC

Fabric has been used to cover walls for centuries, first in India, the Far East and the Middle East, and then in Europe at least since medieval times. By the late seventeenth century it had been somewhat eclipsed by wallpaper but was never entirely replaced by it. Samuel Pepys, the famous seventeenth-century diarist, writes of visiting Cornhill in London and having a wretched time trying to buy his wife 'a chintz, that is painted Indian calico, for to line her new study which is very pretty'. John Evelyn, another diarist of the period, mentions 'dining out in a room hung with *Pintado*', which was another name for chintz.

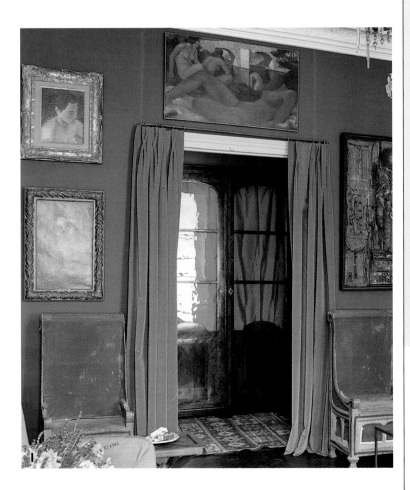

SHORT CUTS TO 'WALLING'

As a short cut to achieving the softly luxurious effect of 'walling' (upholstered walls – see below), you can use panels of fibrebrand, which is quite soft. Obviously you will need to have measured the room and made a scale drawing of it (see page 16), in order to work out how many panels to get made. Don't forget the spaces over doors and fireplaces, over and under windows, and so on. You will also, of course, need to work out the right amount of fabric. Allow extra for wrapping the fabric around the panels – about 1m (1yd) all around each one.

Wrap the fabric around the panels, securing it with staples, then either screw the panels to the wall or attach them with wall-bound adhesive. You can conceal the joins if you want by covering them with braid, but the panels, if well-sized and fitted, can actually look quite neat in their own right.

There are also wall-upholstery systems, which rely on heavy-duty plastic tracks with adhesive backing. The panels of fabric are inserted into the channels of the track. For a really padded appearance, polyester padding can be placed on the panels before the fabric is stretched over them.

Walling

Today, fabric-covered, or 'upholstered', walls are still very much in evidence, particularly in Europe, and especially in France, where a surprising number of hotels and private homes have soft

1 *Dark green fabric and matching curtains make a distinguished background for a collection of paintings, as well as giving a timeless quality to these old rooms.*
2 *Green checked cotton walling above a plain painted dado looks agreeably crisp. The cotton is also used on the closet doors. The smaller red check on the charming painted chair creates a counterpoint to the green.*
3 *A large red check hanging looks arresting behind the table and striped chairs and contrasts with the flagged stone floor. Note the empty picture frame on the table.*

padded walls. I say surprising, because 'walling', as such treatments are called, is both expensive and extremely labour-intensive.

The process involves fixing a framework of thin battens to the wall, lining between them with wads of fire-retardant polyester wadding known as 'bump' and then stretching seamed fabric over the battens. The results are often original and usually luxurious,

1

1 *Lengths of white cotton sewn together are gently suspended from brass door knobs fixed just below the ceiling, softening the walls in this otherwise graphic black-and-white bedroom. Curtains and bedspread are made from the same soft cotton, but the bedspread is quilted.*

2 *In this subtly coloured room, single widths of fabric are hung individually to puddle on the floor in an unusually tailored manner.*

as well as providing excellent insulation against both cold and noise.

Walling is something the inhabitants of medieval Europe would have found a great deal more comfortable than their panelling or their tapestry, wool, leather and canvas hangings. Ironically, the method is similar to that employed in the late sixteenth and seventeenth centuries for displaying wallpapers. If only our ancestors had thought to do the same thing with fabric lined with sheep's wool, instead of just hanging it, they would have been a great deal warmer.

Hanging fabric from rods
Another way of using fabric on walls is to treat it like curtains hanging from just below the ceiling. As long as the fabric is fairly voluminous (it needs to be about three times each wall's width) and looks graceful, you can use cotton sheeting, voile or muslin, which are not only inexpensive but can be taken down and tossed in the washing machine at intervals. Alternatively, you could use more tailored fabrics, like wool, flannel or camel hair, or sumptuous silk or velvet, which all need to be dry cleaned. The advantage

of this approach is that even if the fabric is not washable, it can at least be removed and cleaned.

Continuous rods on brackets are fixed all around the room at ceiling height. Each curtain, which should be long enough to just touch the floor or to 'puddle' onto it slightly, is made with a casing at the top, so that it can be slotted onto the rods. The curtains are allowed to hang loose, but the hems will probably need to be weighted.

Where there is a door, window or fireplace, the curtains are simply held back with tie-backs. If the fabric is

2

fabric. The battens are then fixed to the walls just below the ceiling and above the skirting boards, to keep the fabric fairly taut and tightly gathered or in neat pleats. Short panels are used above and below windows. Roller blinds can be used at the windows, or the fabric can hang loose there and be tied back. Panels should be positioned so as to give easy access to light switches and electric sockets.

Sticking fabric on walls

If the fabric is firm, like good-quality felt, tweed or other wool, hessian, corduroy or imitation suede, it can be stuck to the walls rather like wallpaper. As wide a fabric as possible should be used. It is cut into the required lengths, allowing for overlaps at top and bottom and any pattern matching. The paste is brushed onto the walls, and then each fabric length is unravelled, aligned to a plumb line and gently smoothed down with a large roller. This clearly will not look as soft as walling, but it will still look distinguished and add an interesting texture.

Tenting

If ceilings are in a bad state of repair, or really undistinguished, or if you would like to finish off walls covered in fabric in an exotic way, you could try tenting the ceiling. The idea is to allow fabric to hang in dramatic folds from a fixed point, or points; at the other end, each length of fabric is fixed to the angle of the ceiling and wall. You could use a circular rail, or a corona (designed for bed hangings), fixed in the centre of the ceiling, and swoop from it however many lengths of fabric are needed to conceal the ceiling.

permanently tied back at the windows, roller blinds could be used behind it, in a fabric that is matching, contrasting or 'negative' (in the same two-colour design, but with the colours reversed). Where fabric is tied back at the mantelpiece, the wall can be painted where the curtains part, or something large, like a mirror or painting, can be put there.

Hanging fabric from battens

An alternative way to hang fabric 'curtains' on the walls is to slot battens of wood into hemmed casings at both the top and bottom of each length of

part two: the specifics

MIRRORING

Floor-to-ceiling mirror can be relied upon to give a room added length, width and height, as well as extra light. It is a somewhat expensive way to gain this extra visual space, but there are tricks by which the effect of mirror can be maximized:

- Fixing mirror literally from floor to ceiling doubles the apparent size of a room by creating the illusion of an opening going through to another room.

- Used on one wall, preferably at right angles to a window, mirror will seem to double the size of the room, and the extra reflected light by day will be stunning. Curtains or blinds, when drawn at night, will also seem to double in size.

- Fixing mirror in the space between two tall windows will make an enormous difference to light and brightness.

- Lining an alcove with mirror will increase the feeling of depth, adding perspective to a room.

- In a dark or somewhat dreary room, lining the recesses at either side of a chimney breast with mirror will make a huge difference. If you stand tall, bushy plants in front of each, with up-lights behind, the effect will be even airier.

Do be sure to take accurate measurements so that the large piece, or pieces, of mirror required will fit through your doors and if necessary will go up the stairs (including being transported around any bend or turn in the stairs) or fit into a lift. If the space to be mirrored is large, you will almost certainly be better off with panels of mirror.

Some people find blank mirror cold-looking, and tinted mirror glass is one way of counteracting this, and it will add to the room's ambience. Alternatively, glass shelves can be fixed across the mirror to display a collection of glass, or a mixture of books, *objets* and small plants. The display can be lit from above by a recessed down-light, or from below by an up-light, or both.

I *A door in this bedroom has been completely mirrored, to reflect and seemingly enlarge the space as well as to provide good all-over personal reflection. Note the round mirror placed on the wall to allow an efficient view of the back when the door is at an appropriate angle.*

TILING

Tiled walls can look splendid, and not just in bathrooms and kitchens, as demonstrated by ancient buildings in the Far East, Iran, Turkey, Italy, Spain, Holland and South America.

No one can fail to be impressed by the magnificent completely tiled rooms (floors, walls and ceilings) of the Alhambra in Granada, Spain, and the splendours of Istanbul's Topkapi

tip

OLD GROUT CAN GET VERY DIRTY, BUT LUCKILY THERE ARE SOME STAIN-RESISTANT VARIETIES TODAY WHICH LOOK MUCH BETTER, AND YOU CAN CAREFULLY MATCH GROUT COMPOUND TO TILE COLOUR, OR TO THE BACKGROUND COLOUR IF THEY ARE PATTERNED, TO MAKE THE GROUT ALMOST DISAPPEAR.

Palace and Blue Mosque, with its 20,000 blue-glazed tiles covering the inside walls.

In cooler climates, a wealth of tiled surfaces will generally seem too cold, but they can be used to good effect in smaller amounts. Many western and northern European countries used the tin-glazed, painted maiolica tiles produced by Italy and Spain from the fifteenth century onwards. And the blue-and-white Delft tiles, first produced in Holland in the seventeenth century, were – and still are – as popular in America as in Europe.

Today there is an enormous choice of tiles, not just machine-made ones but also hand-made or hand-painted tiles from all over the world. Moreover, it is still possible to find beautiful antique tiles, particularly Victorian and Edwardian examples.

Economical ideas

If you cannot find enough of a particular antique tile, or cannot afford many expensive tiles, you could always use them as a border, like a chair rail, or in a square or diamond shape, or as randomly placed tiles in a wall of plain, less expensive ones.

Inexpensive plain tiles can be effective without any adornment if they are laid on the diagonal or in a

2 *Two separate designs of highly decorative blue-and-white tiles are used on the walls of this kitchen, cleverly divided by an edging of slim white border tiles. In contrast, plain white tiles with a dark bull-nosed edging have been used for the worktop.*

part two: the specifics

herringbone or basket-weave pattern. Or they can be delineated with a border of tiles in a contrast colour or special edging tiles.

Other decorative tiles

There are a great many pictorial tiles available – that is to say, tiles made to form part of a picture or design, like an urn of flowers, a fountain, an arch or bower or some sort of landscape.

These need very careful measuring of the space they are to fill, to make sure that the design will fit, quite apart from expert tile-laying. (You could achieve a similar effect by getting an artist to paint a design on a wall of pale-coloured plain tiles – see right for advice on painting on tiles.)

Don't forget about mosaic tiles and glass bricks, both of which can look highly decorative. Glass tiles can

also be found, though they are not widely available. Make sure that whatever you use is appropriate to the style of room.

Painting tiles

If you are stuck with tiles you hate, remember that you can disguise them with paint. A good paint shop might recommend an epoxy enamel paint (see page 94), but an oil-based paint

should do, particularly if you apply a proprietary tile primer first. You can either just paint them a plain colour and leave it at that, or you can then embellish them with stencils or an all-over design.

An alternative is to tile right over the top, provided they will not stick out too far; this is generally cheaper than ripping the old tiles off and starting all over again.

WOOD PANELLING

Wood panelling looks good in virtually any style of interior, particularly as there are so many different ways to use it. It can be left plain, stained with a natural shade or a colour, painted, or grained to make it look like more expensive wood.

If it is not already in place, new panelling can be added, either from floor to ceiling or to chair-rail or picture-rail height. Traditional fielded panelling can look good in a period home – architectural salvage yards are good places to look for this. Tongue-and-groove is a less expensive, widely available option, and even plywood can look good if given an interesting finish. Another option is the thin 'matchstick' panelling that looks so charming in many houses on the East Coast of the United States.

Panelling needs to be hung by a carpenter, as it is fixed to a framework of battens screwed to the wall. New wood will need to acclimatize to your home for a few weeks before being installed, to reduce the risk of cracks and gaps opening up over time. If you are having new hardwood panelling installed, make sure that it is from an ecologically farmed plantation.

1 *Leather tiles look handsome with a similarly coloured leather-covered stool and chair.*

2 *Multicoloured tiles are used here for walls, ceiling and floor, thus giving the impression to anyone entering the room of walking into a bright, hard-edged box of Smarties.*

3 *Light, modern panelling in different subtle tones resembles a series of shoji screens applied to the wall. There is certainly no need for art.*

4 *A dado of genuine old panelling in a hallway is repeated in paint in a room leading off. Note how the same sludgy green is used to paint the door architrave.*

5 *Tongue-and-groove panelling on a stairway is painted a cool grey and white. The effect is pleasantly cool in conjunction with the painted white stairs.*

part two: the specifics

SECTION FIVE

Floors are the bottom line, so to speak, of any room and have tremendous decorative, as well as practical, potential. They anchor a scheme, hold it together and give it a crucial steadiness, richness, simplicity or glamour, according to the function, mood and style of the space. Because they are also walked on, sometimes danced on and very often sat or lounged on, they take a tougher beating than any other surface. The first choice in any space, however, is between hard, soft and the in-between flexibility that vinyl or linoleum offers. Fortunately, you don't have to limit yourself to just one type – wood, tiles or stone of any sort softened by rugs or squares of carpet gives you the best of both worlds.

Floors

Flooring Options

Whether you decide to go for carpets or rugs, hard floors or flexible flooring, or a combination, you need to consider your options first. In particular, this involves thinking about the existing floor and any future flooring – ideally, not just in the room (or rooms) you are decorating but in the rest of the home, too.

EXISTING FLOORS

Do not make any radical decisions on floor coverings before studying existing floors carefully. They might not need to be covered at all.

Wood floors

Parquet and timber floors in reasonably good condition – without gaps, splits and frayed, splintered ends – could just be polished and then either be left bare or have rugs laid on top, with some non-slip backing to prevent them from slipping.

If a floor is worn, the first task is sanding it down. This can be done professionally or you can hire a sander with a dust-bag attachment and sand it yourself (which is messy and hard work, but a great deal cheaper). It can then be either stained a different colour – say, much darker, or maybe even a dark green or bronze – or bleached, or whitened.

An alternative is to paint it with floor, deck or marine paint; or just flat oil, acrylic or emulsion paint. Or you can give it a more ambitious, decorative paint treatment, perhaps marbling it, combing it, painting it in chequerboard squares or stencilling it. In fact, an otherwise plain floor can look extremely effective with a stencilled border or design.

Whichever treatment you choose – plain, stained, bleached or painted – the floor will need to be sealed with two or three coats of protective varnish afterwards. Acrylic-based varnish needs 12 hours' drying time, but for other types, each coat must be allowed to dry for 24 hours before being walked on. As well as protecting the surface, this will give it a sheen, with the degree of gloss depending upon the varnish, and it will bring out the graining (except on painted floors, obviously).

Vinyl and linoleum floors

These are best disguised using oil-based paints, rather than emulsion which does not grip as well on their surfaces. (Even oil-based paint will eventually peel off from vinyl, but it is still worth doing, as it can simply be painted again when that happens.) Before applying any paint, it is essential to wash the floor thoroughly with a sugar-soap solution (sugar soap is available through most good hardware and DIY shops) then rinse it well and allow it to dry completely.

Concrete floors

Paint is surprisingly effective on concrete floors. A special concrete paint (from a speciality paint shop or good hardware store) can be painted straight onto it. Alternatively, oil paint can be used, and provides a better choice of colours, but it must be applied over a diluted PVA seal and then overpainted with an acrylic varnish when dry. In fact, with either type of paint, you should finish off with an acrylic floor varnish.

I once saw what I thought was a splendid old flagstone floor in a converted barn. In fact, it was concrete, which had been scored to look like flagstones, pitted here and there with a chisel, then rubbed all over with clear floor polish in many patient applications, and finally sealed. Patches of tan and reddish-tan shoe polish, artfully superimposed in random areas, provided realistic variations in tone. It was impressive.

Tiled floors

Existing tiled floors with unsightly stained or cracked grout can be prised up, cleaned and relaid with fresh new grout. Since grout comes in many tones and colours, choose one that will camouflage wear and tear, and that will not be so noticeable that the grid pattern becomes too dominant.

JUXTAPOSITIONS

When planning flooring for a room, don't think about it in isolation. Remember the vistas that are constantly opened up in a home. Doors that lead off corridors and hallways are often left open, and glimpses of upper storeys can be seen from stairways. For the space to flow naturally, the floor coverings need to be coordinated, at least in colour. And, of course, a small apartment or house looks better if one colour is used throughout, though it need not be of uniform quality.

Where different textures or colours meet at doorways – say, carpet with tiling or parquet, or chestnut brown with apricot – the effect is neater if a threshold strip is inserted between the two. This is also practical, since it will protect the edges of the different materials, as well as delineating the contrasting areas.

1 *Paint was used to make this concrete floor look like flagstones with a terracotta border and inlaid centre design. Realistic pits and crevices were achieved by pressing sheets of newspaper onto wet paint and quickly removing them.*
2 *A pale-coloured kilim softens an expanse of coir matting in this house. It is always best to use some sort of gripping device or underlay when adding a rug to any soft floor covering, otherwise it will ruck up or creep. Note how well the Arts and Crafts occasional table balances the staircase.*
3 *The wood floor in this kitchen with its interesting storage wall has been painted clear blue and protected by several coats of acrylic varnish.*

part two: the specifics

Carpets

As well as being soft and warm underfoot, fitted carpet, also called close carpeting, is very practical, providing good sound insulation and draughtproofing and also hiding floors that are in poor condition. There is an enormous range of close carpeting in every price, colour and texture.

Most modern carpets are either woven or tufted. Although woven carpet has a reputation for durability, good-quality tufted carpet will work well in any area of the home and is a good deal less expensive. The main aspects you should look at in either type are density and pile height.

DENSITY

A carpet's density is measured by the number of stitches per centimetre or inch, and is the most important aspect of carpet construction to understand. A very closely tufted or woven carpet will assure years of wear, whatever the height of the pile.

PILE HEIGHT

The term 'pile' refers to the tufts or loops of pile above a carpet backing. They form the surface of a carpet, and although many people think that a deep-pile carpet looks more expensive, this is not necessarily so. In fact, high pile on a carpet often means that it is rather loosely woven and that the pile will flatten easily when walked on.

CARPET TEXTURES

The surface finish of a carpet depends to a great extent on which type of pile it has. Here are some of the most common types.

Velvet or close pile: A short, dense and deeply smooth finish. In this kind of pile, all the loops formed in the manufacturing process are sheared at the same height. Some people do not like it much because it can show footprints, while others like it because of the feeling of light and shade. Because the loops are cut, velvet does not have the resilience to dirt that a more tightly woven loop carpet will have. However, it does look particularly elegant and is therefore recommended for formal living rooms, and rooms where there is not too much traffic.

Twist pile: This is a sturdy, hard-wearing finish. It is much less prone to shading than the more luxurious smooth velvets. Because it is tough, it is good for stairs and other high-traffic areas.

Loop pile: This pile is formed by loops of yarn. It looks good but can snag. An example is the elegant Brussels weave, which can look extremely good in living rooms that do not get high traffic, as well as master and guest bedrooms. If the carpet does snag, you can either cut off the offending tag

Interesting wide stripes have been inset in front of the fireplace in this otherwise plain Wilton carpet, forming a kind of rug between the two facing sofas. The stripes also echo the parallel lines of the fire surround.

tip

WHEN CHOOSING CARPET, GIVE IT THE 'GRIN TEST' BY FOLDING IT BACK ON ITSELF. IF A LOT OF THE BACKING SHOWS, THE CARPET IS NOT GOING TO BE VERY DURABLE. IN THE TRADE, THIS GLIMPSE OF BACKING IS KNOWN AS 'GRIN' BECAUSE IT LOOKS A BIT LIKE A SMILE BREAKING THROUGH.

very carefully or, if the carpet is loose-laid, turn it back and pull the snag through the backing.

Long or shag pile: This has an informal, rough-and-ready look. It is made in the same way as velvet, that is to say, tufted in high loops. But the loops are then cut through with a shearing knife (as if shearing a sheep's coat) to give it its distinctive thick, shaggy look. Shag pile carpet comes in many densities, and the less tightly the yarn is packed, the more it is likely to flatten. Because of its long length, it is not easy to clean. Since shag is difficult to look after (unless you intend to spend a good deal of time raking the pile through in order to get it to stand up again), a good compromise is a similarly textured rug, like the Greek flokati, which is woven in a natural white.

WEAVES

The various weaves of carpet are Axminster, Wilton, Brussels weave, cord and wool 'sisal'.

There is often a good deal of confusion between the first two. Briefly, they are both smooth-piled and woven on a loom, which means that surface pile and backing are woven together for strength and durability. The size of an Axminster loom, however, allows greater variety of colour in patterned carpets than in Wilton, where the number of colours in any design is limited to five. Thus, Axminsters are generally patterned, while many people favour plain velvet Wilton. In Wilton, the colours not appearing in the surface pile are carried along the back, to form an extra pad of fibre that cushions against wear – hence Wilton's greater reputation for hidden value.

The neat looped pile of Brussels weave makes it a good texture for crisp geometric designs.

Cord is woven in much the same way as Wilton carpet but the strands are pulled tight to form the ridges. It is similar to Brussels weave in that it has an uncut pile, which gives it its recognizable looped appearance. It is an effective construction for those cheaper fibres that would otherwise become flattened. Hair cord, for example, is made from animal hair, and there are nylon and jute cords, as well as cheap wool cord.

Wool 'sisal' delivers the interesting texture of sisal matting (see pages 127 and 135) with a much softer feel. It is also easier to clean than sisal and comes in a good choice of colours.

TUFTING

Tufted carpets, in which the pile is punched into a backing and glued, are more common and less expensive than woven ones.

FIBRES

There are actually only four generic families of fibres generally used in carpets: wool, acrylic, nylon and polyester. All the various brands and trade names fall into one of these four families. They can be mixed with each other, can be woven or tufted and are available in any of the textures described above. Which fibre you choose is really a matter of common sense and suitability.

Wool is not only good-looking, hard-wearing and warm but also resistant to water and stains. It has a

part two: the specifics

natural resilience, which means that the pile springs back into place easily. It is also the most expensive fibre.

Nylon, in its various guises, is the strongest, but the average home does not require maximum strength. It is easier to clean than anything else and is less expensive than wool or acrylic. On its own, however, it does not adapt quite so easily to colour, texture and pattern. A favourite mixture is 80 per cent wool, 20 per cent nylon, because it has all the softness and subtlety of wool, takes dyes well, and is extremely hard-wearing.

Acrylics accept dye well, are very soil-resistant and are getting softer to the touch all the time.

Polyester is the least expensive of any of the fibres. It soils more easily but takes dyes well and so comes in a rainbow of colours.

WIDTH

The terms broadloom and body carpet refer to a carpet's width. Broadloom is woven on a loom more than 2m or 6ft wide, and common widths are 2m, 4m and 5m or 6ft, 12ft and 15ft (in multiples of either 1m or 3ft because of the loom or machinery sizes). Obviously, the closer a room's measurements approximate to these widths, or their multiples, the more economical a carpet will be, since there will not be so much wastage.

Body carpet is made in narrow strips, such as 69cm (27in) or 91cm (36in) wide and is generally used for stairs, passageways and awkwardly shaped rooms. It is easier to get more subtle colours in body carpet, as well as the more expensive dense, smooth piles, like velvet Wilton.

1 *Cord carpet is an effective construction for cheaper fibres.*
2 *Brussels weave is woven in much the same way as cord, with a recognizable crisp looped appearance.*
3 *Twist pile has a sturdy, hard-wearing finish and is good for stairs.*
4 *Axminster looms allow a greater variety of colour in a design (as here) than Wilton.*

ALTERNATIVE FLOOR COVERINGS

Natural matting, such as sisal, coir, woven rush and seagrass, provides an attractive alternative to carpet. Available in broadloom, body carpet and rug form, it has a traditional feel and can look very good in either the city or the country. An excellent background for rugs, matting is also a good common denominator for a mixture of furniture periods. It is, however, tough on the feet and occasionally somewhat slippery on stairs, and its roughness makes it less suitable if young children will be crawling around. Nevertheless, matting certainly looks more appropriate in the country than carpeting and is useful where wood floors are beyond redemption.

5 Loop pile carpet is the same construction as the elegant Brussels weave. The snag is literally that it can snag easily.

6 Seagrass has a nice crisp texture.

7 Coir makes a good background for furnishings.

8 Wool sisal is here contrasted with stone.

9 Sisal fibres can be dyed easily and are available in herringbone as well as ribbed and bouclé patterns.

part two: the specifics

Rugs

The popularity of area rugs is not surprising, given their infinite versatility. Not only do they provide a soft, comfortable surface underfoot, but they soften hard floors visually, too, and add colour and texture to a scheme. They are particularly useful for helping to demarcate zones within a room and to draw disparate items of furniture together.

Another distinct advantage that rugs have over fitted carpets is their adaptability, as they can easily be moved around or changed, without having to be replaced as carpet does.

Oriental rugs are the aristocrats of area rugs. Equally elegant are the beautiful, large, antique needlework rugs like the French tapestry-woven Aubussons, as well as the excellent modern Roumanian, Portuguese and Chinese copies of these.

There are also the non-politically correct, but nevertheless striking, animal-skin rugs (though many people prefer the *faux* varieties) and dramatic contemporary rugs with their bold, often graphic designs.

A considerable number of ethnic rugs are widely produced around the world. Most of these fall roughly into one of three categories: ethnic cottons, such as traditional Moroccan or Greek weaves and Indian dhurries; dense woollen piles like Finnish ryas and Greek flokatis; and the luxurious, thick woollen weaves produced by the Spanish, Portuguese, South Americans and Irish.

All rugs should be secured to prevent them from either slipping on a wood or tiled floor or 'walking' when laid on top of carpet or matting. Use a non-slip mesh backing or Velcro, cut to the appropriate size.

tip

TO CHECK WHETHER A RUG IS HAND-KNOTTED, PART THE PILE AND LOOK FOR ROWS OF KNOTS AT THE BASE OF THE TUFTS. LOOK AT THE BACK, TOO – THE PATTERN SHOULD BE VISIBLE.

Handsome area rugs not only soften the polished stone floor but, with their geometric design, make a good foil for the eclectic collection of furniture, light fittings and other furnishings. They also define the sitting and working areas.

ORIENTAL RUGS

'Oriental rug' is the umbrella term for rugs, carpets, prayer rugs, runners and kilims made by nomadic tribesmen and village craftsmen to furnish their tents. The rugs were draped over seating and hung on the walls as well as being laid on the floors.

Antique rugs are the most prized, but oriental rugs are still produced today to the designs of the past, which relate to the area from which they come. Some of the rugs are hand-made and others mass-produced in cooperatives based in towns and cities.

Kilims are made using the technique of flatweaving, also known as tapestry weaving, in which long threads are woven in and out of the warp and weft. They therefore do not have a pile.

Other oriental rugs are produced by knotting short lengths of wool around the warp threads of a loom. Knotted rugs thus have a pile and are more durable than kilims.

Designs are all based on traditional patterns and reflect the life, culture and customs of the Islamic and Far Eastern worlds. Most rugs or carpets have a central 'field' or 'ground', which is surrounded by a border. The designs in the centre range from the geometric and abstract to the figurative and floral.

Experts can tell which small production centre any rug comes from. The six traditional carpet-producing regions are Persia, Turkey, Turkestan in Central Asia, the Caucasus, India and China. The carpets from each of these regions have distinctive, recognizable features, which are described on the following pages.

tip

AN ORIENTAL 'RUG' IS REGARDED AS BEING SMALL ENOUGH TO HANG ON THE WALL AND SO IS LESS THAN ABOUT 2M (6FT 6IN) LONG; AN ORIENTAL 'CARPET' IS LARGER THAN THAT. IN PRACTICE, HOWEVER, THE TERMS TEND TO BE USED INTERCHANGEABLY.

part two: the specifics

Persian rugs

These are considered to be the finest of all oriental rugs.

- Persian rugs are almost always rectangular or elongated, rather than square.
- They are generally woven in wool, using the special *Senneh* knot. (Exceptions are the rare, beautiful and extremely expensive silk rugs – which explains the old Persian saying, 'The richer the man, the thinner the rug'.)
- Their colouring is rich and often has a central field of crimson or indigo, with figurings of warm browns, greens and yellows.
- The Persians were the only Muslim people to include men and animals (in hunting carpets), which are realistically represented.
- The majority of designs, however, are based on floral motifs. Some of the most popular are used in the *garden* rugs and carpets, so called because they are laid out in the form of gardens with paths, flower beds, pools and streams.
- *Vase* rugs are a more formal version of floral motifs, with vases holding flowers or plants.
- Other designs include prayer rugs with the pattern of a Moorish arch, sometimes pointed at the top, called *mihrab*; and geometric medallion pieces with a large central design and canted corners.
- Persian rugs made before the eighteenth century are usually classified according to their design: *garden, vase, animal, medallion*, etc. Only those made after then are attributed to specific towns, such as Feraghan, Schina, Herat, Heriz,

Silk Tabriz prayer rug, c.1890, from north-west Persia

Isfahan, Joshaghan, Kashan, Qum, Shiraz or Tabriz.

- If you are lucky enough to see an early *animal* carpet, there is a very good chance that it came from Isfahan, just as *vase* carpets probably came from Joshaghan,

and *medallion* carpets from Herat. Herat carpets are considered to be the very best Persians and are particularly associated with small, recurring leaf patterns (sometimes thought to be fish) and rosettes.

PRECIOUS COMMODITY

Oriental rugs started to be exported to Europe via enterprising Venetian traders from the Middle Ages onwards. For several hundred years, these rugs were generally considered too rare and expensive to walk on and so were mainly used as table or wall coverings.

In the sixteenth century, the German portrait painter Hans Holbein, recognizing the status and prestige associated with owning oriental rugs, used Turkish Bergama rugs in so many royal portraits that these rugs became known as 'Holbein rugs'.

Early nineteenth-century Turkish Ghiordes prayer rug

Turkish rugs

These come from the Anatolian region of the country and are often referred to as *Anatolians* by dealers. Popular in Europe long before Persian rugs, they differ from them not only in design and colours but also in the type of knot used. This knot is known as the *Ghiordes*, named after one of the major rug-producing areas. (Other centres of production include Bergama, Hereke, Kula, Kum Kapi, Kirsehir, Konya, Ushak and Ladik.)

- The pile in Turkish carpets is almost always longer than in Persians, and fewer colours are used in Turkish carpets.

- Patterns are bold and tend to be geometric, but there are stylized flowers like the rhododendron, pomegranate and hyacinth.

- In the *mihrab* mosque pattern on prayer rugs, there is a lamp, or ewer, suspended from an arch. This is sometimes flanked by two pillars of wisdom. More sophisticated versions have Arabic script.

- The most usual background colours are red and blue, although prayer rugs are sometimes woven in green, a sacred colour.

- Some of the major rug-producing areas have their own distinctive designs. For example, rugs from Ghiordes – which makes the finest rugs, often considered the equal of the best Persians – have attractive arabesques, floral designs, borders and stripes.

- Because most Turks are Sunni Muslims, they observe the Koranic prohibition against the depiction of people or animals, so you will rarely see these on Turkish rugs.

part two: the specifics

Indian carpet, c. 1900, probably from Lahore

Chinese carpet

Detail from Chinese rug

More examples of various oriental rugs. The detail (left) of a dragon rearing up against a stylized blue sky is taken from an old Chinese rug, and the carpet (far left below) showing scalloped roundels containing imperial dragons is also Chinese.

Caucasian runner

Tekke carpet, c. 1880, West Turkmenistan

Indian rugs

Though generally made in the Persian tradition, Indian rugs also have definite characteristics of their own. They were originally introduced to suit the royal tastes of the Indian princesses, and of the merchants who set up the early workshops.

- Many designs feature animals, birds, trees, and flowers.
- The colours are lighter than those of Persian rugs, with an extensive use of rose.
- The pile is noticeably longer and coarser than Persian rugs.

Chinese rugs

Knotted rugs were being made in China two thousand years ago in organized workshops, much as they are still being woven in factories today, although there was not a real rug industry until the eighteenth century.

- The colours are generally subtle blues, yellows, peaches, roses and apricots, in complete contrast to the ubiquitous reds and greens of the Persian, Turkish, Caucasian, Turkoman and Indian rugs.
- The designs incorporate the motifs common to most Chinese art. Buddhist and Taoist symbols are used extensively. The designs include animals, especially dragons, and flowers like the lotus, peony, daffodil and pomegranate.
- They have a much longer pile and are tied with an asymmetrical knot, which is often cut around the edge of a motif to give greater emphasis to the pattern.
- The famous *pillar* designs are found only in China. They were made to wrap around a pillar, so the pattern is continuous.

Caucasian rugs

These come from the Caucasus, which is the mountainous area between the Caspian Sea and the Black Sea. Although the region is now part of Russia, it has been home to many different tribes from Turkey, Armenia and Persia, all of whom have contributed to the region's rich heritage of rugs.

- The rugs are distinctively coloured in red, blue, green and beige.
- The designs, though varied, are always severely rectilinear.
- Animals, birds, flowers, crabs, beetles, etc, are highly stylized.
- Other designs include medallions, also composed in geometric arrangements, with decorated borders of stars, rosettes or running dog patterns (the Caucasian equivalent to the Greek key pattern).

Turkoman rugs

Turkoman, or Turkman, rugs come from the region between the Caspian Sea and north-west China, which includes Turkmenistan, Uzbekistan, Afghanistan and Pakistan.

- Red is the predominant colour, although different tribes and areas can be identified by the various hues that they introduce into their designs. For example, rugs from the Beshire area of Afghanistan use yellow and green as well as red. Baluchis use a lot of dark blue with rust reds, bluish mauves, and occasional touches of camel, ivory and cream.
- Golden Afghan rugs are really the ubiquitous red rugs, washed until they have become a distinctive apricot-gold colour.
- Designs are almost always geometric, and generally feature the octagonal *gul*, or stylized rose motif.

part two: the specifics

Vocabulary of Carpet Terms

Acrylic: This synthetic looks very like wool and is non-allergenic, but is slightly less stain-resistant and resilient than wool. However, it is also lower-priced.

Axminster: Axminster is a woven carpet, named after the loom on which it is woven, which positions the pile tufts at the same time as it weaves the backing. Because the threads are not carried along the back of the carpet, it is possible to weave Axminsters in a great variety of colours. Although it has a CUT PILE, it can be woven long and shaggy, stubby or sculpted, as well as short or smooth. The strongest weaving quality is generally 80 per cent WOOL, 20 per cent NYLON, but it can also be woven in ACRYLIC or a blend.

Berber carpets: These are made of natural, undyed sheep's wool, with a dense, looped pile, named after the original hand-woven squares made by North African tribes. They are now made by machine in white, cream, beige, fawn, grey and dark brown.

Body carpet: The term for narrow widths of carpet, of less than BROADLOOM width, such as 69cm (27in) or 91cm (36in) wide. It is generally used for stairs, corridors and awkwardly shaped rooms where there will be less wastage than there would be from broader widths. The denser, smoother, more expensive velvet piles are most often only available in body carpet.

Bouclé: The pile formed by uncut loops of yarn in BRUSSELS WEAVE carpet.

Broadloom: The term for broader widths of carpet than BODY CARPET, which are woven on a loom more than 2m or 6ft wide. Common widths include 2m, 4m and 5m, or 6ft, 12ft and 15ft. Clearly, the closer the room size to these widths, or their multiples, the less wastage there will be.

Brussels weave: Tightly looped carpets with a neat, crisp appearance, which lend themselves to clean-cut and geometric designs. They do, however, snag easily, so loose ends need to be carefully snipped when they appear.

Carpet tiles: Squares of carpet, in woven, tufted or bonded form and in various combinations of wool and synthetic fibres. The standard size is 50 x 50cm (20 x 20in). They do not require padding or underlay and are flat, thin and comparatively hard-wearing, although they lack the softness underfoot of fitted carpet. They can be laid by amateurs quite easily, all in one colour, or in chequerboard fashion, or made into random designs. Their advantages are that they are reasonably inexpensive and that, if one or two get stained or worn, they can be removed and replaced.

Coir matting: A great favourite for many rooms because it is a good background for rugs and seems to unite an eclectic mixture of furnishings. Made from coconut-husk fibres, it is inexpensive and hard-wearing. Coir comes in area-rug sizes, mats, tiles and in BODY CARPET and BROADLOOM forms. It is mostly available in natural colours but is sometimes made from dyed fibres. Latex backing prevents dirt falling through.

Cord: A low-loop, woven carpet which, with its ribbed appearance, looks a little like corduroy. It is woven in much the same way as plain WILTON but is much cheaper and not particularly soft underfoot.

Cotton: Cotton rugs have the advantage of being machine-washable and hard-wearing, but one drawback is that they get flattened easily.

Cut-and-loop pile: Also known as high-and-low pile, this is a combination of CUT and LOOPED pile, which gives it a sculpted appearance.

Cut pile: As the name implies, the strands of yarn are cut rather than left looped. All AXMINSTER carpets and some WILTON carpets have cut pile.

Dhurrie: A FLATWEAVE COTTON rug, the Indian equivalent of the kilim.

Felt: Felt is a very good option for short-term rentals or holiday houses, and infrequently used guest rooms, when it is bought in carpet thickness. It comes in a good range of colours and is inexpensive.

Flatweave: A term applied to both carpets and rugs that are woven and

have no PILE. They are generally cheaper than pile carpets and are usually made of COTTON, WOOL or LINEN, although occasionally SILK is used. The two main types of traditional flatweave are KILIMS and DHURRIES.

Frieze: Hard-wearing carpets with tightly twisted yarns which form a thick, low-pile surface. They are good for stairs and any area that gets a lot of use.

Fusion-bonded: Fusion bonding produces a very dense CUT PILE available in mostly plain colours.

Hand-knotted: Oriental rugs (apart from KILIMS) and American Indian rugs are produced in this way. The yarn is hand-tied with a woven backing using individual knots. Since the process is labour-intensive, it is expensive.

Indian carpet: This is always off-white, is comparatively inexpensive and can be bought in rug sizes and BROADLOOM widths. The WOOL PILE is looped and knotted into the backing, so it wears well.

Jute: The fibre of an Asian herbaceous plant, jute is used for matting. It feels

relatively soft and looks almost silky, but it is not particularly hard-wearing.

Kilim: A traditional FLATWEAVE rug from Turkey or Afghanistan. The fibre is usually wool, and the pattern is geometric. The vegetable dyes used produce warm, rich colours that mellow with age.

Linen carpet: This has an interesting texture and looks very handsome, with much of the natural feel of sisal and coir. It is expensive and not at all hard-wearing, so it is best for decoration rather than practicality. It needs a rubber pad or underlay at least 5mm (¼in) thick underneath.

Long pile: See SHAG PILE.

Looped pile: A surface formed from uncut loops. How well it wears depends on the density of the construction – ie, the number of loops per square centimetre or inch. It can be either shaggy or smooth.

Low pile: See VELVET PILE.

Nylon: The most popular man-made fibre used for carpeting. It is non-allergenic, resistant to water-soluble stains, very easy to clean and easy to dye. In fact, it takes colour more clearly than wool. The latest nylons cost more than the older varieties because they have built-in static control and are more resistant to soiling.

Pile: The tufts or loops of pile above the backing of either a WOVEN or a TUFTED carpet or rug. The quality of the pile is affected by the fibre size and weight, the ply of the yarn (the number of strands twisted together to form one strand) and the density of the tufts.

Polyester: The advantages of polyester are that, like NYLON, it is non-allergenic and is moisture- and abrasion-resistant. It makes up into thick CUT-PILE carpets that have a luxurious feel, but it can pill like a sweater.

Polypropylene: Also known as olefin, this man-made fibre is strong, resists moisture and mildew and is reasonably priced. It is a good choice for bathrooms, family rooms, children's rooms, basement rooms and even kitchens, but it has a tendency to fade.

Rag rugs: Rugs made from fabric strips that are plaited or woven together, or hooked or prodded onto a backing.

Rush matting: Rushes can be woven into thickly textured or plaited lengths or sold in squares. One big advantage of rush matting is that it can be laid loose over concrete and other hard floors without underlay, and it has an interesting rustic texture. It is not, however, very hard-wearing.

Saxony pile: A particularly soft, mid-length wool PILE.

Seagrass: A plant fibre grown in paddy fields and used for matting. Naturally water- and stain-resistant, it is suitable for areas of medium traffic.

Shag pile: Carpet with a 2.5–5cm (1–2in) cut pile. Once deemed the height of luxury, it is much less used nowadays. It was, and can be, used in living rooms and bedrooms, but should never be used on stairs, since heels could get caught in the pile. It gets dirtier than short pile, and the cheaper varieties tend to flatten easily.

Silk: Silk yarn can be made into extremely expensive and exotic rugs. It is one of the best of all fibres, and is usually hand-loomed. If the silk is not colourfast, it tends to fade in sunlight.

Sisal: Tough, durable, white fibre which can be dyed easily and looks crisp. Sisal matting looks neat on any floor. It is softer than COIR but not as soft as JUTE.

Tufted: This is the most widely produced type of carpet, in which each fibre is punched into a base material rather than woven on a loom. It is then secured with adhesive and usually sealed with a waterproof backing. It can have a LOOPED PILE or a CUT PILE.

Twist: A sturdy, hard-wearing finish which keeps neat and is less likely to 'shade' than the more expensive and luxurious 'VELVETS'.

Velvet pile: Velvet is a short, smooth, luxurious cut pile and is usually found in WILTON and AXMINSTER carpets in a vast range of colours, designs and textures.

Wilton: A woven carpet which, like AXMINSTER, gets its name from the loom on which it is woven. Unlike Axminster, Wilton is woven in one continuous length, so that the surface pile and backing are woven together for a special strength. Patterned Wiltons are somewhat rare, since the number of colours in any one design is limited to five. But they do come in a very large range of plain colours. They are available in VELVET and other CUT PILES, as well as LOOPED and CUT-AND-LOOP piles.

Wool: Extremely hard-wearing as well as luxurious, wool is the only natural fibre used in any quantity in the carpet business. Wool carpets, however, are much more expensive than those made from man-made fibres, and really need professional cleaning when allowed to get dirty. Although 100 per cent wool is available, a mixture of 80 per cent wool and 20 per cent nylon is more common.

Wool sisal: A wool and sisal carpet which is woven to give the neat sisal effect but is much softer underfoot and more expensive than sisal. Wool is often combined with JUTE in the same way.

1 *Rag rugs were much favoured in the nineteenth century, when they were made – often as a hobby – by a great number of people. Modern versions are available today (look out for the Portuguese rugs in particular) and their texture provides a nice contrast to any hard floor.*

2 *The crisp texture of Brussels weave is a natural background for interesting geometric and other graphic designs.*

part two: the specifics

Hard Flooring

Brick, tiles, stone (such as flagstones, slate and marble) and wood – the so-called hard floorings – have been used in homes over the centuries and have enjoyed renewed popularity in recent years. Handsome and hard-wearing, they are generally best if used with area rugs.

BRICK

Brick is an unexpectedly good floor treatment, especially in the country: as useful for halls, kitchens and cloakrooms as for living rooms and dining rooms. Along with old brick tiles known as pavers or paviours, brick is comparable in price with a good wood

1 Large, white ceramic non-slip tiles used both for floor and staircase make this space look particularly graphic. The grey paint on the side of the stairs looks good with the black table and the pale sand of the dining chairs.

2 Well-waxed old floorboards in a hallway lead onto equally well-worn flagstones in the living room of an old farmhouse. If a hard floor meets a softer texture, they will generally require a metal or wood strip between them. But here the two hard, time-worn materials converge quite happily while providing an interesting textural contrast.

or ceramic tile floor. It should be laid on top of a solid, level base or concrete screed, and regular bricks can be arranged in various patterns, from basket-weave to herringbone. Modern bricks, custom-made for floors, are thinner and lighter than conventional building bricks and come pre-glazed to combat stains. However, if the sub-floor is strong enough, you may prefer to use old bricks, which have a more mellow look and are often quite a bargain. Architectural or salvage companies and local builders interested in old houses are good sources.

Once they have warmed up, bricks maintain a comfortable temperature yet are agreeably cool in summer. If you are laying a brick floor and you live in a seasonal climate, consider first installing under-floor heating.

All old bricks should be sealed for easier maintenance. Then all you need to do after sweeping is to pass a damp mop over them.

FLOOR TILES

Versatile, hard-wearing and decorative, tiles have been a deservedly popular hard flooring for centuries.

Ceramic tiles

Non-slip, floor-weight ceramic tiles can look highly decorative in the right setting and climate and are pleasantly smooth to walk on, though cold. They come in a wide variety of colours and styles. Either hand- or machine-made from clay, they are fired at high temperatures. For outside use, choose the frost-proof, vitrified variety.

Terracotta tiles

These unglazed tiles come in several varieties. The most handsome, such as the kind produced in Mexico, are hand-made out of natural clay and kiln-fired. Like bricks, they retain heat. They are easily scratched, notably by grit on the bottom of shoes, but they develop a very attractive natural patina. Machine-made terracotta tiles are also available, and these are more regular in appearance.

Quarry tiles

Unglazed quarry tiles are tough and dense, and non-slip, but somewhat absorbent. Glazed quarry tiles are a little more slippery but tougher. Made from unrefined high-silica clay, all quarry tiles look rustic. They come in a range of terracotta tones but also a variety of greys.

part two: the specifics

Encaustic tiles

Inlaid with a pattern, encaustic tiles have a soft, matt look. They look particularly stunning used in conjunction with plain 'geometric' or terracotta tiles. Widely used in Victorian and Edwardian halls, corridors and conservatories, encaustic tiles are now popular for restoration work. They are generally smaller than other floor tiles – about 7.5–10cm (3–4in) square.

Laying and maintaining tiles

All these tiles, like bricks, need a solid, level base or concrete screed. If you want to tile over a wood floor, cover it in hardboard first or find a malleable glue that can be mixed into the adhesive, allowing movement without breaking the adhesive. If these precautions are not taken, the inevitable movement of the floorboards will some day crack the bond of the adhesive, causing the tiles to rise up.

When tiles are laid, a grout is used to fill the gaps. It is made from ground Portland cement and sand, mixed with water to form a quick-drying paste. Modern grouts are much improved, with acrylic latex additives which help prevent cracking and staining.

Most new tiles come complete with the manufacturer's instructions about sealing. Unglazed tiles, whether new or old, will benefit from a liquid resin sealant that acts like a heavy-duty polish. Alternatively, the traditional finish of one part boiled linseed oil mixed with three parts white spirit can be applied at regular intervals.

Like bricks, tiles can be kept clean by sweeping then passing a damp mop with mild detergent over them.

MOSAIC TILES

These come not only in squares but in numerous other shapes and in a flooring weight. They lend themselves to all sorts of designs. There are three types – clay, marble and glass silica – but they all act and feel much the same as conventional ceramic tiles.

Mosaic tiles are normally supplied back-mounted with a peel-off mesh or plastic backing, or solid face-mounted with paper, in 30 x 30cm (12 x 12in) squares or 30 x 60cm (12 x 24in) oblongs – so you don't have to stick each piece in place or grout between them. Maintenance is as for ceramic tiles, but they are easier to clean if the flooring is continued up the wall for about 15cm (6in).

1 Old encaustic tiles in a late nineteenth-century house are original to the building. Note the small black-and-white diamond-tile border at each side.

2 Aged flagstones are invariably a plus in a room, and will look as good with modern furniture as with old. If laying new ones, however, in whatever stone, try to install underfloor heating first. Warmth and comfort allied to charm is always the best possible combination.

STONE

Stone floors, whether in the form of slabs or tiles, lend elegance and a timeless quality to a home. They will last practically for ever but are cold underfoot and usually quite heavy.

Flagstones

As attractive inside as outside on terraces, flagstones are mainly used in hallways or some other room on the ground floor, on top of a concrete screed or slab floor or a plywood sub-floor. They can be custom-cut or bought in irregular slabs, and although somewhat cheaper than ceramic and terracotta tiles, they are more expensive to install. The term 'flagstones' refers to 'flagging', or slicing, stone into thin slabs. They are mostly cut from blue stone or slate, but sandstone (such as York stone) and limestone can all be used in slabs. Some flagstones, such as limestone, are porous and need to be sealed, while others cannot be sealed at all.

Slate

This is often used as an alternative to marble, especially as it is much more stain-resistant. Available as slabs or tiles, it generally looks best in squares or rectangles, and colours range from pale grey, green and blue-grey to darker green, bluish-purple and black. The slabs should be laid on a concrete screed or slab floor or a plywood sub-floor downstairs, but the thin tiles are light enough to use upstairs over a plywood sub-floor. Slate can be left untreated but it can equally effectively be sealed and waxed. Either way, it looks solid and handsome and is fairly easy to maintain, though it is not cheap.

Marble

This looks expensive, and it is. It usually comes in 30cm (12in) and 45cm (18in) square tiles, although slabs can be ordered too. The most fragile grades are usually the most decorative, with the most interesting veining and coloration, but they are also the most costly. The more solid grades are usually classified A and B, while the more delicate are C and D. The disadvantages of marble are that it scratches and stains easily, but to some people the aesthetics outweigh the impracticality. Lay it on a cement bed, on a concrete sub-floor or, if using the very thin tiles, on very flat plywood, blockboard or chipboard.

Terrazzo

Consisting of marble chips set in a cement base and polished to a high sheen, terrazzo is reasonably non-slip, as well as being durable and handsome. Like marble, it is available in tiles or slabs, and is usually best laid in panels of about 8m (26ft). Because it is very heavy, it should be laid on a cement screed on concrete.

Granite

Cheaper than marble, granite has an attractive grain and is less likely to stain or scratch, as well as being less slippery. Like marble, it comes in slabs but is also available in very thin tiles, which means that it can be used in upstairs rooms, set on plywood, as long as the floor is level and firm. Granite comes in some 50 different colours and in either a matt or a polished finish. The former is safer, in the sense that it is much less slippery, but the latter does look splendid.

part two: the specifics

CONCRETE

Although concrete was invented by the ancient Romans, it is still considered to be one of the most modern and malleable of materials, as it is able to take on any shape or thickness. It will make a good-looking floor in tile form, if it is painted or stained and waxed (see page 123). Concrete is also extremely practical, since it is both heat- and cold-resistant, as well as scratch-proof, and it is reasonably priced. However, concrete floors do take a month of curing to set properly, so they are best used in homes that are being built from scratch or in major renovations.

WOOD FLOORING

Now that wood flooring is available in every price bracket, tone and finish, it can be used anywhere in the house with impunity. As well as new wood, consider reclaimed beams and boards from old industrial and farm buildings. Pine, cypress, spruce, Douglas fir, chestnut and oak are some of the species available.

Types of wood

Softwoods and hardwoods are both used for flooring, with softwood being somewhat cheaper. However, because softwood is butt-joined, it can shrink and leave gaps if it is not carefully installed. It can also be dented easily by high-heeled shoes and heavy furniture. Softwoods include spruce, fir and pine, and should be finished with a polyurethane or oleoresinous sealer, then polished if desired.

If you choose hardwood, make sure that the wood comes from an ecologically managed plantation. Until quite recently, the most easily available choices of hardwood have been maple, afrormosia, walnut, cherry, beech and red and white oak. Red oak and beech are the most common and generally the cheapest of this group. Maple is particularly tough and is therefore often used for contract work. Teak, ebony, iroko, mahogany, Australian ironwood and rosewood look splendid but are double the price of oak.

In addition to all the above, many new tropical hardwoods are now coming on the market, and they are generally cheaper. They are also ecologically acceptable, since they are often produced by groups who are determined to minimize damage to the environment, as well as to provide trade for under-developed countries.

Exotic new tropical woods to enquire about are taun, planchonia and calopyllum from Papua, New Guinea; these are excellent mahogany substitutes. Two more woods from Papua are kamarere, a strong red wood that dries quickly, and turupay, which is a yellow-chestnut colour and enormously tough. Another reddish wood is chontaquiro, from Peru, which is very easy to work with. Merbau is a lovely chestnut colour and dillenia is a substitute for rosewood. Celtis looks like pine but has all the properties of a hardwood and is as cheap as beech, while viltex looks like teak but costs less than ash. Kwila, a handsome black-brown colour, from the Solomon Islands is more expensive – however, you can splash it with impunity without marking it, so it would be excellent in kitchens and bathrooms.

1 *Gleaming polished concrete makes a stunning underpinning to the neutral colour scheme in this idiosyncratic loft. The flow is interrupted only by an insert of flagstones in the kitchen area – a nice textural and spatial contrast to the overall smooth monotones.*

2 *Bamboo floors are comparative newcomers to the increasing choice of natural wood flooring. They are both durable and handsome.*

3 *Nicely fitted parquet flooring made from oak.*

4 *Wood is as much a feature of this study as polished concrete is in the loft on the left. The light wood floor blends beautifully with the finely reeded and plain panelling and bookshelves.*

Wood flooring comes in various forms: planks, which are 7.5–20cm (3–8in) wide; strips, which are 4–6cm (1½–2¼in) wide; parquet, which comes as interlocking oblong wood blocks; and mosaic panels, consisting of small hardwood strips pre-assembled into square tiles on a backing.

Wood flooring is available in either solid or laminated wood. The laminated type consists of a thin layer of hardwood veneer, laminated to underneath layers of plywood, block-board or even cork. The hardwood

part two: the specifics

means taking delivery of the boards or parquet well before installation. A solid wood floor, as opposed to the laminated variety, can be nailed directly to a wood sub-floor. If the new surface is on the ground floor, it is a good idea to install some sort of moisture-retardant material, like bitumen, felt or building paper, between the sub-floor and the new surface. If the wood is to be laid over concrete, a vapour-retardant should be used on top of the concrete, in order to act as a barrier against any moisture.

Laminated flooring, however, can be set straight over concrete. And if it is one of the types that consist of interlocking pieces and are glued together rather than nailed, it should be set over a foam pad laid on the sub-floor.

It is most important that installation nails are not knocked through electric cables or water pipes, so services should be mapped out with care and accuracy.

If you are attempting to lay the floor yourself, fix a line of string along the front of any fireplaces, or any

layer may be as thin as 1–2mm (1/16in), but thicker grades are harder-wearing and can even be sanded and refurbished a few times before the surface gets too frail. Both solid and laminated floors are sometimes used in kitchens, but neither is recommended for bathrooms.

Laying a wood floor

Even if you are employing professional floor-layers, it is useful to know what they should be doing. First, you should make certain, if you can, that the wood becomes adjusted to its new atmosphere before it is laid, which protruding walls or cupboards, then work backwards from these into the recesses. Since wood expands and contracts with changes in temperature and humidity, this slight movement must be allowed for, with a narrow expansion gap around the edge. If necessary, it can be covered with beading or filled with cork. Removing the skirting boards allows the new floor to be slipped underneath before they are put back, which covers the expansion gap and makes the job look neater. However, this is not always possible.

1 *Polished chipboard is an unusual but durable and practical surface for both general living and play space.*
2 *Wide, bleached floorboards provide a contrast to the high-beamed ceiling and tall, painted bookshelves in this mellow French living room.*

4

3

3 *Large grey diamonds painted over white have been given several coats of acrylic varnish for toughness. Such painted finishes are an inexpensive but decorative solution for battered old floorboards.*
4 *The slatted boarding used for this bathroom is more usually connected with outdoor showers, gardens, decking and paths. It is rare to see it used inside.*

Finishes

All hardwood floorings, except pre-sealed laminated floors, need a sealer to repel moisture and dirt.

If you are finishing the floor yourself, it is much easier and more comfortable, as well as swifter, to use a water-based finish, like a urethane/acrylic combination or an organic primer with a citrus-oil base. These dry in 30 minutes and do not yellow the wood like many polyurethane finishes do.

The traditional finish for most hard floors is tung oil and wax, and this can still be used, though the floor will need to be rewaxed once a year or so and polished regularly with an electric polisher, an essential machine for any large areas.

part two: the specifics

Flexible Flooring

Hard-wearing, easy to maintain and relatively inexpensive, flexible floorings not only are practical but are often extremely decorative and are warmer underfoot than tiles or stone.

LINOLEUM

Made of a compound of linseed oil, pine resins, wood, ground cork and pigment pressed onto a jute backing, linoleum comes in sheets or tiles. Non-slip, burn-resistant and reasonably priced, it is making a big comeback. One of its biggest plusses is that the material can be inlaid and spliced to make handsome and distinctive customized designs that are a far cry from the rather sticky old brown 'lino' that covered the floors of so many dreary rooms in the early twentieth century. Whether you are using the sheet form or tiles, linoleum should be glued to a spotless, level, preferably plywood underlay.

CORK

Durable and economical, cork is warm, soft and quiet underfoot. This very resilient material is made of compressed and baked pieces of the bark of the cork-oak tree. It lasts well, especially when combined with vinyl, and is efficient in bathrooms, play-rooms, kitchens and hallways.

It comes in sheet and, much more commonly, tile form. The tiles are usually pre-sealed. If they are unsealed, they will need to be varnished after laying. Cork is available in a range of colours as well as light to dark browns.

As with wood, cork should be left in the room in which it is to be laid for at least three days prior to installation,

to allow it to become acclimatized. If the cork is being laid on old wood, cover the sub-floor first with latex-fill, hardboard or plywood. If the sub-floor is concrete, install a moisture-proof membrane first in order to prevent

moisture rising up from the slabs and lifting the flooring.

It is important to sweep cork flooring carefully to ensure that there is never any residue of grit or sand to score the surface. Avoid abrasive or alkaline cleaners. As with most floors, sealed surfaces are easily cleaned with a damp mop and mild detergent.

VINYL

Made from PVC (polyvinyl chloride), vinyl flooring is comfortable to walk on, tolerably reasonable in price, easy to clean and available in a huge choice

of colours and designs. Like linoleum, plain colours can be combined to form good-looking patterns.

Basically, the choice is between the more expensive, longer-lasting, solid variety, and the cheaper, composition vinyl which is a mixture of fillers and pigments with a thermoplastic binder. Composition vinyl can be either cushioned or flat. The cushioned variety is slightly 'bouncy' and more resilient underfoot, making for a softer tread, and it provides some sound insulation. The flat variety is very flexible, moulding itself easily to the floor.

Solid vinyl comes in plain colours but also in realistic copies of marble, granite, terrazzo, limestone, brick, terracotta tiles and wood. If you are purchasing composition vinyl, it is usually best to get the inlaid variety, in which the design runs through all the layers, as opposed to the rotogravure type, in which the design is merely printed on the surface.

Vinyl is available in either sheet or tile form. It can be laid on existing wood, tiled or linoleum floors (if smooth and in good condition) or on a concrete screed.

RUBBER

Rubber flooring is more hard-wearing as well as softer, warmer and quieter underfoot than linoleum or vinyl. It is resistant to burns and dents, and, because in some cases it has inbuilt self-releasing wax, it can often cure itself of scratches and minor damage. It is available in sheets and tiles, in either industrial or domestic quality.

It comes in a range of colours, including primaries, pastels and industrial black, which lends itself to a high-tech decor. Studded patterns of varying sizes are the most common, but ribbed and slate-like effects are also available. The studded and ribbed versions are very non-slip, which makes them useful in bathrooms, but they are also more difficult to clean and so not really suitable for kitchens.

1 *Cleverly cut and inlaid linoleum in quite an ambitious design makes an inexpensive but exotic and easily maintained bathroom floor.*
2 *Studded industrial rubber flooring is a perennial favourite for many minimalist installations, being non-slip, reliably tough and relatively noiseless.*
3 *Vinyl tiles laid in a classic diamond pattern (and looking similar to the painted wood floor on page 143) are a practical choice for kitchens, dining areas, halls and corridors. They are comparatively soft underfoot, are easier on breakages than regular ceramic, terracotta or quarry tiles, slate or concrete, and are very easy to keep clean.*

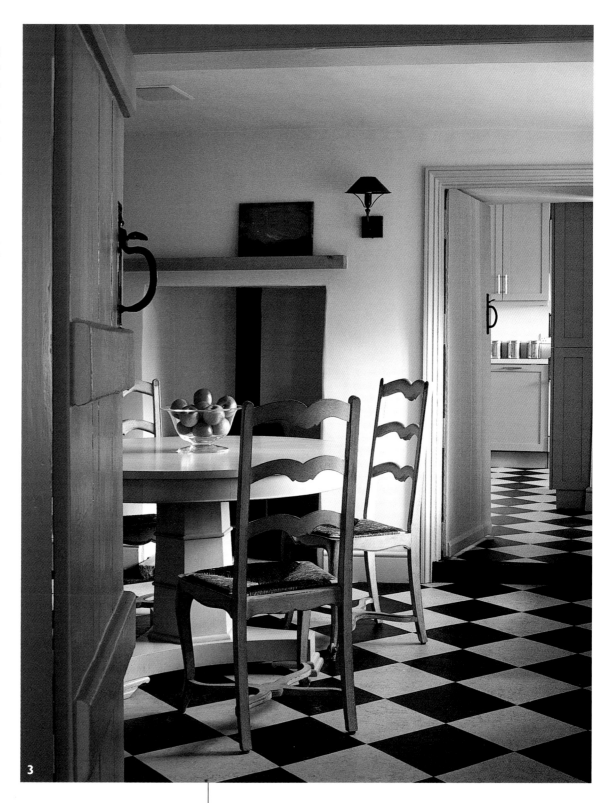

part two: the specifics

SECTION SIX

Beautiful windows that provide equally beautiful light while looking out over an agreeable view are clearly desirable – but they are also comparatively rare. Happily, there are numerous ways to cover, treat, disguise and enhance less-than-perfect providers of light and air. They range from the most elaborate use of fabric, tassels, fringes, edgings, tie-backs and headings to the simplest of treatments. There is a formidable choice of blinds, made not only from fabric but also from aluminium, vinyl, pinoleum, split bamboo, paper and wood. And then there are alternative treatments like screens, shutters, shelves of wood or glass, trellis, stained glass, painted glass and windows treated like paintings.

Windows

Choosing Window Treatments

It is a good idea to make a window treatment an integral part of a room, rather than designing it to stand out from everything else. I don't mean that windows should not be a focal point. Indeed, large windows, and unusual or particularly handsome window treatments, make very fine focal points, and in a room that might otherwise be lacking in architectural detail or interest, they can add a special quality. But curtains should be seen in the same context as the rest of the room scheme.

tip

TEST HOW MUCH LIGHT WILL BE LOST IN A PROPOSED WINDOW TREATMENT BY APPROXIMATING THE EFFECT WITH PINNED-UP SHEETS.

1 *Camel-coloured roller blinds at these long windows so exactly match the painted walls that they look like a panelled continuation of them.*
2 *Elaborate curtains are used at the entrance to this room, while simpler, light-coloured ones are hung at the French doors, to allow some light to filter through.*
3 *Storage shelves are a bold and practical solution to this awkwardly shaped window.*

It would obviously not look right if you installed the elaborately fringed and/or swagged curtains so beloved by the Victorians in a minimalist room (though, paradoxically, it is perfectly possible to put simple but well-made curtains in an otherwise elaborately furnished and decorated room). Nor would it look good to have very bright curtains in a gently or subtly coloured room. As in most things to do with decoration, it is a question of achieving a reasonable balance with all the rest of the components of a room.

Often the most decorative or unusual windows, such as arched, bay or dormer windows or French doors, are the hardest to treat. Suggestions for their treatment are given on pages 168–71. There is, however, a vast choice of ideas for ordinary windows, ranging from curtains or blinds in various styles to completely different treatments. It is easier to make a choice if your rooms are a specific period or style, or if you have already chosen the way you want a particular room to look. Much also depends, of course, on practical considerations, like how light the room is, what it is to be used for and, the money available.

1

with roller or Roman blinds or shades, fitted underneath the curtains. This should cut down satisfactorily on heat loss, insidious draughts and road noise.

- **Do windows face east or north (or west or south in the southern hemisphere) in rather dark rooms?**
  If so, you should ensure that you choose window treatments that will obscure as little of the light you get as possible. This rules out tied-back curtains that meet in the middle, deep pelmets and other elaborately draped styles.

- **Do windows face south or west (north or east in the southern hemisphere)?**
  If they do, you are likely to get a lot of light and sun, so avoid using fabrics that will fade or rot easily, like silks and very bright colours. Consider filtering the light with translucent blinds or sheer curtains.

- **Do you live in a town or city, or in a place where there is a lot of pollution in the air?**
  If so, avoid using light colours or treatments involving a lot of elaborate folds, so that the fabric does not need to be cleaned too often.

PRACTICAL ASPECTS

If you want to ensure that your curtains are practical, here are some of the questions that it is important for you to ask yourself.

- **Are your windows draughty, cold or inclined to let in road noise?**
  Apart from the drastic and expensive measure of changing your present windows for good-fitting double-glazed windows, or at least treating them to draught-excluders, make sure that any curtains you order are heavy and interlined. Even better, introduce a further layer of fabric between you and the outside world

part two: the specifics

I *Translucent panels threaded on battens at the top and bottom have a pleasantly airy feel. They also use little fabric and are inexpensive to make. However, they provide scant privacy at night when the lights are on.*
2 *Painted double-hung old shutters are good-looking and effective in their own right, which is just as well since they would be awkward to use in conjunction with most curtains or blinds.*

• Are your windows overlooked by passers-by or by houses or apartments opposite?

Do not forget that net, muslin, voile, lace and otherwise translucent curtains or blinds that provide privacy during the day without cutting off light are transparent at night. As an alternative to sheer curtains, café curtains (curtains hung from a rod fixed halfway up a window) provide considerable privacy. Another way of providing some privacy is to fix several glass shelves across windows on which you can display a collection of glass or china or plants, or all three. Densely planted window boxes can also provide a degree of privacy.

- **Do your windows have radiators under them?**

  Unless a window is tiny, curtains generally look better if they are just puddling on the floor, yet covering radiators with curtains causes heat loss. Therefore, if you decide to use curtains at windows with radiators, you will almost certainly want to tie them back at each side and use a blind or shutters as well. Or you could omit the curtains completely and just use the blinds or shutters on their own.

- **Do your windows have deep recesses?**

  If so, it is preferable to hang the curtains outside the recesses because this will let in the maximum amount of light by day.

3 *These toile de Jouy curtains with matching low-slung tie-backs are prettily suspended from a pole covered in the same fabric. The juxtaposition of the toile with the striped love seat is effective and, together with the miniature topiary trees on the sill behind, forms an attractive little vignette.*

4 *Swedish cotton curtains are also hung from a self-covered pole, but with the addition of silvered finials and hold-backs, as well as a deep window seat. This seat is comfortably scattered with cushions in various patterns.*

part two: the specifics

151

Curtains and Top Treatments

Whether you are a full-scale curtain and trimmings person or prefer the simpler, modern styles, the fact remains that most rooms benefit from some sort of softness and decoration at the windows, even if it is only in the form of a top treatment.

Provided curtains are appropriate for the style of the room and home and fulfil the practical considerations discussed on pages 149–51, they can today be as sumptuous or minimal as you like. But during the nineteenth century, the great age of curtains, the treatment in the main rooms of most respectable houses consisted of a pelmet *and* a valance, the over-curtains and under-curtains, and a blind or shutters. The boxed-in pelmet was often blended in with the cornice of a room. It supported the valance

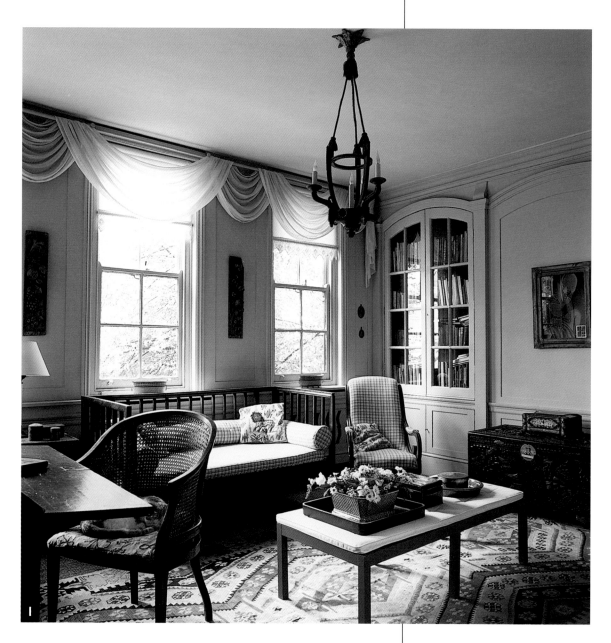

1 *A very long, slim rod with an elaborately swagged length of sheer fabric runs the full width of the window wall in this living room. The lightness of the fabric, allied to the pale aqua of walls and ceiling, serves to exaggerate the sense of coolness.*

2 *A curtain made from a heavily ridged fabric is here suspended by stitched leather loops from a trim steel pole. It is an unusual but effective treatment.*

3 *Breezy voile is contrasted with black rings and a twisted iron pole. The rings are spaced far enough apart to form graceful deep scallops.*

4 *Here, another light curtain is suspended by slim tabs from a rod that is held well away from the window. Note the bracket, which packs quite an interesting punch in itself.*

and also the pole or track from which the curtains were hung. Alternatively, the valance was sometimes draped around a pole, ending in a swag and tails, which obviated the need for a pelmet. Generally the curtains and valance had fringing in contrasting or toning colours. Tie-backs or ties were used to loop the curtains back by day, and sometimes by night, too, if a blind or shutters were used.

Today, such elaborate curtain treatments are seldom seen except in the most formal rooms – indeed, the opposite, a bare or minimally dressed window is much more common. But properly made curtains can still make all the difference to a room scheme. What is more, the top treatment – whether an elaborate swag with tails,

a pelmet or valance, or simply an attractive heading on curtains suspended from a pole – is as basic to the overall effect as the fabric is.

POLES AND TRACKS

All curtains are suspended from poles (with rings), rods (with or without rings) or tracks of one kind or another. Poles – whether made of polished wood, painted wood, wood covered with fabric, brass, wrought iron or steel – stand on their own merits. They do not need to be hidden by swags and tails, pelmets or valances.

The thickest poles, generally known as cornice poles, are around 35–38mm (1⅜–1½in) in diameter and come in standard lengths with rings and brackets. You can contrast wooden

poles with brass brackets or use slimmer architrave brackets. If you have very wide windows, you might need to join several poles together.

Some poles are supplied with decorative ends such as knobs or finials, but you can also buy finials

separately. They are now available in all kinds of fanciful shapes, as well as the more traditional designs such as spears and pineapples.

Slimmer poles, or rods, can be used without rings for cased or tab headings (see pages 158–9) or café curtains.

3

2

4

part two: the specifics

Tracks are always purely functional and meant to be hidden, which can be done with swags and tails, pelmets or valances (see right, and pages 155–6). Some types are designed to support curtains *and* valances. Tracks can be either corded (providing the means to draw the curtains as well, thus preventing wear and tear on the leading edges) or uncorded. They can even be bought specially curved to fit bay, bow or arched windows.

They are generally made of white plastic or metal, with a choice of brackets, depending upon how far away from the windows you need the curtains to hang.

CREATING ILLUSIONS WITH CURTAINS

Small windows with poor views can be made to look much larger and more elegant than they are, with no sacrifice of light, by using several layers of cream or white voile, muslin or lace.

For example, you could hang one layer straight over the window, suspended from the upper part of the window frame and descending to the floor, to hide the shape of the window. You could then add two separate curtains, gathered onto an overlapping rod suspended over the top of the window frame, and caught back with tie-backs at each side. The fabric could be edged with a bobble fringe or ribbon trim for added interest. Or you could simply top the first layer with a gently draped valance in similarly coloured silk. If you require more privacy than the several layers of light fabric can provide at night, you could always mount a roller blind under the first curtain.

Another way of creating a long, graceful-looking window out of a nondescript rectangular or square one is to build a window seat. Fix a wood frame around the top and sides of the window and down to the floor. Next, fix a length of wood between the sides as a seat. For comfort, it should be about 35cm (14in) deep, which means it will project beyond the frame at the front. Now mount a pole across the top to hold two floor-length curtains, tied back at each side of the window. Put a foam cushion on the seat, and use scatter cushions to hide the wall between the window sill and seat.

If you have two or three such windows on a wall, you can make this arrangement look an integral part of the room, as well as adding useful storage, by building in shallow cupboards and/or shelving between the new window frames.

LININGS AND INTERLININGS

Unless you are deliberately using sheer or lightweight curtains to filter rather than block light, you should certainly line curtains. They will hang better and look much more sumptuous if you interline them as well, quite apart from preserving heat.

Lining protects the main fabric from sun, dust and pollution, encloses hems and raw edges and can provide decorative contrast wherever a curtain is caught back. A good lining makes curtains look better from the outside too. All these points also apply to swags and tails, valances and pelmets.

If early-morning light is a problem in bedrooms, curtains (and fabric blinds) can be lined with special

'blackout' linings which, though not necessarily black, will make the window treatment much more opaque. They can also be lined with milium, a thermal fabric which not only blocks out light (though not quite so well as 'blackout' lining) but also helps insulation.

SWAGS AND TAILS

These are most often used for elaborate, formal treatments, and although they look as if they are made from one beautifully draped length of fabric, they usually consist of a number of different pieces that have been skilfully joined together. They are frequently trimmed with braid, piping, fringing, cord or fabric borders, and often have contrast or patterned linings. It is essential not to skimp on fabric, but it is equally important not to overdo it.

Proportions are crucial for this treatment. At its deepest part, the swag needs to be between one fifth and one sixth of the overall height of the window, while the tails should fall at least halfway down the window. The grander styles look best on large windows in rooms with high ceilings, but relatively simple treatments are quite versatile. Indeed, swags and tails do not have to be partnered only with curtains – simple swags can also be used effectively over blinds or shutters, or on their own.

A swag with tails is fitted to a pelmet board using drawing pins or a staple gun. Instead of a pelmet board, a swag and tails can be draped over a pole, extending beyond the window on either side so as not to obscure too much light. If the fabric needs to be fixed in place, use a wooden pole, which will take drawing pins, small nails or staples from a staple gun.

As a simple alternative to a swag and tails, a length of fabric can be casually draped over a pole. To make it easy to remove for cleaning, it can be held in place with Velcro dots.

PELMETS

These are decorative cover-ups for the tops of curtains (or blinds), disguising any unsightly tracks or fittings. To avoid a top-heavy look, they should not be deeper than one sixth of the overall curtain drop.

It is possible to find splendid carved, gilded or painted pelmets in antique shops. If they fit or can be made to fit the windows, they can be a great asset to a period room.

part two: the specifics

This soft cotton valance has a frivolously puffy knot at each side. Such extravaganzas are generally stuffed with tissue paper to keep the shape if the fabric is very light. The gauzy fabric is edged with a fringed trim.

Generally, however, pelmets are made from plain wood, which is either painted or covered in a suitable fabric, or from a stiff material like buckram, which is again covered in fabric. A shaped pelmet is very effective in disguising an ordinary straight curtain track fixed across an unusually shaped window, like an arched window (although an equally arched track is better).

Another variation of the shaped pelmet is the lambrequin, which reaches right down the sides of a window, sometimes as far as the floor, making an undistinguished window look a great deal more interesting.

Both pelmets and lambrequins can be trimmed, edged, piped, rosetted, ruched, fringed or corded, according to taste and the style chosen.

VALANCES

Softer than pelmets, valances are made entirely of unstiffened fabric. Unless intended to look light, they are usually lined and interlined. They can be gathered or pleated, by hand or using heading tapes, as in many of the methods described for curtain headings (see right). They can be decorated to match the curtains, perhaps with a contrast band or frill, piping or some other trimming.

Valances can be hung from a special valance track aligned to the main curtain track. Alternatively, they can be attached to a board, which is either above the curtain track or has the curtain track attached to the underside. Such boards are usually fitted either to the top of the window frame or above the window, by means of strong, evenly spaced brackets. The boards should be at least 5cm (2in) longer than the track at each side.

A valance known as an attached or integral valance looks much the same as the conventional variety when the curtains are drawn, but is actually attached to the top of each curtain so that the two halves move apart when the curtains are opened. This avoids blocking incoming light but, because the curtain track is not covered when the curtains are open, it is best used with a pole.

CURTAIN AND VALANCE HEADINGS

Headings determine the style of curtains and valances, and they affect how they hang. Many are meant to be paired with decorative poles rather than being hidden. Traditionally, pleated headings are made by hand, but the job is quite labour-intensive, and heading tapes are much faster.

For some curtain treatments, the curtains are left permanently drawn at the top. The sides are held back with tie-backs, which are simply released as necessary to close the curtains. This treatment is sometimes known as a fixed heading. Any curtains can be treated in this way, but some headings have to be fixed because they are not easy to move and may look unsightly when open. They are therefore more suitable for rooms that either are very light or are used mostly at night.

French pleats

Also known as triple or pinch pleats, this heading allows the curtains to fall into gentle but precise folds. You can buy French pleat heading tapes but they sometimes sag, so it is generally better to hand-sew them. A single tuck is made at regular intervals which is then divided into triple pleats. It is important to work out the right number of pleats and spaces to fit neatly and symmetrically into the given space. This heading is fixed to a track or curtain pole or rod by pin hooks placed at the back of each pleat.

Goblet pleats

This handsome heading is formed and secured in much the same way as French pleats. However, instead of small triple pleats being formed from a fold, this time each fold is secured at the base to form a small 'goblet'. To help them keep this goblet shape, they are usually stuffed with a suitable filling or interlining, and they are often further distinguished by a contrast binding or lining. Like French pleats, they are best hand-sewn, although appropriate heading tapes are available.

Flemish pleats

This handsome treatment, which needs to be treated as a fixed heading, looks infinitely better if hand-sewn. It is

tip

FOR AN EVEN MORE LUXURIOUS AND PROFESSIONAL-LOOKING EFFECT ON LINED AND INTERLINED CURTAINS, PAD EACH LEADING EDGE WITH AN EXTRA STRIP OF INTERLINING ROLLED LENGTHWISE AND INVISIBLY HAND-STITCHED INSIDE THE CURTAIN LINING.

2 *French pleats (also known as triple or pinch pleats) are here attached by rings to a classic wood pole complete with finials. Loose cord tie-backs hold back the fabric just behind the sofa.*

3 *Small goblet pleats are closely attached to a slim, slightly curved pole. The low-slung tie-backs form a good frame for the high-backed and graceful chair.*

part two: the specifics

157

formed from goblet pleats (see pages 156–7) which are bound or trimmed at the base of the heading with a hand-sewn cord, sometimes twisted into decorative knots.

Alternatively, instead of going right across the base of every 'goblet', the cord can be attached to the base of, say, every third one, so that it falls into large loops. They are usually fixed to a track or board.

Box pleats

Box pleats look crisp, tailored and elegant. They can be formed by hand, but they can also be achieved very satisfactorily by simply sewing a box-pleat heading tape, which has a pair of pull-up drawstrings, to the top of the curtain or valance. Box pleats should be treated as a fixed heading.

Smocked

This is another very handsome heading, as good in formal living rooms and dining rooms as in bedrooms, but it does involve a good deal of careful workmanship. Even with a special 'smocking tape', which gives the heading a smocked outline, the smocking still has to be hand-sewn. If the whole heading is hand-stitched, it is best to plot out the smock design on paper first, before transferring it to the top of the curtain. A smocked heading should be treated as a fixed heading.

Pencil pleats

These are the most functional but the least decorative of the various headings, so may be better concealed beneath a pelmet, valance or swag. They are usually formed with the help of a pencil-pleat tape with three rows of pockets for positioning hooks, as opposed to the narrower tape used for gathered headings, which has only one row. Pencil-pleat tapes come in different weights and depths to accommodate various types of fabric.

Gathered

An informal heading, mostly used for sheer and lightweight fabrics, and made with a narrow tape sewn about 5cm (2in) from the top of the curtain. When the integral drawstring is pulled, it forms a frill of fabric above the tape and soft gathers below.

Cased

This method, though casual and capable of many variations, suits most window types, but it should be treated as a fixed heading and so will not be suitable for dark rooms.

A pole or rod of the appropriate size is simply pushed through a casing sewn at the top of the curtain, or near the top if a stand-up frill is liked as a finishing touch. The pole or rod is thus completely covered except for the very ends.

Tab

This is a variation of a cased heading, in which a series of tabs, like individual casings, are attached to the top of the curtain pole or rod. The pole or rod is pushed through them.

The tabs can be in the same fabric as the curtain, or in a contrast fabric. Both ends of each tab can be stitched to the curtain like a loop, or just one end can be stitched and the other buttoned in place.

Scalloped

A good, casual treatment, particularly for lightweight or café curtains, is simply to hang the curtains from a pole using sew-on or clip-on rings. The

3 *Here a simpler tab heading in the same sheer cotton as the curtains is attached to a steel rod. The curtains puddle gracefully onto the white-painted floor.*

4 *A bold perspex pole is pushed through reinforced overscale eyelet holes in this tailored, contemporary eyelet heading.*

spaces between adjacent rings will automatically take on scalloped shapes. For more pronounced scallops, a series of shallow semicircles can be stitched and cut along the top edge, which has been faced, and rings are attached between the scallops.

Eyelet

This contemporary heading involves inserting jumbo eyelets along the top edge of the curtain. The curtain is folded concertina-fashion and a pole is slotted through the eyelets.

part two: the specifics

159

TIE-BACKS

Curtains can be caught back in a number of different ways, and at various heights. The usual height at which to position the hooks for a tie-back is two-thirds of the way down the window, but of course they can be placed higher or lower, depending upon what seems in proportion to the window. A well-placed tie-back, or pair of tie-backs, can give a splendid swoop to curtains, revealing interesting glimpses of a contrast lining if desired.

One of the most commonly used shapes of tie-back is a long, narrow oblong, stiffened with buckram or interfacing. It can be casually tied around a curtain or given rings, sewn in at the ends, each of which is then attached to a couple of hooks judiciously placed behind and to the side of the curtain. Other stiffened shapes, such as crescents, are also possible.

Another type of tie-back is made from interlined tubes of fabric plaited together. The fabrics might incorporate, say, one strip of the curtain fabric and two others.

Other styles include tie-backs with bows; thick cords with tassels made from silk or cotton, or a mixture of both; metal tie-backs, also known as hold-backs; and brass or silvered 'roses' on a long stem, behind which you can tuck the curtains.

ITALIAN STRINGING

Another method of holding curtains back when they meet at the top is called Italian stringing, or reefing. A diagonal line of rings is sewn at the back between a point about one fifth of the way down the outside edge, and a point about one third of the way down the leading edge. Cording is then run through these rings (and, for one curtain, along a batten at the top). Pulling on the cords at the side pulls the curtains apart in much the same manner as the curtains on a puppet theatre. Italian stringing looks effective and lets in more light than tie-backs placed lower down.

CURTAIN TRIMS

Most curtains look more 'finished' and elegant with some sort of trim, even if it is only a self-trim – a slim roll of the curtain fabric finishing off the edges. An inspiring selection is available in every price range.

Contrast linings are a wonderful way of finishing off curtains, particularly those that are tied back or

160

1 A three-part twisted brass hold-back.

2 Fringed tassels on a cord tie-back.

3 A handsome gilded screw-in 'rose' hold-back, which is easy to use and enables the curtain to be looped back as fully as desired.

4 Goblet-pleated interlined linen curtains are Italian strung, with a tassel suspended just below the centre of the fixed heading. Note the effective inset border matching the white paintwork.

Italian strung. They can include the same design in a different colourway, or even the same fabric used back to front, which can be very subtle. (I find that the back of a fabric is sometimes much more interesting than the front, so always examine both sides.)

Sometimes when I want a contrast fabric to show on tied-back curtains, I just face the inner half of each curtain with the contrast fabric over the top of the normal lining material. If the contrast fabric is quite expensive, and the curtains large, this works out a lot less expensive than using the contrast fabric for the whole curtain.

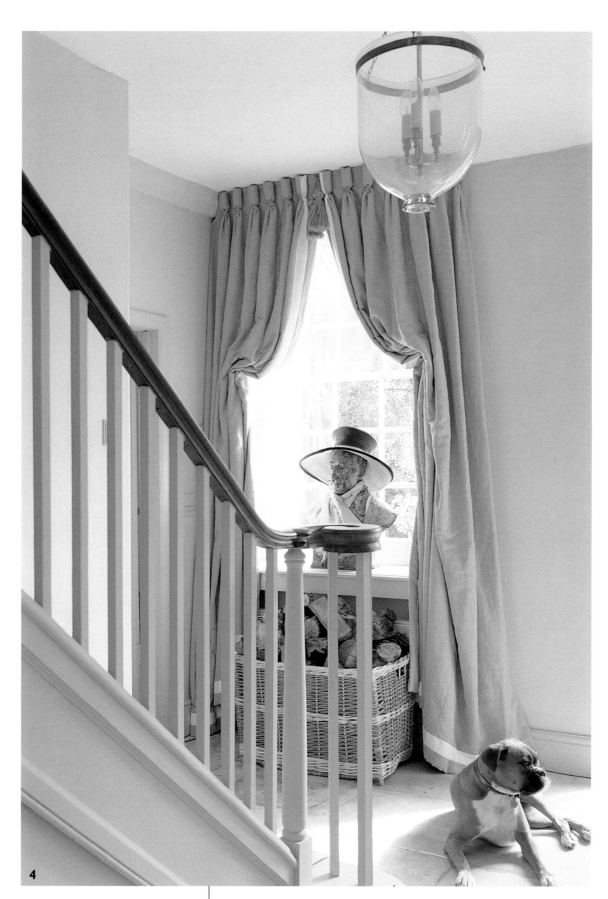

part two: the specifics

Blinds

Window blinds, used as either alternatives or adjuncts to curtains, have many advantages worth considering. Since a blind is basically just a single piece of fabric, it will show off the design of a patterned fabric much better than curtains. Also, a plain fabric with a border, either inset or on the edges, looks very crisp and architectural. Romans and rollers, in spite of sounding like a 1960s pop band, have clean lines, so are suitable for every sort of room, whether modern, period or eclectic.

If you have a good-looking window frame, you can install a blind inside the recess to show it off, rather than hiding it with curtains. Most types of blind are good alternatives to curtains for small windows or windows with radiators or window seats underneath. You can also use them effectively in conjunction with permanently tied-back curtains, which you cannot, or do not want to, disarrange. Apart from being a practical cover-up for a window, a blind adds an interesting sense of perspective to a room.

All blinds are lowered and raised by either a spring mechanism or a cording system which allows the blind to lie flat against the window, to be ruched or to be pulled up in neat folds or pleats. Since blinds can be lowered

1 *Plain off-white roller blinds on a pair of bathroom windows look pleasingly geometric behind a scarlet-painted bathtub. Frivolous tassels attached to the roller blinds repeat the colour of the bath in miniature.*

2 *White silk Austrian blinds provide quite a contrast to the dark oriental table and collection of baskets below. But the juxtaposition of textures — silk, wood, bamboo, succulent leaves, stone and terracotta, velvet upholstery and differing basket weaves — works well, creating a modern mood. This space is compact and utilitarian, as well as attractive to the eye.*

2

tip

MAKE A WINDOW
LOOK LONGER AND
MORE GRACEFUL BY
POSITIONING A BLIND
SO THAT THE BOTTOM
OF THE BLIND, WHEN
PULLED UP, JUST COVERS
THE TOP OF THE FRAME,
THUS DISGUISING ITS
PRECISE WHEREABOUTS.

and raised at will to any desired level, they can be made either to filter light or to block it out altogether.

FABRIC BLINDS

There are five main types of fabric window blind: Austrian, festoon, pull-up, roller and Roman.

Austrian blinds

These were a great favourite in the Rococo period of the eighteenth century. In spite of being considered by purists as fussy, they can look entirely suitable in certain situations. Austrian blinds have fullness in the width – the type of heading chosen is a matter of taste, though pencil pleats are most often used. The blind is pulled up and let down in a series of ruched, scallop-like folds. When it is completely down, the only fullness in the length is at the base, where it is still ruched.

An Austrian blind has a series of rings, usually as part of Austrian blind tape, attached to the back of the blind in vertical lines. Each line of rings is threaded with a cord that is attached to the lower ring. The top of the blind is attached to a wooden batten or an Austrian blind track which is fixed to the top of the window frame or just above the window. Screw eyes are attached to the underside of the wooden batten for the cords to pass through, so that they will all hang together at one side. These cords are knotted together, so that when they are pulled, the blind is raised.

A tailed Austrian blind is made in much the same way, except that the cording is omitted from the sides, causing the fabric to droop into a tailed shape. It is possible to have as many scoops as liked between the tails, but just one looks less fussy.

Both kinds of Austrian blind are normally made in light, airy fabrics, but they look more tailored and 'serious' in heavier fabrics, like heavy cotton or linen union; this is especially true of the tailed variety.

part two: the specifics

Festoon blinds

Festoons are often confused with Austrian blinds since both have a good deal of fullness in the width. However, while an Austrian blind falls flat like a curtain, with its ruches or scallop effect only along the base, a festoon has the fullness distributed along its entire length. (It needs twice the length of fabric of the finished drop.) It is gathered onto cords which are inserted between the fabric and lining while it is being made, rather than at the back as in an Austrian blind.

Pull-up blinds or curtains

These were much in use in the eight-eenth century in the grander houses. Robert Adam included them, for example, in his wonderful interior for Osterley Park, near London, so they have an excellent provenance. They look somewhat like Austrian blinds and also work on much the same principle, but they are made to lower right to the ground, when they look like an elegant closed curtain.

Roller blinds

The earliest of all blinds, these are also among the most useful. They were originally known as Holland blinds because 'Holland' was the name of the

highly glazed, finely woven, buff- or Manila-coloured linen with which they were made. Now they can be painted, stencilled and made in almost any fabric that can be stiffened or laminated, or that is firm enough (without being too thick) to roll satisfactorily. They can be common-or-garden practical or highly decorative, depending upon the design of fabric or the trim at the bottom. They are wound around a roller that has either a spring mechanism or a 'sidewinder' cog mechanism.

Reverse roller blinds

With this type of blind, the rolled fabric is at the bottom. It works very simply with a pair of cords and screw eyes without the benefit of a roller or any mechanism. The fabric should be lightweight so that it rolls up easily.

Roman blinds

A Roman blind is flat, with no fullness across the width. When down, it has no fullness in the length either. It draws up into horizontal pleats. The fabric is backed by a series of thin battens sewn parallel to each other in casings or pockets; the battens are pulled up by cords to form crisp folds.

A Roman blind can be lined and interlined, or backed with blackout lining or not lined at all, depending on the fabric and whether it needs to block out light and draughts, just filter the light or retain privacy. The blind can be edged, bordered or trimmed with fringe or cording, and either left on its own or dressed up with a pelmet, valance or lambrequin (see pages 155–6).

It is a good idea not to make Roman blinds any wider than just under 1.5m (5ft). Otherwise, they will be heavy to pull up, and it is really important to pull them up neatly so that they do not look lop-sided. If windows are much wider, make two or three narrower blinds and hang them side by side.

OTHER TYPES OF BLIND

Blinds that are not made out of fabric look very striking and can provide the keynote for a decorative scheme.

Bamboo blinds

These are made from strips of bamboo of varying sizes and often have an interesting tortoiseshell appearance.

Louvre blinds

Louvres are slats or strips of metal, wood or stiffened fabric, which are designed to pivot open or shut. Vertical louvres, which both pivot and draw to one side, are a good solution for an entire window wall in a modern building. The type with thin horizontal slats are known as mini-blinds, while those with wider horizontal louvres are Venetian blinds.

Matchstick or pinoleum blinds

These are made from slim spills of wood (hence the name matchstick) sewn tightly together with cotton. They are generally rolled up and held in place with cords (like reverse roller blinds), although sometimes they are sold with a spring mechanism like a conventional roller blind. They are usually sold as untreated wood which can be either left natural, varnished or spray-painted.

These blinds are useful for filtering light, perhaps behind a more conventional treatment like drawn-back curtains, since they can be seen through at night. As they are cheap, they could act as a stop-gap until more expensive ideas can be fulfilled.

Paper blinds

These are flat blinds that roll up and down like rollers but are made of soft, thick, pliable paper. They are another good temporary measure.

Proprietary blinds

There are various proprietary blinds on the market with different degrees of solidity or transparency, and some types have slats. Made from a variety of materials, they work effectively, can look handsome and are excellent for modern buildings.

Proprietary blinds come in a range of sizes to suit all shapes of window, or they can be custom-made to order by the manufacturer. Most types are frequently advertised.

1 *Graphic fabrics like stripes lend themselves well to Roman blinds.*
2 *Narrowly striped Roman blinds, which are half let down on these long windows, look neat and tailored set right against the glass, inside the reveals. A small amount of light creeps through the sides, but the blinds would not have looked nearly so graphic if they had been hung outside the frames.*
3 *Wide-striped Roman blinds coordinate effectively with the series of multicoloured drawers fitted below the wide window sill in this child's room.*
4 *Thin-slatted Venetian blinds cover a wall of windows and make intriguing striped patterns of light and shade.*
5 *Detail of an inexpensive matchstick, or pinoleum, blind. Though not particularly strong, they are useful as under-blinds or as protection against sunlight.*

part two: the specifics

Alternative Window Treatments

In addition to curtains and blinds, there are various other good-looking ways to treat windows.

SHUTTERS

These are always neat and effective, whether they are louvred and folding, or the old solid variety, which were almost *de rigueur* on late eighteenth- and nineteenth-century houses. Old wooden shutters can be stripped; and louvred wood shutters can be left as natural wood; both types can be painted any colour. The old solid kind can also be painted with designs or have their panels picked out or outlined in different colours, to give an updated geometric look reminiscent of paintings by Mondrian.

1 *American louvred 'plantation' shutters in natural wood.*
2 *A pair of free-standing screens front the translucent Roman blinds on this enormous window with its tall integral French doors. The screens lend gravitas to the area as well as literally screening some of the superabundance of light.*

3 *Solid shutters at this small window have been covered in fabric and, unusually, pierced with tiny diamond shapes. The juxtaposition of colours and the grouping of glass on the sill add charming detail.*

4 *Chains of irregularly shaped coloured glass strung across a deep-set window reflect the sun in rainbow colours.*

5 *Here, frosted glass provides the simplest of window treatments, while the recess created by a deep window embrasure has been used to form a dressing table area complete with storage and sink.*

- Glass shelves stretched across a frame are always a successful treatment for small, odd windows; windows that are difficult to open for one reason or another; corner windows at right angles to each other; and kitchen, bathroom and cloakroom windows. Like this, the window becomes an open display cabinet for items such as clear or coloured glass, plants and ceramics.

- Small windows on a stairway, landing or corridor look chaste but interesting with one sculptural object, bud vase, plant or small collection of objects on the sill.

- A window that frames a stunning view and is not overlooked can be treated like a painting, by making much of the window frame. This can be done by painting the frame an interesting colour (which goes with the rest of the room, obviously) or even by aggrandizing the existing window frame.

- An internal window or a small window in a hall, up the stairs or in a bathroom can be made to look highly decorative, either by replacing the glass with stained glass or engraved glass, or by painting the existing glass.

part two: the specifics

Problem Windows

Ironically, some of the most interesting windows are actually the most awkward to dress. They need to be framed and shown off rather than obscured, which gives rise to the perennial conflict between aesthetics and practicality. Here are the most common problem windows, together with some possible solutions.

BAY AND BOW WINDOWS

Though mostly considered an asset in a room, a bay window – or a bow window, with its continuous curve – is often a problem if it has a window seat or a radiator underneath. The answer (as, indeed, for any type of window above a window seat or radiator) is to hang some sort of blinds against the glass. Permanently tied-back curtains can be hung at the sides, or the blinds can be left on their own if you want a crisper look. Add a contrasting or complementary fabric element, when

1 *Quantities of reasonably priced heavy Indian cotton have been made to look quite grand with elaborately fringed swags. In order not to hide the shape of the bay window, they are permanently looped back, and only the Roman blinds are pulled down at night. The bay has been elegantly filled with a bolstered chaise longue.*

2 *The difficulty in finding a suitable treatment for a triangular window has been avoided here by not doing anything – the shape makes quite enough of a statement on its own.*

there is a window seat, with scatter cushions covered in a variety of materials and textures.

You can make this type of window look as grand or as simple as you like according to the top treatment you use. There is no reason why you cannot suspend quite elaborate swags and tails either across the front of the bay or on a curved track along the top of the window.

If there is no impediment around the windows, a corded track can be bent around them. The track is best suspended from a pelmet board. Use either one pair of voluminous curtains drawn back during the day or a tied-back pair at each section of window. In this case, the treatment is probably more expensive than awkward.

FRENCH DOORS

Many French doors open inwards, which creates a problem if you want to use them while curtains are closed, but there are various ways you can overcome the problem.

If there is space, you could hang curtains from a pole, which should be wider than the frame so that they can be pulled to either side to allow the doors to be opened.

If there isn't room to do this, you could hang blinds on the glazed part of the doors themselves, together with a good-looking top treatment fixed above the window. Or create sash curtains as for skylights.

Alternatively, for each door, hang a curtain on a Victorian-style *portière* rod, one end of which fixes to the door frame and the other to the far side of the door; the rod swivels, so that the curtain opens with the door.

2

WINDOWS WITH SHUTTERS

You can easily leave shuttered windows as they are, or you can just add a splendid pelmet or valance. Alternatively, hang Italian-strung curtains or curtains permanently held back with tie-backs, closing the shutters at night. Security shutters can be a problem, though. If you have these, it is best to forget about fabric treatments and simply paint them.

ARCHED WINDOWS

Try not to lose the effect of the arch at night – or during the day, for that matter. The traditional way to treat a Venetian, or Palladian, window (a rounded, arched window with narrow rectangular windows at each side) was to have a festoon shade in two parts

on the centre, leaving the side windows undressed or simply shuttered.

Rounded tracks can be installed to follow the arch, keeping curtains permanently closed at the top and held back underneath during the day. A Velcro-like pencil-pleat heading tape can be used in a similar way.

A simpler and cheaper approach, though it means losing the arch at night, is simply to fix a pole or track well over the top of the arch so that at least you see it during the day. Another alternative is to fix a pole across the window below the semicircular portion, and curtain the window beneath, leaving the arch bare. Austrian and festoon blinds and pull-up curtains can also be hung from a curved or arched track, though they will have to be stationary within the arch itself.

PICTURE WINDOWS AND WALLS OF GLASS

You probably will not want to obscure a picture window by day (although you will need somehow to filter or control the amount of sunlight). However, if it is a gloomy, black space at night, you will almost certainly want to cover it then. (Exceptions include high-up city apartments, where the city lights many floors below can look magical, and windows looking out onto a garden that is beautifully lit.) Roman blinds, or vertical louvres, chain or other sorts of proprietary blinds are often the best solution for a whole wall of glass, where curtains would most often look rather fussy. However, you could hang a single, dramatically looped-back curtain at a picture window, if there is room to loop it back to the side.

DORMER WINDOWS

Because there is no room to the side of these windows to hang curtains, roller or Roman blinds are one of the neatest solutions.

Alternatively, run hinged, slim rods through casings at the top of a pair of short curtains – the rods and curtains can swing back against the reveals during the day, minimizing light loss.

SKYLIGHTS

You can buy special Venetian blinds from the manufacturers of skylights. Or use normal Venetian blinds or mini-blinds, a roller blind or a blind that can be held against the wall by cup hooks fixed below the window sill.

An alternative is a sash curtain. Slip expandable slim tension rods or expandable plastic-sheathed curtain

part two: the specifics

wires through narrow casings at the top and bottom of a lightweight curtain, and attach it to the frame.

CIRCULAR WINDOWS

These are really best left bare – or you could replace clear glass with etched, painted or stained glass.

CLERESTORY WINDOWS

The best treatment for these long, narrow, horizontal or vertical strips of glass is blinds. Alternatively, fit glass shelves across the frame to make a display area.

SIDE-BY-SIDE WINDOWS

These should generally be treated as one window. Hang curtains from a pole or track within a pelmet that goes across both windows, and draw the curtains to the side. Alternatively, use blinds of one kind or another.

CORNER WINDOWS

When two windows are at right angles to each other in a corner, use either blinds or glass shelves which you can light from above or below by a recessed down-light or an up-light.

DIFFERENTLY SHAPED WINDOWS ON THE SAME WALL

If one of the windows is particularly small, just leave it untreated with a shelf across it or a sculptural object on the window sill. Otherwise, curtain the whole wall, tying the curtains back at either side if it is a small wall. If it is very long, you might need to have some fixed-headed curtains on the walls between the windows.

PIVOT WINDOWS AND WINDOWS THAT OPEN INWARDS

If you need privacy, mount lightweight curtains or sheers on the window itself. For windows that pivot horizontally, attach a slim rod to the inner frame and hang café curtains from it. For vertical pivoting windows, fix sash curtains to the frames, as for skylights (see pages 169–70) or use *portière* rods as for French doors (see page 169).

1 *Fixed roller blinds above with Roman blinds below is the solution to the oversized windows in this cathedral-ceilinged room.*
2 *Old-fashioned* portière *rods open with the windows or can be folded away to the sides of the frame. The curtains themselves are slung from slim tabs.*

3 *Awkward, shallow, horizontal windows are notoriously hard to treat. This one has simply been hung with Venetian blinds and balanced with a deep storage shelf of the same length.*

4 *A classic oeil de boeuf window has been left severely alone and looks rather like a landscape painting in a round frame, nicely balancing the portrait above.*

5 *An unusually shaped window – arched and slim, with a roundel tucked into the arch – has again been left untreated, and rightly so. Note how the severe 'greige' walls, the bookshelves and the single stone vase all enhance the graphic architectural look.*

part two: the specifics

Fabrics for Windows

Almost any fabric can be used at a window, though clearly some fabrics are more appropriate for particular rooms and climates than others. But just because chintzes, light cottons, silk taffetas and *failles* are conventionally suited to bedrooms, there is no reason why flannels, wools or weaves of one sort or another should not be used there. By the same token, heavy textures such as wools, tweeds and velvets, as well as chintzes, silks, *moirés*, damasks and brocades, are thought good for living rooms – but these spaces could just as well be a riot of airy textures if it seems appropriate for the situation and climate.

Most fabrics look and hang better and last longer if they are both lined and interlined. If you specifically want the floaty look of unlined curtains,

tip

IT IS FAR BETTER TO USE A GREAT DEAL OF AN INEXPENSIVE MATERIAL, PERHAPS SMARTENED UP WITH A BORDER OR TRIMMING LIKE CORD OR BRAID, THAN A SKIMPY AMOUNT OF EXPENSIVE FABRIC.

perhaps for a delicate room scheme, or to combine with contrasting blinds, use an interesting texture such as wild or watered silk, silk taffeta, softly printed voile, embroidered muslin or light linen. Try to ensure that lightweight curtains are three times the width of the window, with deep hems, both to help the fabric hang better and to allow for shrinkage.

Roller blinds need an easily rolled fabric, though it is possible to get a variety of fabrics specially stiffened or laminated. Roman blinds, which are raised (into neat folds or pleats) and lowered by cords, can be made in literally any material, as long as it is not too thick to pull up and pleat evenly. Austrian, festoon and pull-up blinds need very light, soft fabrics to work well and look good.

1 Simple, inexpensive checked cotton has been lined and interlined, and beautifully designed so that the curtains look infinitely more expensive than they were. The Victorian chair and the window seat have been covered in the same bold check.

2 Translucent blinds are hung behind much heavier curtains in a panelled bay window so that the look can vary from light and airy to warmer and more enclosed.

3 Deliberately filmy curtains have been designed to blow around in romantic fashion in this country living room.

part two: the specifics

3 *A curved track holds these voluminous voile curtains well away from the French doors. These curtains, too, are as generously puddled onto the floor as a sweeping bridal train.*

1 *Double curtains in green and yellow gossamer fabric have been hung one above the other and left to puddle deeply on the floor in a nicely negligent way.*

2 *In complete contrast, crisp, deeply pleated curtains only just graze the floor and are kept rigorously in place by weighted hems. Note how the exaggeratedly large hems add to the dramatic panelled effect.*

Vocabulary of Fabric Terms

Acrylic: A SYNTHETIC FIBRE, or a fabric made from this fibre. The properties of this fabric make it adaptable to many uses. It is stronger than NATURAL FIBRES and will not shrink or crease, but it does attract dirt.

Aniline: Term applied to dyes derived from coal tar; used in colouring fabrics.

Baize: A coarsely woven, reversible fabric with a felt-like surface. It was often used to cover doors between domestic and living quarters, but it can be used for curtains and blinds.

Bark-cloth: A woven fabric with a rough texture, primarily used for curtains.

Batiste: A soft, sheer fabric, usually in white. It can be woven of COTTON, SILK, LINEN, WOOL or SYNTHETIC FIBRES.

Bedford cord: Lengthwise, corded material of COTTON, WORSTED or SILK.

Bengaline: A finely woven fabric with a raised horizontal rib.

Bobbinet: Curtain material made with round-hole mesh. The closeness of the mesh and the fineness of the thread determine the quality. Usually used for sheer curtains.

Brocade: Originally heavy SILK but now made from SYNTHETIC FIBRES, with elaborate pattern in silver or gold threads. A JACQUARD WEAVE, brocade has an embossed appearance.

Brocatel: A variation of BROCADE with a higher relief, or *repoussé*, effect, with WARP and FILLING yarns unequally twisted, and an extra set of yarns for backing. The JACQUARD pattern stands out in raised, or blistered, effect.

Buckram: Once a rich, heavy woven cloth but now a stiffened material, usually COTTON with glue SIZING, which can be used to stiffen curtains, pelmets, valances and tie-backs.

Bump: Thick, loosely woven, blanket-like cotton or polyester interlining for heavy curtains. Also used as a backing for fabric walling (see page 112). It is heavier than DOMETTE.

Butcher's linen: A coarse, HOMESPUN linen-weave cloth, originally used for French butcher's smocks.

Calico: A PLAIN-WEAVE, lightweight fabric which is very inexpensive.

Cambric: A fine, closely woven, white or plain-coloured COTTON fabric with glazed appearance on the right side. Primarily used for curtains.

Canvas: A closely woven cloth, usually of LINEN, hemp or COTTON.

Casement cloth: Broad term which covers many curtain fabrics, usually of a light, plain, neutral colour. The weave structure is plain TWILL, satin-striped.

Challis: Soft fabric of SILK, WORSTED or RAYON, available in plain colours or printed with small figures.

Chambray: A fine-quality PLAIN-WEAVE fabric with a LINEN-like finish that is woven in plains, checks and stripes.

Chenille: Fabric made by weaving a thick, soft WEFT and a small, hard WARP, which binds weft threads tightly together. Split into strips, this forms the chenille yarn used for weaving the fabric. The cut edges of yarn form a PLUSH-like surface.

Chiffon: A thin gauze fabric of PLAIN-WEAVE construction, made of SILK. Used mainly for curtains.

Chino: A coarse cotton fabric woven of combed yarns in a TWILL WEAVE.

Chintz: Originally any printed cotton fabric, but now a curtain fabric, which usually has a GLAZE. It is principally associated with large floral patterns but plain chintz is also available.

Cotton: The fibre, or fabric made from the fibre, from the seed-case of a cotton plant. Cotton is an incredibly versatile fabric and comes in a wide range of weights and textures.

Crash: Term applied to several fabrics having coarse, lumpy, uneven yarns or rough TEXTURE. Made of jute, RAYON, LINEN or COTTON, or a combination of them, it is available in natural or colours and is used for curtains.

Crêpe: General term covering many kinds of crinkled or unevenly surfaced materials, such as wool crêpe or crepon.

Cretonne: Printed curtain fabric of COTTON or LINEN in a variety of weaves and finishes; may include CHINTZ.

Crewelwork: Embroidery worked in coloured WORSTED yarns with long, loose chain-stitch on cream-coloured COTTON, LINEN or WOOL fabrics.

Damask: Named for the ancient city of Damascus, where elaborate floral designs were woven in silk. Today this JACQUARD WEAVE is available in SILK, COTTON, WOOL or SYNTHETIC FIBRE mixtures. Flatter than BROCADE and reversible. The pattern changes colour on the wrong side.

Denim: Heavy TWILL made of coarse COTTON yarn. The name, originally *serge de Nîmes*, comes from the French town of Nîmes. Furnishing-weight denim is finer and has a softer finish than that used for jeans. It is usually YARN-DYED.

Dimity: Crisp, lightweight, COTTON fabric usually woven with a stripe or check pattern.

Dobby weave: Cloth with small geometric pattern woven on a loom with a special attachment.

Domette: Light brushed-cotton interlining for lightweight curtains and for swags and tails; lighter than BUMP.

Duchess: Curtain material with an appliqué design.

Dupion: A slubbed yarn made from silk; also known as douppioni.

Embossing: Pressing fabric between engraved rollers with heat to give a raised effect, similar to embossed stationery. Washing or steaming removes the design. Embossed VELVET, or PLUSH, is a fabric made by weaving the pile high then shearing it to different levels.

Embroidery: A decoration in needle-work executed by hand or machine on fabric already woven.

Faille: Ribbed fabric of SILK, RAYON or COTTON, with stripes produced by alternating fine and heavy WARPS.

Figured: Fabric with a woven-in pattern.

Filet: Square-meshed NET or LACE. Once hand-made, it is now mostly machined.

Filling: Same as WEFT or WOOF. Yarn for the shuttle. Each crosswise yarn is called a pick.

Flannel: A soft fabric of PLAIN or TWILL WEAVE with a NAPPED surface on one or both sides.

Flock: Short, clipped fibres, glued to wood, paper or fabric, to provide a suede-like surface.

Gabardine: A firm, tightly woven fabric with a close TWILL-WEAVE surface and a flat back.

Galloon: Narrow binding of COTTON, WOOL or SILK, usually showing fancy weaves.

Genoa velvet: A FIGURED VELVET with a SATIN ground and multicoloured PILE.

Gingham: Checked PLAIN-WEAVE fabric made from COTTON yarns dyed before weaving. Originally a clothing fabric, it is used now for curtains and also for loose covers.

Glaze: A finish on fabrics such as CHINTZ, which are treated with paraffin and calendered (pressed between rollers). Used for curtains, and also lampshades and loose covers.

Grass cloth: Coarsely woven fabric of vegetable fibres used as curtains, and also as wall coverings.

Grenadine: Loosely woven curtain fabric of leno weave, plain or with woven dots, in SILK, RAYON or WOOL.

Grenfell cloth: Closely woven, water-repellent cloth for curtains, and also upholstery.

Hand-woven: A term indicating that some part of the weaving has been done by hand.

Herringbone: A pattern that is made up of rows of parallel lines which, in any two adjacent rows, slope in opposite directions.

Hessian: Coarse cloth woven from jute. Though used to cover furniture springs and for wall coverings, it can also be made into curtains.

Homespun: Loosely woven fabric made to resemble hand-woven, Colonial material.

Hopsacking: A rough-surfaced COTTON, LINEN or RAYON fabric with a plain basket-weave pattern.

India print: Cotton fabric with hand-blocked (or simulated) designs in bright colours.

Ingrain: Flat-weave cloth made of multi-coloured threads dyed before weaving.

Irish point: Net curtain material with appliqué design, similar to DUCHESS.

Jacquard: DAMASK, TAPESTRY, BROCADE and all elaborately FIGURED cloths woven on a Jacquard loom.

Jacquard weave: Weave structure of complex patterns produced on a Jacquard loom by combinations of PLAIN, TWILL and SATIN weaves on a plain or satin-weave background.

Jaspé: French term for streaked or striped; applied to fabrics having various coloured WARP threads which give a streaked appearance.

Lace: A fine, open-work fabric with patterns of knotted, twisted or looped threads on a ground of NET or mesh.

Lambelle: A lightweight DAMASK texture having fine MERCERIZED WARP threads and slightly coarser WEFT threads of contrasting colour.

Lampas: Originally an East Indian printed silk. Now applied to decorative fabric having REP ground with SATIN-like figures formed of WARP threads and contrasting WEFT figures.

Lawn: Light, thin, very smooth fabric of highly polished yarn. Originally of LINEN but now of COTTON.

Linen: A fabric made from the bark of the flax plant. Woven into cloth, it is noted for its smoothness, strength, coolness and lustre, as well as its tendency to crease.

Linen union: See UNION.

Lisère: French silk cord fabric, made with a WEFT of BROCADED flowers and a WARP of JACQUARD figures.

Lustre: Gloss finish applied to fabric by heat and pressure.

Madras: A strong COTTON fabric from India, woven with a brightly coloured check or stripe pattern.

Marquisette: A type of open weave, used for curtains. Marquisette fabrics are made of RAYON, NYLON, SILK or COTTON.

Matelassé: French, meaning cushioned or padded, hence a quilted surface produced on the loom. A FIGURED or BROCADED cloth with a raised pattern.

Mercerized: Treatment for thread or fabric to give strength and lustre.

Metal cloth: Any fabric with decorative interwoven metallic threads.

Moiré: A fabric, especially SILK, having a watered or wavy pattern.

Monk's cloth: Rough, canvas-like curtain material, made of heavy COTTON yarns, often containing some flax, jute or hemp. Also called friar's cloth, it wears unusually well and is used for wall hangings, loose covers and upholstery.

Mousseline: A lightweight, MUSLIN-LIKE cotton with a crisp finish which is closely woven of highly twisted yarns.

Mummy cloth: Light, textured COTTON or SILK fabric with an irregular WARP figure.

Muslin: A PLAIN-WEAVE fabric made from COTTON, sometimes printed and varying in fineness.

Nap: Not to be confused with PILE. The downy, or fuzzy, appearance of cloth produced by raising the fibres to the surface, as in flannel. When lengths of a nap fabric are joined, the nap must run in the same direction.

Natural fibres: Fibres produced from natural sources (such as SILK, WOOL and COTTON) as opposed to SYNTHETIC FIBRES.

Nets: Fabrics of loose, open construction with threads that are tied where they cross.

Ninon: A type of light, transparent PLAIN-WEAVE fabric that is often used for sheer curtains.

Noil: Short fibres removed during the combing of a fibre, and spun into yarn.

Nottingham lace: Flat LACE used for curtains and tablecloths. Originally hand-made, now machine-made.

Nylon: A SYNTHETIC material adapted for fashioning into filaments of extreme toughness, strength and elasticity, then knitted into fabrics.

Oiled silk: A thin, waterproof SILK fabric, which has been soaked in oil and dried.

Olefin: A trade name, this fibre is a product of the petroleum industry. It is lightweight and highly durable.

Organdie: A fine, LAWN cloth, chemically treated to produce crispness and stiffness. It is used for curtains and also for clothing.

1

2

1 Two different kinds of blue-and-white stripes have been used for a particularly unstructured blind treatment. A batten is thrust through a casing at the top, then the blind is rolled up and kept neatly in place by buttoned tabs. Buttons are sewn to the sides for symmetry.

2 Roman blinds in Indian cotton mask the strong glare of sunlight while allowing its warmth and light to filter through.

Organzine: A thrown SILK of continuous fibre made from the unbroken cocoon of the silkworm.

Paisley: A multicoloured design of Indian descent, woven or printed, usually on natural fabrics.

Panné: A term applied to PLUSH, VELVET, mohair or SILK that has been flattened by steaming and pressure, so that the PILE lies close to the back, giving the fabric a shiny appearance.

Peau de soie: French term for soft, closely woven SATIN with a gentle lustre; usually made of SILK.

Pick: The WEFT weaving; comes from one passage of the loom's shuttle.

Pile: Fabric having a surface made of upright ends, as in fur, as distinct from NAP. It may be cut or uncut. Pile may be made of extra WOOF yarns, as in VELVET and PLUSH, or of extra WARP yarns, as in VELVETEEN. Warp pile can have loops on both sides, as in towelling. When lengths of a pile fabric are joined, the pile must run in the same direction.

Plain weave: Weave structure in which the WEFT goes under one and over one WARP. Examples include GINGHAM, VOILE, MUSLIN and TAFFETA.

Plissé: French term for COTTON fabric that has been chemically treated to give a crinkled surface.

Plush: Cut or uncut PILE fabric having a pile of greater depth than VELVET.

Point d'esprit: French term for a BOBBINET with a small dot or woollen figure, similar to SPOTTED MUSLIN.

Polyester: A SYNTHETIC FIBRE which is strong and durable, but pills and soils easily. It blends easily with NATURAL FIBRES, such as COTTON, for both strength and versatility.

Pongee: A PLAIN-WEAVE curtain fabric of SILK or COTTON.

Poplin: Fine, cotton-ribbed fabric, usually MERCERIZED. Launders and wears well, unless the weave is loose.

Ramie: A NATURAL FIBRE similar to flax, obtained from the stalk of a plant native to China.

Ratine: TAPESTRY-woven fabric with knobbly or bumpy surface.

Raw silk: See WILD SILK.

Rayon: A lustrous SYNTHETIC FIBRE made by converting cellulose (wood pulp or cotton linters) into a filament by means of a chemical and mechanical process. It is stiffer, more lustrous and less expensive than SILK, but not so strong.

Rep: Closely resembles POPLIN but rep has a heavier cord (FILLING yarn) and is wider; it is used for curtains and upholstery. When a JACQUARD figure is introduced on a REP background it is called armure.

Repeat: One complete repetition of a pattern in fabric (also in wallpaper and in rugs).

Sailcloth: Light COTTON CANVAS or other material of close weave.

Sanforizing: A patented pre-shrinking process.

Sateen: MERCERIZED COTTON fabric of SATIN WEAVE. Better grades resemble SATIN made of SILK. True sateen has FILLING on the surface.

Satin: A lustrous surface fabric with broken TWILL WEAVE. Usually woven of SILK threads but may be made of RAYON.

Satin weave: Weave structure in which the WEFT is 'floated' over more than one and under one WARP thread.

Seersucker: COTTON or RAYON fabric with crinkled surface.

Selvage: Tightly woven edges that prevent fabric from unravelling.

Scrim: A coarse type of VOILE used principally for sheer curtains.

Shantung: Knobbly fabric, originally woven from Chinese SILK, now made also from RAYON or COTTON.

Sicilian silk: A DAMASK fabric with a SILK WARP and a COTTON or LINEN WEFT, forming a PLAIN-WEAVE ground with a SATIN-WEAVE figure.

Silk: Soft, NATURAL FIBRE obtained by unravelling the cocoons of Japanese silkworms. Also applied to fabrics woven of silk thread.

Sizing: Any chemical substance applied to a fabric to provide greater stiffness, a smoother surface and increased strength. Can be permanent (glue or clay) or temporary (starch).

Spotted muslin: Sheer, PLAIN-WEAVE COTTON fabric embroidered or woven with dots at intervals. Used for clothing as well as curtains.

Suede cloth: Cloth with a NAPPED surface made to resemble suede.

Synthetic fibres: Fibres made through chemical and machine processes, as opposed to NATURAL FIBRES; also called man-made fibres. Examples include RAYON, ACRYLIC and POLYESTER.

Taffeta: A name applied to several types of fine, crisp, PLAIN-WEAVE fabrics. May be made of SILK, COTTON, LINEN or RAYON in mixed fibres.

Tambour embroidery: Machine embroidery in chain-stitch to resemble hand-work done on tambour frames.

Tapestry: Originally a HAND-WOVEN fabric made with a bobbin worked from the wrong side on a WARP stretched vertically or horizontally. A machine reproduction of tapestry is a YARN-DYED, FIGURED fabric composed of two sets of WARP and FILLING yarns woven on a JACQUARD loom.

Tarlatan: Thin, gauzy fabric of COTTON that has been glazed for stiffness. Used mostly for curtains.

Ticking: A striped COTTON fabric. Originally used to cover mattresses, it now comes in a finer grade for curtains.

Toile: A finely woven COTTON or LINEN with translucent qualities.

Toile de Jouy: Originally an eighteenth-century copperplate-printed COTTON fabric, printed with pictorial scenes in a single colour on a white or cream background. Modern versions are widely available today.

Towelling: An absorbent fabric, woven or knitted, with a loop PILE.

Tricot: A low-priced COTTON or RAYON TAPESTRY where the right and wrong sides are different.

Tweed: Rough-surfaced WOOL fabric of mixed, flecked colours.

Twill: A heavy COTTON fabric.

Twill weave: Weave structure in which the WEFT moves one step to the right or one step to the left with each line, producing a diagonal texture.

Union: Sturdy LINEN-and-COTTON fabric, also known as linen union.

Vat dye: A process of dyeing any material to obtain permanent colour.

Velours: Fabrics with a short PILE.

Velvet: All WARP-PILE fabrics, except PLUSH and TOWELLING.

Velveteen: A fabric with short COTTON PILE made in approximate imitation of SILK VELVET.

Vinyl: A non-woven plastic, which is capable of being embossed or printed to produce any desired finish, such as a leather or wood grain, floral pattern or textured design.

Voile: A translucent PLAIN-WEAVE fabric, often of COTTON, made of yarns that have more than the normal amount of twist. Used for sheer curtains and blinds.

Warp: Set of yarns which run length-wise of cloth, across the WEFT.

Weave: The characteristic structure of a fabric produced from interlocking strands of yarn. Common weave structures include PLAIN, TWILL, SATIN, JACQUARD and DOBBY WEAVES.

Weft: Set of yarns running crosswise, and interlaced with the WARP, to produce a woven fabric. Also called woof, filling, pick or shoot.

Whipcord: A ribbed material formed by floating the WARP threads over several large WEFT threads.

Wild silk: SILK fibres as they are taken from the cocoon of the silkworm before the natural gum has been removed. Sometimes called raw silk.

Wool: NATURAL FIBRE from sheep; also fabric woven from yarns of wool fibre. Each breed of sheep produces its own unique type and grade of wool, but all wool shares the qualities of warmth and elasticity that make it adaptable to blending with other fibres. It can be combined with natural or SYNTHETIC FIBRES for strength, beauty and smoothness.

Worsted: Smooth, tightly woven WOOL fabric made from exceptionally long fibres. Gabardine and serge are examples of this.

Yarn-dyed: Fabrics woven of yarn dyed before it is put on the looms.

part two: the specifics

SECTION SEVEN

It is easy to become so involved with the complexities of a room's paint effects, window treatments and flooring options that the furniture is all but forgotten. Yet remove the furniture from a room and you are left with an empty shell. Furniture, more than anything else, is what makes a home comfortable, convenient and livable – and so should be considered carefully, whether you are about to choose new furniture or to reuse existing furniture in a more effective way. This section, therefore, deals with the most important aspects of furniture, from arranging it to choosing upholstered furniture, beds and other modern pieces, with a brief guide to antique furniture.

Furniture

Furniture Arrangement

Apart from its style and practicality, the way furniture is arranged is of paramount importance, so your starting point should be to think about how the pieces will work together.

It might seem odd to consider furniture arrangement before discussing the actual furniture, but it is important to learn how best to place furniture, for two reasons:

1 If you are redecorating, renovating or generally trying to improve an existing room, you need to have a sure idea of what to keep, what to discard and what extra pieces, if any, you must acquire.

2 If you are designing a room from scratch, you must have a clear idea of exactly what furniture you will need, how you want to use it, what sizes will work best and where you want to place it. All this must be decided before you go out and buy anything.

ESTABLISHING PRIORITIES

If a room does not function well, it is a failure, however good it might look. And in order to function well, the room has to be well arranged. It is as simple as that.

- If people do not feel comfortable in a room . . .
- If there is nowhere to read . . .
- If there is nowhere near at hand to place a glass or coffee cup . . .
- If there is no easy, natural way to walk through a room without having to squeeze by and dodge pieces of furniture . . .
- If the furnishings are not appropriate . . .
- If there is no real focal point . . .
. . . then the room is not a success.

The ideal in every room is for each piece to be placed where it works *and* looks best, but there is often a conflict between the aesthetic and the practical. An armchair, for example, might look particularly good in a corner and help to balance the other furnishings visually – but it might never actually get used there.

Therefore, if you are forced to choose between aesthetic and practical considerations, the practical must take priority. Armchairs are meant to be *sat on*, and sat on in comfort. Find something else of comparable visual bulk, like a large, bushy plant, or a side table, to give the needed balance.

Although people's needs obviously vary a good deal, there are some general criteria to follow with regard to furniture arrangement.

SEATING GROUPS

You cannot really consider any piece of seating on its own merits alone, unless it is an occasional chair, or a desk and chair. Seating should be considered as part of a group. A chair on which you can sit comfortably and read easily should be partnered by a side table and a light source, preferably a lamp at the right level for reading. For deep comfort, you might also want a footstool. This arrangement, in turn, should be considered as part of a larger seating group (unless it is positioned in the corner of, say, a

1 *Upholstered pieces are arranged around a big coffee table to form a comfortable conversation area in this large space. The dining area is by the long windows.*

2 *A useful breakfast/quick-snack/ reading/writing surface has been built in on one side of a galley kitchen. The stools, which have cane tops and steel bases, are light and easily manoeuvrable and take up little visual space.*

3 *In this obviously comfortable bedroom, club armchairs are positioned for reading or conversation. Their scale also balances the bed..*

2

study, as a relaxed place for reading and thinking). Usually, this larger group is a conversation group and includes a sofa, at least one other armchair and possibly a love seat as well, depending on space.

These different seats will all need good lighting, as well as some sort of nearby table surface. You could, for example, combine end tables with a large upholstered stool or a good-sized coffee table in the centre of the grouping. In addition, the seating should be grouped around some sort of focal point (see page 183).

MANIPULATING SPACE

Space is as much an element in a room as the objects in it. I am not, in this case, talking about the size of a room but about the space around each item – the balance between solid objects and empty space. In general, rooms that have a lot of space around the furnishings look much better than overcrowded rooms, because they seem lighter and airier.

As well as improving the aesthetics of a room, the manipulation of space plays an important part in its traffic patterns. Traffic patterns must be established when planning the positions of furniture, so that there can be easy movement throughout the room. Establishing these is mostly a matter of common sense, but there are a few guidelines to keep in mind.

- A major passageway through a room should be at least 1.2m (4ft) wide, and preferably 1.5m (5ft), to allow enough room for two people to walk side by side. For subsidiary traffic routes, allow at least 45cm (18in).

- Allow 30–45cm (12–18in) between a sofa or armchair and a coffee table, so that people can get up gracefully from a sitting position, without having to twist and sidle. At the same time, the table should not be so far away as to make it awkward to reach out and pick up, or put down, a glass or book.

- Allow about 45cm (18in) between dining chairs and at least 60cm (2ft) to pull a dining chair back from a table. There should be at least 120cm (4ft) between the dining table and a wall, to enable people to walk behind diners when serving and clearing away.

- In front of a dresser, bureau or chest of drawers, 90cm (3ft) is necessary to allow the drawers to be pulled out. In front of a wardrobe, at least the width of the door should be allowed for opening the door. Between beds or between a bed and a wall, 45cm (18in) is needed for bed-making.

A SENSE OF BALANCE

Before you start thinking about side tables, occasional chairs, storage units, desks, dressers, pianos, and so on, you need to consider scale and balance. This involves the ratio of vertical lines (tall pieces) to horizontal lines (low pieces) and the proportion of light items relative to solid ones.

- If a room consists of mostly tall pieces, such as a wall unit or armoire, with large pictures, mirrors, tall plants and high-backed chairs and sofas, it will look too stiff, formal and uncomfortable.

- If it is all low lines, with low-backed seating, low storage, small plants,

part two: the specifics

The light, elegant dining table here is balanced by more solid upholstered dining chairs. The twisted wire chandelier echoes the table base, as do the tall, skinny candlesticks by the wall. The large painting nicely fills the space between the two windows.

low-hung horizontally shaped mirrors, and paintings hung low on the walls, a room will look incomplete and somehow disturbing.

- If most of the objects in a room are solid and heavy-looking – for example, a lot of upholstered pieces with a piano and an armoire – a room will look stodgy and decidedly ponderous.
- If all the furnishings are very light – say, several occasional chairs, a cane or wicker sofa and love seat, and an *étagère* (a piece of furniture with open shelves) – a room can look worryingly insubstantial.

There has to be a happy medium in a well-arranged room. This does not mean having half vertical lines and half

horizontal; half solid and half light – that would look too set, too *meant*.

On the whole, most rooms look best with a predominant number of low pieces, set off here and there by taller pieces of varying heights. They could progress, perhaps, from a low, upholstered stool or sofa to a wing chair, then to a side table and lamp, and finally, to the really tall lines of an armoire, a bureau-bookcase, or a painting or mirror over a side table, chest or fireplace, and tall plants.

Similarly, a sofa and armchairs, which are solid, should be balanced by the openness of occasional chairs; the lightness, perhaps of a glass table; the height and massiveness of a storage unit. A dresser or a bureau-bookcase

can be balanced with tall but light and leafy plants, or indoor trees. Densely painted canvasses can be juxtaposed with the reflective qualities of mirrors.

Planning a room is much easier if you start with the larger, anchor pieces (the pieces you cannot move around much), balancing them carefully with permanent features, such as doorways, fireplaces, windows, bookshelves or panelling. When all that is clear in your mind, you can decide where to fill in with the smaller pieces.

Remember that other features you have already planned for the room, like the floor, wall and window treatments, will also count strongly in the general balance of the room. Elaborate window treatments will have much more visual weight than casual ones. A patterned fitted carpet or densely patterned oriental rug will be visually heavier and have more importance in a room than a plain wood or tiled floor with simple bordered, geometric or needlework rugs. Dark-coloured walls will look heavier than pale colours. All these factors need to be considered when you are working on the furniture arrangements, and deciding how it should be balanced with the decoration of the room as a whole.

SUITABILITY OF POSITION

The final, and most important, key to success is how well the arrangement takes into account the environmental factors and also ease of use.

Environment

Extremes of climate, heat and cold, dryness and humidity all need to be taken into account when positioning furniture. Strong sunlight will make both wood and fabrics fade, so fabrics used for upholstered pieces placed near windows should be as fade-resistant as possible. If furniture is covered in a fabric likely to fade, do not place it near a window unless you want it to fade, or you have fitted some sunblinds (or if the glass is the specially treated type suitable for exceptionally sunny areas, or it has been covered with a sun-filtering film).

Over-zealous central heating can make antique furniture (made at a time when there was no central heating) split, warp and lose bits of veneer, as well as making doors and drawers difficult to open and shut. To help counteract this, fit a room with a humidifier. In addition, make sure that good pieces of furniture are not placed too near radiators or heating vents.

Pianos and other large musical instruments should, if possible, be placed near an inside wall, rather than a window, and away from radiators, heat vents, sunshine and obvious draughts. Apart from the case, which in older pianos is as vulnerable as antique furniture, sound mechanisms can be affected by extreme humidity.

Listening and viewing

Stereo equipment should be placed near, or against, a hard wall, facing soft surfaces like curtains and upholstery, or an upholstered wall (see page 112), because the combination of hard and soft surfaces produces the best acoustics. A television screen should not, except in the case of a media room, be a dominant part of a space. Nevertheless, it should be placed so that it can be seen easily by at least four people.

Creating a focal point

If a living room does not have a natural focal point, like a fireplace or window, you will need to create some central interest around which you can form various furniture groupings. A large painting or a group of smaller ones, a tapestry or a rug mounted on a wall might be suitable. If there is a suitable outside wall, you might be able to put in a decorative wood-burning stove; it is worth finding out.

Other possibilities include an interesting bookcase or a 'media wall' (an attractive built-in storage system for television, video recorder, sound system and videos and CDs). Even a low table holding an assortment of interesting objects could be a suitable focal point. Whatever you choose, it will help to draw people in and unify the whole seating area.

CREATING ARRANGEMENTS ON PLAN

The next stage is to check that your proposed arrangement will work, by drawing it to scale on a floor plan. Do not be tempted to skip this stage, as it is an invaluable way to check that the arrangements will work. Living rooms are by far the most difficult to do – most other rooms more or less arrange themselves, unless they are particularly large. Therefore, planning out your own living room will be good practice, whether it is for real or just for experimentation.

Start by drawing your room plan on graph paper (see page 16). Most pieces of furniture have fairly standard measurements, and so you can use the templates of the most common furniture pieces, all drawn out to scale; these are available as kits from paint and DIY shops. You will need to supplement them with templates you make yourself (to the same scale) for non-standard items – or you could make them all yourself.

Look at the photographs in this book to get ideas for possible arrangements. Analyse why some are more suitable for your room than others, taking into account the points covered in this chapter.

Try your hand at some arrangements. There is no need to think in terms of style at this stage – just scale, comfort, practicality and suitability. Move the templates around on the

FURNITURE PLACEMENT CHECKLIST

Before finalizing the furniture placement in a room, use this checklist to remind yourself of all the factors you need to take into account. With just a little practice, you will find yourself thinking of all these aspects automatically.

PRACTICALITY – Will it work well?

AESTHETICS – Will it look good?

ORGANIZATION OF SPACE – Have you allowed enough space around individual items of furniture?

TRAFFIC PLANNING – Can people move around easily?

SCALE AND BALANCE – Will the furnishings look interesting and varied, and without any individual item dominating?

ENVIRONMENTAL ASPECTS – Will furniture get too much sun, heat, cold, humidity, dryness or draughts?

EASE OF USE – Will people be able to hear music and see television properly, and is there a good focal point?

plan until you find the best arrangement, then trace their outlines onto the final plan.

Doing a floor-arrangement plan helps you to see if there is anything left out, what should be left in and what should be purchased new. If you abide by such a blueprint, you are less likely to go astray later with unsuitable impulse purchases.

Upholstered Furniture

The most important point to learn about upholstery is that what you see is not necessarily what you get. What you *cannot* see is the key to the piece's comfort. An upholstered piece should *feel* as good as, or better than, it looks, because the inner construction is what counts. Therefore, always look at the label detailing the construction of an upholstered piece before you are beguiled into buying it; in most countries, the law requires that the contents be listed in detail. More often than not, the label will detail care instructions as well.

CONSTRUCTION METHODS

To ensure that you know what to look for and whether the construction is all it is made out to be, it helps to understand a little about how upholstered furniture is constructed. There are two types of upholstery:

1 Fully upholstered pieces, such as sofas, love seats, armchairs, slipper chairs and upholstered stools. These are completely covered with upholstery, with no frame showing, except possibly the lower part of the legs.
2 Exposed-frame pieces, like occasional chairs, *chaises longues* and stools that have parts of the frame showing.

The *frame* is constructed first. A good-quality piece of furniture should be made from oak, teak or walnut, or some other kiln-dried hardwood, not from softwood such as pine. It should be straight, with no warpage. The joints should be glued, and double- or triple-dowelled, corner-blocked and screwed.

Next comes the *webbing*, which is the bottom-most material used on an upholstered piece, to hold the other layers. Good strong webbing should be made from jute, flax or a synthetic material, and woven into a basket-weave design, which is tacked to the bottom of the frame.

In top-quality furniture, after the webbing come the *springs*. Such furniture incorporates coil springs which are set close enough together to provide good support without actually touching each other, and which are hand-tied in place. About eight springs are used for one chair seat. Cheaper furniture makes use of more rigid 'sagless' springs, which are far more cost efficient because they do not need to be hand-tied; or else it eschews springs altogether, as in the case of foam upholstery.

On top of the springs goes a tough layer of *canvas* or *hessian*, which is firmly sewn in place as a base to hold the *padding*. This padding consists of polyurethane foam, polyester, rubberized hair, foam rubber, feathers or down, according to the quality of the furniture. Down is the most expensive type of padding, but a popular filling nowadays is a 'sandwich' which consists of down with a layer of foam in the middle. This prevents the soft down from sagging too much and gives it a certain firmness.

The best-quality furniture then has a final layer of *fibrefill* or *cotton felt*, which is eased just below the upholstery fabric. Sometimes even that layer has a protective covering of muslin to reduce the tension on the covering and thus maintain the shape.

When the *upholstery fabric* is stretched over the piece of furniture, it is often trimmed with self- or contrast piping to give it more 'fit' and definition. Loose cushions are treated in the same way.

COMMONLY USED FABRICS

The upholstery fabric itself has to be firm and durable, since it will have to withstand a great deal of wear and tear. The toughest-wearing upholstery fabrics are densely woven cotton, sailcloth, denim, ticking, cotton rep, twill, brocade and corduroy, which are all cotton-based; linen union, which is linen mixed with cotton and is the most traditional loose-cover material; velvets, which can be either cotton or linen-based; and woven, textured or plain damask.

Wool is a softer but still excellent upholstery fabric and is the basis for tweeds, wool reps, jacquards and some tough, shaggy textures. Never buy a loosely woven wool, or a loosely woven texture of any sort, for upholstery. Leather and suede, while expensive, always look luxurious and are extremely long-lasting, so they remain enduringly popular. Ultra-suede (imitation suede) is cheaper and can be easily spot-cleaned, so it is a good substitute.

To prolong the life of upholstery fabric, it is advisable to have it treated with one of the protective finishes available, like Scotchgard or Teflon's Zepel. It is better to have such a finish applied by the upholsterer or the fabric producer, since the do-it-yourself aerosol finishes, in less than skilled hands, can be something of a disaster. In any event, such a treatment should be tested on a small portion of the fabric first. A further refinement is to get the fabric quilted, which also prolongs its life.

CHECKING FOR QUALITY

First test for comfort. Are there firm cushions to give back support? Is the chair or sofa of standard height? (Too low seats are difficult for the elderly, people with back problems and those who are overweight.)

If the piece is covered in a patterned, striped or checked fabric, make sure that the designs are centred, lines and checks are straight and the pattern matches at the seams. All seams and piping should be neat and straight. Any buttons should be sewn right through the filling, not just attached to the fabric. You can test this by gently pulling on the button; if there is a slight tension, it has been properly done.

Check any loose seat cushions (these are a good idea because they can be regularly reversed, thus prolonging the life of the seating). Good-quality items should be stuffed with feathers or down and should be closely fitted to the chair or sofa.

Now run your hands over the piece to be sure there are no lumps or bumps. You should not be able to feel

1 Brightly checked cotton upholstery matches the various colours of the collection of glasses and finger bowls on the shelves next to the chairs.

2 A 1920s modern classic leather and steel sofa has a useful filing cabinet placed beside it as a side table.

3 A grey-painted frame on a piece of French furniture. Note the studs edging the upholstery fabric.

4 A pair of luxurious-looking French fauteuils upholstered in nicely worn linen velvet. Again, notice the finishing touches of the metal studs edging the material.

the wooden frame through the padding, nor should you be able to feel any of the springs when sitting – although you can check that they are there by feeling for them through the 'deck' or 'platform', which is the surface beneath the seat cushions.

Check that casters are smooth-running and sturdy. Finally, as mentioned earlier in the book, don't forget to check measurements – of both the piece you are thinking of buying and your doorways, lifts and any turns in stairs and passageways. Make sure the piece can actually be delivered into its destined room.

part two: the specifics

Non-Upholstered Furniture

Whether in beautifully grained wood or sleek modern plastic, tables, chairs and storage pieces have a wonderfully tactile quality. However, it is important to check the quality behind the beguiling surface.

1 Red and black curved Italian plastic chairs look good set around a pale wood dining table.
2 A painted dresser with glass-fronted bookshelves goes well with the Louis Seize-style chair covered in a small check, and with the white-painted iron bedhead.
3 Light steel chairs around a refectory table in a pale natural wood tie in with the steel-fronted range in the background.

WOOD FURNITURE

Wood furniture, whether new or old, is made either of hardwoods, such as mahogany, rosewood, oak, maple, walnut, teak, yew or cherry, or of softwoods such as pine.

Wood veneer is generally a thin sheet of fine, attractively grained wood glued to a base of inexpensive solid wood, plywood or chipboard. While old wood veneer on antique furniture is inclined to crack and come loose from its base in hot, centrally heated rooms, modern veneers rarely do so. Nevertheless, antique furniture is often in very good condition and has a beauty, patina and rarity value that everyone will appreciate.

All wood furniture, whether new, antique (technically, over a hundred years old) or – that nebulous third category – second-hand, should be checked for stability and quality of construction and finish.

Chairs

It is important to check the joints of chairs, new or old. They should be constructed with corner blocks, preferably with ribs; these are meant to strengthen the joints, which come under considerable pressure. There should be no gaps, and the joints should be smooth. Dining chairs, because they come under daily strain, generally have stretchers (cross pieces connected to the legs) to reinforce them. Straight legs have the greatest strength.

To test the stability of a chair, lean on the piece to see if it tips easily.

4 *A large-scale Colonial-style chair of the kind made in Indonesia looks both comfortable and sculptural. It also appears very much at home against the white-painted floorboards and the floaty white voile curtains.*

Next, push it a little to see if it wobbles. Finally, inspect the finish, which should be perfectly smooth with no bubbles or streaks.

Tables

Like chairs, these should be constructed with corner blocks to strengthen the joints, and the legs should be secure. The grain of the wood should be well-matched, and if there are extending leaves, they should obviously match the grain and colour of the main part of the table. Check, too, that any extending leaves are easy to fit and to remove.

Case goods

These are storage pieces like wardrobes, armoires, breakfronts, dressers, desks, bureau-bookcases, sideboards and chests of drawers. (They are called case goods, incidentally, because, up until the eighteenth century, people kept all their clothes and personal belongings in wooden cases or chests.)

Examine any inset panels in doors, in drawers and on the sides of the piece, to see that they feel solid. Doors should swing freely and fit well. Apply slight pressure to the tops of doors to make sure that they do not sag when they are pressed. Drawers should slide smoothly and fit well, and their bottoms should be firm enough not to buckle when pushed upwards. The insides should be smoothly finished and the corners joined by dovetail or tongued-and-grooved joints. Fine-quality furniture has thin layers of wood, or 'dust panels', between drawers to protect them from dust. Check too for matching colour and wood graining on the fronts, tops and sides of all pieces.

HARDWARE

Another important item to examine carefully on both new and old furniture is the hardware (the knobs, handles, hinges). Make sure it is of an appropriate scale, shape and material, and, in the case of old furniture, that it is right for the period. Good hardware is cast mainly from heavy metal, such as brass, and the edges must be smooth. Knobs also come in porcelain, wood, glass, copper, brushed steel, chrome and resin.

GLASS, PLASTIC OR METAL FURNITURE

Furniture, particularly occasional pieces, can also be made from glass, perspex or other plastics, metals or combinations of these materials. Well-designed pieces are deservedly popular, because they can fit in any room alongside most periods of furniture with a pleasing anonymity and will generally take up less 'visual' space than wood pieces.

Glass

This is particularly used for table tops and shelves. (Some nineteenth-century Indian and Far Eastern princes and potentates actually had entire suites of elaborately chased, completely glass or mirrored furniture for their palaces.) The glass should have a thickness of at least 5mm (⅛in), preferably 1.2–2cm (½–¾in) for practical use. It must be smoothly ground and bevelled at the edges.

Plastics

These include fibreglass, perspex, laminated plastic, polystyrene, polyvinyl and acrylics. The disadvantages of plastic are that it collects dust (although you can polish or spray it with an anti-static solution which helps that problem) and scratches easily. Always choose pieces that are thick enough to stand up to heavy use. Joints should be smooth and bonded together with a heavyweight adhesive or sturdy bolts.

Metals

Brass, copper, stainless steel, chrome-plated tubing, plastic-covered steel tubing, angle iron and wrought iron are all used for furniture, mainly in conjunction with canvas, heavy cotton, or open-weave plastic in the case of seating, and glass in the case of tables. Always check metal to make sure it is smooth, with no bubbles, and free of weak spots along seams. If the piece is collapsible, test the mechanism for durability, safety and easy operation.

CANE, WICKER, RATTAN AND BAMBOO

This is a useful category of furniture for porches, conservatories and garden rooms, bedroom occasional furniture, and fill-ins. Check that it is sturdily constructed, that joints are bound well and that it is not shedding too many little 'tails', which can later unravel. All of these materials take paint well and generally age gracefully.

part two: the specifics

Beds

Because you spend around a third of your life in bed, it is hardly extravagant to buy a good-quality one. But because they all look much the same, it is sometimes difficult to know what to look for.

Like upholstery, beds have 'hidden' value, and the more expensive the mattress and divan, the better it should be. Obviously, divans should be steady, sturdy and non-squeaky, and mattresses should both support and 'give' easily, with the degree of firmness that best suits the user (who, incidentally, should always try out a bed by lying on it first).

Bed length is usually determined by adding 15–25cm (6–10in) to the height of the user. In the case of a couple, the length is dictated by the taller person. As with other large pieces of furniture, remember to check the sizes of doorways, lifts and narrow turns on stairs, and corridors before ordering a bed. If a large bed will be impossible to get into the house or apartment, you could substitute twin-bed divans, set side by side with mattresses that zip together.

MATTRESS TYPES

There are several types of mattress, all of which are quite different from each other, though the first three types are all covered in ticking and look similar. Like upholstery, mattresses should bear a label describing their contents and construction.

Inner-spring mattresses

This type of mattress, like a good over-stuffed chair or sofa, consists of 800 or so coiled springs, covered with insulating cotton, polyester or foam. Usually

you buy one in conjunction with a box-spring divan, which is about 18cm (7in) thick, as is the mattress. This is the most popular type.

Foam mattresses

This lightweight mattress is made of urethane or latex foam. It should be 10–15cm (4–6in) thick, and firm. Usually foam mattresses are sold with slightly deeper box-spring divans.

Stuffed mattresses

These mattresses are for beds not large enough to hold inner-spring or foam mattresses. They are much thinner and consist of polyester or cotton topped by foam.

Water beds

As the name implies, the mattress on a water bed is filled with water. The mattress sits inside a plastic lining set within a wooden frame. Water beds are supposed to be especially good for the circulation, to encourage restful sleep and to be effective for burn victims, as well as discouraging bed sores in invalids and the bedridden. Make sure that it has a sturdy frame, a puncture-resistant mattress (many a nasty flood has been sustained without such a precaution) and a thermostatically controlled water heater.

A recently introduced variety of water bed, called a 'soft-side', has a good-quality, high-density polyurethane foam frame instead of the

1 *A black-painted iron bed is softened by the luxurious-looking white bed linen. The heart-shaped chair back beside it echoes the bed's design.*

2 *A French lit en bateau, so-called because of its boat-like shape, dates from the French Empire period. Such beds look extremely elegant and are certainly pieces to reckon with in their own right, but they are always somewhat tough to keep tucked in and tidy.*

3 *An exotically framed daybed looks handsome in any room, whatever the style, as well as being relaxing to lounge around on.*

4 *Another twentieth-century classic chair and matching stool balance the low, modern bed in this room. Notice the length of yellow cotton used as a decorative panel behind the bed.*

wooden variety, and is covered with padding and ticking so that it looks more like a normal mattress.

GUEST BEDS

Certain types of bed are particularly useful for the occasional guest:

- A *sofa bed* can be a sofa most of the time, and open out to become a spare bed when necessary. (Make sure the mattress is thick enough for comfort; some are quite thin.)
- A *daybed* can be made into a full-size bed by sliding out a frame from underneath.

- A *rise-and-fall single bed* contains a second bed underneath, which can be jacked up to the height of the first.
- A *Murphy bed* folds up against a wall behind a panel and so is excellent for use in a studio or one-roomed apartment.

HEADBOARDS

Almost all headboards are sold separately, but there is an enormous choice, including padded fabric, wood, brass, perspex, chrome, cane and white- or black-painted iron.

part two: the specifics

Period Furniture

In theory, any piece of furniture over 100 years old can be called antique, but in practice, more modern pieces are also very collectable now. As in styles of architecture and decoration, furniture designs have been cyclical, appearing and reappearing in different guises, in different woods, with different decoration, in different countries. Sometimes styles have coincided exactly with a ruler, at least in the country of origin, but have reappeared some years later in another continent. Leading designers produced pattern books, which were copied, with varying degrees of success, by cabinetmakers all around the world, often decades later. Nor do styles necessarily run in neat chronological order, since many are concurrent with each other or are reactions to a prevailing look. Then, too, there are the umbrella terms, such as Georgian and Victorian, covering a variety of styles over many decades.

RECOGNIZING STYLES

Very early period furniture, and really beautiful pieces from the eighteenth century or earlier, are seldom to be found outside museums, grand houses open to the public, and the more rarefied antique shops. Nevertheless, it is useful to have a shorthand knowledge of the styles, if only to recognize influences, reproductions and re-introductions.

On the following pages you will find capsule descriptions of furniture style-periods for both sides of the Atlantic. To place each furniture style in context, see the Chronology of Style-Periods on pages 76–7, and also see pages 78–83 for details of the style-periods themselves. Technical terms are defined as briefly as possible in the Vocabulary on pages 198–203.

BRITISH FURNITURE

Furniture was minimal until the end of the Middle Ages and the beginning of the Tudor era, when a new peace and stability in the country meant that furnishing a home for comfort and display became more important.

Tudor

Tudor furniture was sturdy and recti-linear – not so much comfortable as serviceable. It consisted of staple pieces like four-poster beds, chests, dressers, wardrobes, stools, benches, settles, chairs and desk-boxes.

- Most tables were still of the temporary trestle type.
- Cabinet furniture was primitively decorated by simple surface grooving, narrow strips of inlay in contrasting wood, a chequered effect or crudely carved patterns.

English Renaissance oak cupboard

Elizabethan

More Renaissance ideas filtered into Britain during this period.

- Oak was the principal wood. Elaborate carving, especially strapwork, was popular and was cut into the solid wood.
- Court cupboards, or buffets, were used for displaying pewter.
- Chairs were either 'turned' or 'wainscoted'.
- Furniture legs were often bulbous, carved at the top with a gadroon and at the bottom with an acanthus leaf. The very top sometimes imitated a Doric or Ionic column.
- Beds for the rich were very grand, with carved corner-posts, a canopy and long velvet hangings. They, too, were often decorated with bulbous ornament.
- Solid-topped refectory tables replaced the makeshift trestle tables of Tudor times.

Stuart (Jacobean and Carolean)

Classicism was now better understood, which was reflected in the furniture. A sense of comfort also crept in, with chairs beginning to have upholstered backs and seats.

- Lighter chairs were made for smaller houses, along with gate-leg tables.
- The farthingale chair and the dresser (initially without the shelf section) were introduced.
- The bulbous turning of the Elizabethan period became more elongated.
- Knobs and drawer-pulls were often carved, sometimes in a caricature of the human head.

Jacobean oak wainscot armchair

Cromwellian

Decoration became less important than function in this period.

- Mouldings were applied rather than carved from solid wood.

- Leather was used for upholstery.
- Exaggerated ornament disappeared.
- The first chests of drawers appeared, and probably the first stick-back (Windsor) chairs.

Restoration

The prevailing feeling of extravagance was reflected in the furniture.

- Walnut veneer replaced solid oak.
- Chair seats, and sometimes backs, were often caned and covered with loose cushions. Spiral turnings for legs and stretchers were used frequently, as was the Flemish scroll.
- Frames were sometimes gilded and were very often silvered. Handsome upholstery, leather and heavy hand-made silk fringes all became fashionable.
- The wing chair was introduced. At that time, its back was capable of being lowered to an almost horizontal level, hence its alternative name of 'sleeping chair'.
- Upholstered stools and benches in elaborate designs were also now popular.
- Round tables appeared, as did gaming tables, smaller occasional tables and bookcases.
- Japanese lacquer ornamentation started to become popular, along with floral marquetry.
- Painted wooden fire screens in the form of life-sized human figures dressed in contemporary clothes became fashionable.

William and Mary

Immigrant French Huguenot and Dutch craftsmen injected a new vigour into British craftsmanship.

William and Mary ormolu-mounted japanned cabinet on stand

- Splendid pieces were made of walnut, with marquetry using holly, ebony, satinwood and ivory.
- Lines became simpler, with more delicate proportions and less carving.
- Thin wood veneers and cross-banding were often applied to flat surfaces.
- Oriental lacquer finishes became more prevalent.
- King William's attachment to his Delft pieces galvanized the incipient passion for blue and white (already started by the new oriental porcelain imports).
- The legs and feet of furniture changed radically once again. They became straighter, and the bun foot made its appearance, although spiral and trumpet legs were still being made.
- The newest piece of case furniture was the tallboy. Fall-front writing

cabinets appeared at this time, along with the first occasional tables, tea and card tables. Lighter armchairs were also made. Other new pieces to emerge were clocks, cabinets, dressing tables, and mirrors.

Queen Anne

Inspired by the Dutch version of Baroque, Queen Anne furniture was nevertheless a uniquely British style. It was based particularly on walnut veneer and subtle curves.

- Furniture innovations were secrétaires and other desks and china cabinets. Card and tea tables were developed further.
- Comfort became more of a priority, and this was the first time that the properly upholstered armchair made an appearance. The wing chair became more comfortable, while the spoon-back chair was a conscious attempt at ergonomics.

Queen Anne walnut wing chair

part two: the specifics

- Almost all pieces had the newly perfected, double-curved cabriole legs ending in Dutch or claw-and-ball feet.
- The hoop-back chair was introduced. Splats in the middle of chair backs had different shapes in the form of fiddles or vases.
- Typical pieces were tall, often double-domed cabinets, such as the bureau-bookcase, bureau cabinet and cabinet on a chest, in walnut veneer with fine mouldings.
- Carved shell shapes were much in evidence, as were elegant brass handles on drawers, and curving swan-necked pediments.

Early Georgian

The gentle curves of the Queen Anne era gradually gave way to the more severe lines and architectural details of classicism. To match the Neo-Palladian architecture, furniture was on a grand scale.

- Heavy carved and gilded pieces were upholstered in velvet and damask. Massive cabriole legs and claw-and-ball feet added to the stately, throne-like look of the chairs. Settees became popular.
- Solid-looking mahogany slowly replaced walnut.
- Bookcases now had pedimented tops, thereby echoing the exterior of the house.
- Fall-front bureaux and small tables on cabriole legs were typical. The drop-leaf dining table appeared.

Mid-Georgian

A time of almost unparalleled experiments in design, this was also the era of the pattern books, nobly produced by great cabinetmakers like Thomas Chippendale (whose *The Gentleman and Cabinet Maker's Director* was first published in 1754) as well as lesser luminaries. They gave inspiration and instruction to aspiring cabinetmakers and joiners in Britain, on the American East Coast and, indeed, all over the world. The various publications gave a choice of fashionable styles to follow, from pure Rococo to its offshoots, Chinese and Gothick.

Chippendale

The master of them all, Chippendale anglicized the Rococo. Having studied many sources – Classicism, Rococo, Louis Quinze, Gothick and Chinese – he combined them and refined them with a stunning sense of harmony.

- Chippendale's early seating made much use of the cabriole leg with carved foot, and splat backs with a yoke form (ie, a frame similar to a yoke used for carrying pails). In ornament he used Rococo motifs such as 'C' scrolls, flowers and foliage, shells and rocks.
- He later turned to the straight Marlborough leg, and intricate imitations of Gothic tracery for chair backs.
- He also worked in a Chinese style, incorporating pierced legs on chairs and fret carving, latticework and *faux* bamboo. His carved and gilt Chinoiserie mirrors were ornately decorated with Rococo scrolls and oriental motifs.

The Adam brothers

Great as Chippendale's influence was, that of Robert Adam, together with his brother James, was probably greater. The Adam period is considered one of the triumphs of the glorious

Early Georgian giltwood mirror

eighteenth century, and although the Adam designs were made exclusively for the super-rich, their ideas eddied out to the mainstream. Spearheading the new Neoclassical style, the Adam brothers were not cabinetmakers, but they cooperated with Chippendale and Hepplewhite, among others. Sheraton was also greatly influenced by the Adam motifs and ornaments.

- Satinwood, and other pale and elegant woods imported from the East, started to come into favour.
- Inlay was used for both wood and marble.
- Dining chairs and tables grew lighter and were supported by slim, tapering legs.
- Desks started to have fitted drawers.
- Very fine mirrors often became an integral part of the decoration or panelling.
- The Adam brothers did not make chairs, but they produced beautiful side tables, cabinets, bookcases, settees and, above all, sideboards.

- Another Adam piece was the console table, which was often gilded, with a top of scagliola or marble set on four straight, tapered legs. It was generally set between tall windows, with a long mirror above it, and often it was decorated with festoons, or with plaques like Wedgwood's Jasper medallions, or with inlaid coloured woods.
- Adam furniture also included commodes, with either painted decoration or marquetry; bookcases with broken pediments and narrow beading; and *torchères* in Etruscan shapes, with tripods of satinwood ornamented with painting, gilding or marquetry.
- Robert Adam is credited with the fashion for flanking a serving table with pedestals supporting classic urns, frequently made of the same wood. These urns were often fitted with lead containers so that cutlery and glasses could be washed between courses, while the pedestals were used as plate warmers or as storage bins for wine. Other pedestals were designed to take classical busts.
- Adam motifs included the Grecian honeysuckle and fret, the fluted frieze or apron, the patera and rosette, and the various urns and corn husks.

Hepplewhite

George Hepplewhite adapted the rarefied Adam designs for a larger, middle market. His furniture, characterized by lightness and elegance, free of unnecessary ornament, bridged the period between the decline of Georgian mahogany and the rise to fashionable prominence of satinwood.

- Hepplewhite's shield-back chairs, with their spade-shaped feet and sober lines, became widely popular.
- His bow and serpentine fronts for sofas, chairs, sideboards and chests of drawers had a wide influence.
- Hepplewhite's carvings, like Adam's, relied mainly on Roman motifs, such as elongated laurel leaves, honeysuckle and pateras. Carving reached its apogee in the 1750s and 1760s – at no age has the woodcarver been more technically ingenious.

Late Georgian

Many changes took place during this period, when formality began to give way to romanticism. Furniture was now arranged not for display but in small, functional groups. The period more or less began with Thomas Sheraton, a designer whose work was to influence much of the best Regency furniture, as well as thousands of cabinetmakers in the New World. Sheraton adapted many French designs, and the French appropriated an equal number of new English furniture ideas including dumb-waiters and tripod tables.

- Sheraton's furniture was light and delicate, with narrow tapering legs. His preferred forms of ornamentation were inlay, cross-banding and stringing, as well as painted decoration.
- Carving practically disappeared in Sheraton's furniture, although it reappeared again in Adam's later designs, and then with Thomas Hope.
- Nautical motifs were popular as a result of Nelson's victories at sea.

- Satinwood continued to be the favourite veneer until around the end of the period, but many other exotic woods were also used.
- Elaborate wood marquetry was briefly revived during this period but was then replaced with cheaper, painted decoration.

Regency

Regency furniture had its roots in the Neoclassicism of the late eighteenth century, but was also strongly influenced by the French Directoire and Empire styles, as well as by Greek classicism, which had taken over from the Roman fervour. Thomas Sheraton, Thomas Hope and Thomas Chippendale, Jr, were all leading Regency furniture makers.

- Mahogany remained the most popular wood and rosewood the most popular veneer, contrasted with inlays of ebony, brass or boxwood. Gilding was only used as a relief.

Regency ormolu-mounted, brass-inlaid rosewood breakfast side cabinet

- There was a revival of japanning.
- Furniture became less sturdy, and chairs were smaller than previously. Often made of cheaper beechwood that had been grained to look like rosewood, they had broad splat backs.
- Large breakfront bookcases gave way to smaller book cabinets.
- Much furniture was based on Greek pieces, as seen on painted Greek vases, and included the X-frame stool and the Klismos chair, with sabre legs and a broad crest rail, often decorated with Etruscan-style paintings.
- The Grecian sofa, with its curved ends, bolsters and carved feet, and the English version of the *chaise longue*, with its sabre legs, are typical Regency pieces.
- Regency carving repeated a lot of Greek and Egyptian motifs, including caryatids and sphinxes, lions and eagles.

- Toilet tables and dressing tables became very popular, along with the sideboard. Occasional tables proliferated, such as sociable round tables, Pembroke and sofa tables, and games tables.
- The writing desk known as a Davenport was introduced.

William IV

The reign of William IV produced some simpler, rather more solid, mahogany furniture. The Grecian sofa, in particular, remained popular. This simple solidity has proved to be especially popular today, since it fits in well with modern pieces.

Victorian

Furniture producers turned indiscriminately to the past for inspiration, sometimes incongruously mixing several styles in one piece. Among the prosperous on both sides of the Atlantic, Neo-Rococo held considerable sway, surrounded by Neo-Gothic, Neo-Elizabethan, Neo-Tudor, Neo-Baroque, Neo-Renaissance, Medieval and Moorish, among others.

- Rooms were much more densely furnished than previously.
- Mahogany was the favoured wood, along with rosewood, ebony and a good deal of gilding.
- Button-back, overstuffed sofas and chairs added to the comfortable and sumptuous atmosphere.
- Characteristic pieces included chiffoniers and sideboards, often carved and inlaid with engraved ivory; large, mirrored hall stands; chesterfields and ottomans; occasional tables of all kinds; balloon-back chairs; and whatnots.

part two: the specifics

Arts and Crafts movement

The first vigorous protest against the mass-produced, machine-made furniture of the Victorian era, the Arts and Crafts movement, spearheaded by William Morris, advocated the re-introduction of craftsman-made furnishings. Morris's company produced sturdy oak furniture (along with wallpapers, fabrics, pottery, and metalwork), of which the 'Sussex' chair was one of its best-known pieces.

- Furniture was simple, robust and rectilinear. Carving was kept to a minimum. Wrought iron decoration was common.
- Pieces were often painted in pale colours, especially green. Painted leather panels might be added.

Aesthetic movement

E W Godwin, a leading figure of the Aesthetic movement, was largely responsible for its two main styles of

Art Nouveau chair by C R Mackintosh

furniture, 'Anglo-Japanese' and 'Queen Anne revival'. Godwin simplified structure and decoration down to their essential elements. Light and well-proportioned, often in ebonized wood, the furniture was easy to mass produce and so was widely imitated. Much of the Queen Anne revival furniture was produced by Collinson & Lock in Britain, and by the Herter brothers in the United States. Typical pieces include the small kidney desk, the overmantel and the glass-fronted display cabinet.

Art Nouveau

Curving, sinuous forms drawn from nature were used for Art Nouveau furniture. Designs were stripped down to elegant

Ebonized Arts and Crafts chair by William Morris with Morris's original 'Bird' woollen tapestry

bare curves, and many pieces were ornamented with carving, marquetry, ivory, gilt or brass. Entire chair backs, arms or legs could be carved to represent plant forms. In Britain, Charles Rennie Mackintosh's furniture, with its exaggerated verticals, lacquered, ebonized or painted finishes and Japanese feel, was a rectilinear version of Art Nouveau.

FRENCH FURNITURE

French furniture had an enormous influence on not only European but also American furniture.

Louis Quatorze

It was Louis XIV who brought French furniture design to a pinnacle of Baroque grandeur and ornamentation. There were many introductions in the seven decades of his reign that were to have a profound influence on the future of furniture.

- The most costly materials were used for furniture, from rare woods to solid silver and lacquerwork.
- Rich brocade fabrics were used for upholstery.
- Carved and gilded furniture was made in walnut as well as the ubiquitous oak. Some pieces were inlaid with ebony.
- Typical Louis Quatorze pieces include rectilinear gilt upholstered sofas; heavy, high-backed chairs with scrolled arms and legs; tall cabinets, bureaux and commodes decorated with floral marquetry.
- Ornamentation on tables and case furniture often consisted of heavy ormolu mounts depicting mythological scenes, masks, lions and acanthus leaves.

- André-Charles Boulle was France's most celebrated cabinetmaker. His finely veneered furniture was elaborately inlaid with tortoiseshell and brass.

Louis Quatorze-style walnut fauteuil

Régence

During this early phase of the Rococo, furniture was lighter but retained some of the Louis Quatorze grandeur.

- The *bergère*, the first really comfortable padded armchair, was developed at this time.
- Chinese motifs such as dragons and parasols began to be used alongside Classical motifs.
- Loose covers for chairs were another innovation of this period.
- Chair armrests were set back and the backs lowered so as not to interfere with the panniered skirts and large, elaborate coiffures.

Louis Seize tulipwood marquetry bureau

Louis Quinze

Rococo is synonymous with the first half of Louis XV's reign. Thanks to the pattern books so prevalent in the eighteenth century, the French Rococo furniture designs were diligently copied in Spain, Austria, Hungary, Portugal, Poland, Bohemia, Russia, Scandinavia, to a lesser extent in Britain, and, most of all, in Germany, where the style was grand, stately and elaborate.

- Rococo furniture was light, with gracefully curving legs and delicately carved floral or shell motifs, and was often gilded.
- Whole sets of furniture would often be made for a room, to create a light-hearted synthesis between fixed and movable decoration and furniture.
- The comfortable, curvaceous Louis Quinze armchairs were agreeable both to look at and to sit on.
- Typical pieces were the serpentine-fronted commode, with ormolu mounts, and the *bergère*.

Louis Seize

Under the reign of Louis XVI, as rooms began to be smaller and more intimate, furniture became simpler.

- The legs were tapered and fluted and almost invariably crowned at the top by a small, square block on which was carved a rosette.
- Cabinet pieces were rectangular, and were enriched with either wood or metal mouldings.
- Many small tables and smaller case pieces were topped with coloured marble.
- For the first time, English taste began to infiltrate across the Channel, especially the designs of Robert Adam.
- Mahogany was used extensively and ebony became more common, as did painted furniture.
- Ornamentation was Greek (eg, scrollwork, Greek fret, palmette, anthemion) but the forms of the furniture were not.

Directoire

This period was characterized by the austere, severely simplified furniture of Neoclassicism.

- Woodcarvers were inspired by military symbols: spears, drums, stars and the Liberty cap of the revolutionary armies.
- Because the French kings had nothing to do with Greece, Pompeii or Egypt, motifs from those sources were still allowed.

- New motifs like scythes and sheaves of wheat were meant to show the growing power of the agricultural workers.
- Greek curves were introduced wherever possible, giving a slight backward roll at the top of a chair back and an outward curve to sofa arms. Front legs on seating often curved forwards, and rear legs backwards. On case furniture, the short supports had a slight outward curve.
- Sometimes Greek or Egyptian heads were used at the tops of legs, which ended with two human feet.
- Bent wrought iron and bronze furniture with tripod supports, also designed in the Greek manner, became popular.

Directoire fauteuil

Empire Style

Furniture, as with other design in this late Neoclassical period, was geometrical in form and Classical in ornament. The principal furniture maker was Jacob-Desmalter, whose patterns influenced many others, both in France and abroad.

- Nearly all tables were round or octagonal with marble tops, and many were supported by a central pedestal leg which rested on a triangular block.
- Beds were usually designed to be placed sideways, military-style, against walls. Boat or sleigh beds appeared, with roll-over ends of swan's necks supporting muslin drapes suspended from above.
- Curved Greek-style chair backs and sofa arms were still popular.
- For the first time, spring seats were used for upholstery.
- The most popular wood was mahogany, but yew, elm, maple and fruit woods were also used, with veneers like amboyna, thuya, amaranth, palisander and rosewood imported from Africa and the West and East Indies.
- Carving was largely eliminated, but there was a prodigious use of ormolu mounts of classical motifs for hardware and details.
- Sphinxes with upraised wings, winged griffins and lions, cobras, vultures, palms, obelisks and hieroglyphics were all motifs taken from Egypt. Caryatids, bees, swans' necks and the ubiquitous acanthus leaves were other much-used motifs.

part two: the specifics

OTHER EUROPEAN FURNITURE

Elsewhere in Europe, the style-periods were much the same as in France and Britain, though each country had its own interpretations and own unique furniture. There are two styles in particular that are of considerable interest today.

Gustavian

This was Sweden's Neoclassical style-period, but the furniture was more pared down than elsewhere.

- Furniture tended to be painted *en suite* with the walls in cool, pale colours such as muted blue, pearl grey and straw yellow. It was usually gessoed before being painted, in order to produce a smoother surface.
- Chairs were straight-legged, with restrained carved ornament.
- Furniture was arranged symmetrically in a room.

Biedermeier

Although contemporary with France's Empire style-period, Biedermeier, which prevailed in Germany, Austria and, to a lesser extent, Scandinavia, was more practical and somewhat less pretentious.

- It is characterized by black-trimmed light-toned wood (elm, ash, maple or fruit wood), though mahogany was used a lot, too, and by solid, clean, geometric lines.
- The discreet, understated Neoclassical detailing comprised mainly columns, pilasters and palmettes.
- Sabre legs or straight legs were used on chairs.

Biedermeier fall-front bureau with decorative urns on top

AMERICAN FURNITURE

The most important influence on the development of American furniture has been the varied social and cultural origins of its people. The English settlers in Virginia and New England, the Dutch in the Hudson River Valley in what is now New York State, the French in Louisiana and South Carolina, the Swedish in Delaware, the Germans in Pennsylvania and the Spaniards in Florida and the Southwest all have contributed to generic American furniture.

Yet despite the disparate backgrounds of the settlers, the North American climate, terrain and natural resources, particularly the plentiful supply of timber, meant that the indigenous furniture, like the architecture and interiors, developed uniquely American characteristics.

Early Colonial

This period was characterized by unpretentious furniture made in local materials by not particularly skilled carpenters. In the North, most were copies of Jacobean or William and Mary styles, or German, Dutch or Scandinavian pieces. In the South, a great deal of English and French furniture was imported.

Queen Anne

By the beginning of the eighteenth century, the country had had a chance to settle, traditions were established and industry strengthened. New settlers began to arrive, among them expert cabinetmakers and carpenters.

The American Queen Anne style tended to be lighter and more delicate than the British original, and the American version often used solid walnut rather than veneer. However, the claw-and-ball foot was not much appreciated until later in the century – instead, the pad or pad-and-discs foot was preferred.

Georgian

In the wealthier homes, furniture became increasingly sophisticated, with skilful copies of Queen Anne, early Georgian, Chippendale, Sheraton and Hepplewhite designs.

- The vase-like outline of solid splats on the back of Queen Anne-style chairs; the claw-and-ball feet based

American late eighteenth-century mahogany elbow chair

on early Chinese carvings of dragons' claws clutching pearls; the carved shells of the Rococo; the acanthus leaves of Rome and Greece – all became regular motifs. Though simpler than the original versions, the pieces produced by the American craftsmen were handsome and very well made.

- Handsome side chairs, tables, highboys, lowboys, bureaux and fall-front writing cabinets were combined with new upholstered sofas, armchairs and daybeds.
- The Martha Washington, or lolling, chair, with its high back, low seat and open arms, was introduced.

Simple country homes, however, were still mostly equipped with solid, rustic furniture, often painted with hearts, flowers, leaves and other Dutch, German or Scandinavian motifs, as well as the roses, thistles and crowns associated with Britain. Numerous pattern books were brought over from London, but regional styles were particularly individualistic because of the variety of colonizing groups.

Federal, Empire and Greek revival

Following the War of Independence, there was a growing demand for more sophisticated home furnishings. In particular, the European devotion to Neoclassicism, together with George Hepplewhite's *The Cabinet Maker and Upholsterer's Guide* (published in 1788), meant that the last years of the eighteenth century and the first years

American Federal mahogany scroll-back chair, c.1807, by Duncan Phyfe

of the nineteenth produced some splendid post-Colonial furniture.

American cabinetmakers revived the habit of using veneer and inlay on predominantly mahogany furniture. Painted furniture, decorated with landscapes, flowers or trophies, also became extremely popular, particularly if it was from Baltimore. Carved motifs included the usual Neoclassical references – caryatids, acanthus leaves, griffins – plus the American bald eagle and other patriotic symbols.

The three leading cabinetmakers of the day were all immigrants: Duncan Phyfe from Scotland, Charles-Honoré Lannuier from France and Joseph B Barry, who was from Ireland but had trained in England. Barry worked out of Philadelphia, and the other two worked from New York. Although

Duncan Phyfe's designs ranged from the Hepplewhite and Sheraton styles through to Empire, and finally to early Victorian, he is mainly thought of as the pre-eminent designer of the Federal style-period, and his lyre-back chairs and caryatid-based consoles were, and are, highly prized.

By the early 1800s, the elegance and purity of the Federal period was giving way to the heavier, more opulent Empire style, with its deeper carving and more elaborate ornamentation, such as stencilling, graining, gilding and ormolu mounts.

Empire style, in turn, evolved into the Greek revival. Americans favoured this style as much as the French did, and Greek revival furnishings and architecture were extremely fashionable, especially on the East Coast.

Simple cherrywood Shaker tripod table, c.1820

Victorian

On the East Coast, there was much the same eclecticism as in Europe. In the Midwest and West, however, very simple pieces were still produced, including unpretentious chests, chairs and cupboards, which tended to be either in the cheerful Pennsylvanian German or Dutch eighteenth-century tradition, or country Windsor, rocking and Hitchcock chairs.

Another profound influence came from the various religious and utopian socialist communities that proliferated in the nineteenth century, particularly the Shakers. Strict rules governed both the decoration and the manufacture of their furniture, and Shaker tables, chairs and case furniture were beautifully crafted, with clean, spare lines.

With the 1876 Centennial, a new spirit of nationalism provoked a Colonial revival, and manufacturers quickly turned from their French-inspired Louis-whatever pieces to the reproduction of simple 'Early American' furniture.

Mission

Produced in the 1890s and the first decade of the twentieth century, Mission furniture was similar to English Arts and Crafts pieces. Strong, straight-lined, with exposed joinery and canvas or leather coverings, it was usually made from oak. Mission furniture was made at the Craftsman workshops by Gustav Stickley, a disciple of William Morris, and at the Roycroft workshops, a craftsmen's community founded by Elbert Hubbard. Like English Arts and Crafts furniture, it is highly prized today.

part two: the specifics

Vocabulary of Period Furniture Terms

Acanthus leaf: The thick, scalloped leaves of *Acanthus spinosus* used since Classical times in stylized form on the tops of columns (notably the capital of the Corinthian column) for architectural mouldings, and, on a smaller scale, as carved decoration on furniture.

Acorn turning: A knob, foot or drawer-pull shaped like an acorn.

Adirondack furniture: Rustic furniture produced in the middle of the nineteenth century in Upper New York State, made from roughly hewn and bent branches and logs. Adirondack chairs are made from slats with a slant back and wide arms (excellent for sitting drinks on) and are much reproduced today for garden furniture.

Angel bed: A bed with a wooden top CANOPY shorter than the bed and no front support.

Anthemion: Decorative motif of Greek origin, the radiating pattern of which resembles the honeysuckle. Often used in Classical ornament.

Apron: A strip of wood at the base of cabinets, seats and table tops extending between the tops of legs or of bracket feet. Also known as a FRIEZE.

Arabesque: Decorative SCROLLWORK or other intricate ornament, using interlaced branches, foliage, abstract curvilinear shapes, etc. The name derives from the fact that it was adapted by Muslim artists around a thousand years ago, becoming a traditional part of Arab ornament. It was used in Europe from the early Renaissance, after arabesques were found in Roman tombs. European versions also included animals and human figures.

Arcading: A series of arches with supporting columns or piers. Used to decorate panels on chairs and chests from the sixteenth century onwards.

Architrave: In Classical architecture, the lowest of the three parts of the ENTABLATURE. It can also refer to a decorative frame surrounding a door, window, mirror or other opening.

Armoire: Large two-door cupboard, originating in France, for storing clothes.

Arrow-back chair: An American form of the WINDSOR CHAIR in which the SPINDLES flare outwards. It was popular after about 1830.

Astragal: A small convex beaded moulding sometimes placed at the junction of a pair of doors on a cabinet.

Ball foot: The rounded end of a turned leg, with a slightly hooded effect.

Balloon back: Chair back in which the uprights merge into the top rail in one continuous curve and there is no upholstery in the back. Very popular in Victorian times.

Baluster: A turned supporting column in a series supporting a rail.

Balustrade: A series of BALUSTERS with a rail along the top forming a low wall or barrier, usually made of stone or wood.

Bamboo: Light, cheap oriental furniture, first popularized in the late seventeenth century by the Dutch East India Company. *Faux* bamboo was sturdier, since proper wood, often mahogany, was used and either TURNED or painted to give a bamboo effect. Particularly popular in the Regency period.

Banding: Decorative INLAY or MARQUETRY with a colour or grain to contrast with the surface it is decorating.

Banister-back chair: American chair often made of EBONIZED maple with vertical split BALUSTERS at the back.

Banquette: An upholstered bench or SETTEE. Also the ledge at the back of a BUFFET.

Barrel chair: A nineteenth-century American upholstered chair shaped like an old rustic chair; it was originally based on half a wine barrel. The back is usually upholstered in vertical ribs.

Bead: A small convex moulding with a nearly semicircular section.

Beau Brummell: Georgian dressing table for men, appropriately named after the early nineteenth-century fop and fashion arbiter.

Bergère: Comfortable French armchair with a rounded upholstered back and sides and a wide seat, which appeared in the Régence period and was popular in the Louis Quinze and Louis Seize periods. It was the antithesis of the majestic, uncomfortable chairs of the Louis Quatorze period.

Bibliothèque-basse: French term for low cupboard fitted with shelves for books, with doors fronted either with glass or with grilles.

Bird's eye maple: Wood of the sugar maple, with small, dark knots, around which the grain forms rings.

Blanket chest: Old English or Colonial chest used for storing blankets and clothes, and often doubling as a bench.

Block foot: A square foot at the base of a straight, untapered leg.

Block front: A chest with a concave centre panel, flanked by two convex panels.

Bobbin twist: Design given to TURNED chair STRETCHERS, backs and legs from the seventeenth century onwards; the name derives from their resemblance to bobbins (reels for winding yarn).

Boiserie: Carved wooden panels used for walls and pieces of French furniture from the seventeenth century onwards. In the Louis Quinze period, they might have been painted white and gilded.

Bombé: French term (literally, 'blown out') for an outward curve or convex front to a COMMODE, BUREAU or ARMOIRE. Particularly prevalent on Louis Quinze furniture.

Bonheur du jour: French term for a small writing table, usually with tall slim legs, and sometimes fitted to hold toilet accessories as well. Very popular in the eighteenth and nineteenth centuries.

Bonnet top: A broken-arch PEDIMENT covering the entire top of a piece of CASE FURNITURE, from front to back.

Boston rocker: An American nineteenth-century rocking chair with a downward curved seat, SPINDLE back and wide top rail.

Boulle: Brass and tortoiseshell MARQUETRY. It is named after Louis XIV's cabinetmaker André Charles Boulle (1642–1732), who perfected the technique. It was highly prized from the late seventeenth to the nineteenth centuries, when the effect started to be reproduced by machine.

Bow back: A type of WINDSOR CHAIR.

Bow front: An outwardly curving front forming a convex curve.

An English oak buffet designed by Thomas Jeckyll c.1865 for The Old Hall, Heath, Yorkshire in England.

Bracket foot: One of the most common of all feet on CASE FURNITURE. It runs both ways from the corner, forming a right angle.

Breakfast table: A small DROP-LEAF TABLE with two hinged flaps below which is a drawer, shelf or cupboard. It first appeared in the eighteenth century.

Breakfront: A bookcase or china cabinet consisting of three sections, with the centre one projecting forward beyond the two end sections. It also denotes an upper bookcase set back from cupboards or shelves beneath.

Brewster chair: Chair with large turned posts and SPINDLES, first made in Colonial America in the seventeenth century and named after a governor of the Massachusetts Bay colony.

Buffet: French term for small sideboard or place for keeping dishes.

Bun foot: A flattened ball or bun-shaped foot with a slender ankle above. Popular in the William and Mary period.

Bureau: A FALL-FRONT WRITING CABINET with a sloping front. The term is French and derives from the Latin *burras* meaning 'red', for the red leather covering originally used on the tops of writing tables. Also known as a secretary.

Bureau-bookcase: Usually bookshelves with glazed doors above a FALL-FRONT WRITING CABINET; introduced in the mid-eighteenth century.

Burjar: A large upholstered armchair originally made by Thomas Chippendale.

Burl: A knot in a tree which shows beautifully patterned markings when sliced. Used for VENEERS and INLAYS, particularly in burr walnut and burr elm.

Butterfly table: A DROP-LEAF TABLE originating in the United States in the eighteenth century.

Cabinet: A display case, usually glass-fronted, resting either on a stand or on another piece of furniture.

Cabinetmaker: Umbrella term for a maker of fine furniture as opposed to a joiner. In the seventeenth, eighteenth and nineteenth centuries, cabinetmakers made CASE FURNITURE, while joiners made chairs and tables.

Cabriole leg: Furniture leg that swells outwards at the knee and inwards at the ankle. Originally used in ancient Greece, it was much in use in the first half of the eighteenth century.

Camelback: A SOFA back with an irregularly curved shape like a hump. This design was much used by Chippendale and Hepplewhite.

Canapé: French word for a SOFA or DIVAN, first associated with the Louis Quinze period.

Cane furniture: Cheap, light, durable furniture made from the rattan palm. It was introduced into Europe and Britain in the seventeenth century by the Dutch East India Company and into North America at the end of that century.

Canopy: A covering, usually of fabric stretched on a frame, used above a bed.

Canterbury: Originally a type of music stand, then a partitioned trolley, said to have been made for an Archbishop of Canterbury. Now mostly used for magazines.

Card table: First appeared in reign of Charles II in England. A walnut version with CABRIOLE LEGS and candlestick corners appeared in the Queen Anne period. Now generally a baize-topped, square, collapsible table.

Carlton House table: An eighteenth-century writing table with an adjustable top, originally made for Carlton House, the London home of the Prince of Wales in the Regency period.

Cartouche: Ornament in scroll or tablet form, usually oval but sometimes rectangular, containing a motif such as Egyptian hieroglyphs or a coat of arms; used on the back of a chair, a fire surround or similar.

Carver chair: Seventeenth-century American armchair usually made of maple or ash, with a rush seat, called after John Carver, one of the Pilgrim Fathers and a governor of Plymouth. Also a dining chair with arms, sometimes called an elbow chair.

Caryatid: Female figure derived from Greek architecture; it is used as a decorative support.

Case furniture or pieces: Pieces used for storage, such as bookcases, cabinets, armoires and sideboards, as opposed to seat furniture.

Cassone: Italian Renaissance chest, elaborately carved, inlaid or painted, and often used as a DOWER CHEST.

Cellaret: A case on legs or a stand for wine bottles.

Chaise longue: French term for, literally, a long chair, like a couch with a chair back. Very popular in France in the late eighteenth and nineteenth centuries. Also known as a DAYBED.

Chamfered: A faceted edge, often on furniture legs which are turned outwards.

Channelling: A grooved or furrowed effect in wood.

Chesterfield: A deep, often button-backed SOFA with high upholstered arms. Called after Lord Chesterfield in nineteenth-century England.

Cheval glass: A long mirror suspended between vertical posts.

Chiffonier: French word for a chest of drawers with a cupboard and doors, which can also function as a SIDEBOARD. It often has shelves and a mirror above it.

Chinoiserie: European designs which freely interpreted oriental motifs. Fretwork, pagodas, dragons, birds, landscapes, trees and rivers were common decorative devices, as was a LACQUER finish. Chinese, Indian and Japan influences were frequently intermingled. Fashionable from the late seventeenth century.

Claw-and-ball foot: A leg, usually on a chair, ending in the shape of a claw holding a ball. In oriental furniture, from which it derives, the claws are talons or dragon's claws. In European and American pieces they are more often an eagle's claws.

Coffer: Box or chest covered in leather or material and banded with metalwork.

Commode: A low chest of drawers which originated in mid-seventeenth-century France and became widely popular in the eighteenth century. During the nineteenth century, the piece was designed for living rooms, but the term

came to apply to a chair that disguised a chamber pot.

Console table: A form of side table that is supported by wall brackets and two front legs.

Corner cupboard: Triangular cupboard that fits into a corner. It can be free-standing or suspended from the wall, and either small or tall.

Cornice: In Classical architecture, the top part of the ENTABLATURE. In furniture, the horizontal moulding that projects from the top of some CASE PIECES.

Cornucopia: The horn of plenty used as a design motif for carved furniture.

Couch: A late seventeenth- and eighteenth-century term for a DAYBED with a single head, usually in the shape of a chair back. Nowadays the term is used for a SOFA as well.

Court cupboard: A low cupboard (the name comes from *court*, the French word for 'short'), used for displaying plate or other precious goods, dating from the late sixteenth century.

Credenza: Italian term for a SIDEBOARD or BUFFET table, usually ornate Italianate or French-style.

Cross-banding: Decoration on furniture using thin strips of VENEER cut across the grain.

Cross-stretcher: X-shaped stretcher found on some chairs and tables.

Curule legs: X-shaped legs used on a folding chair with no back.

Davenport: A small chest of drawers with a sloping top for writing, named after the sea captain for whom it was first made in the 1790s.

Daybed: A COUCH with a single head, usually in the shape of a chair back, sometimes with arms. First made in the seventeenth century. Also called a CHAISE LONGUE.

Dentelles or dentils: A series of rectangular blocks with spaces in between them, used as a moulding on a CORNICE.

Diaper motif: A trellis design of squares or rectangles sometimes containing a carved leaf or flower, or other design.

part two: the specifics

Disc foot: A flat, literally disc-shaped, foot for chairs and tables.

Divan: An upholstered bench of oriental origin, popular in the Victorian era as part of a Turkish, or oriental, style of room. Today it also means a bed base.

Dovetail joint: A right-angled joint with interlocking dovetail or fan-shaped TENONS. From the eighteenth century on, these were often concealed (at least in furniture of high quality) by an overlapping piece of wood.

Dowel: A headless wooden peg used in furniture construction.

Dower chest: A chest made to store a trousseau. Examples include Hadley chests, Connecticut chests and painted PENNSYLVANIA DUTCH OR GERMAN chests.

Dresser: A SIDEBOARD with shelves and sometimes cupboards above, for storing and displaying china; most often made from pine or oak.

Drop-leaf table: A table with hinged leaves, such as a BREAKFAST TABLE, GATE-LEG TABLE, PEMBROKE TABLE or SOFA TABLE.

Drum table: A round table of Neoclassical origins with a TRIPOD base and a FRIEZE beneath the top, sometimes containing drawers. It was normally used for writing.

Dumb-waiter: A dining-room stand consisting of circular trays set on a central column with a TRIPOD base. Diners were able to help themselves to china, cutlery or food from the trays, which diminish in size from bottom to top and may revolve. Introduced early in the eighteenth century.

Dustboard: Thin, horizontal boards placed between the drawers of a COMMODE or chest of drawers to keep out dust.

Dutch dresser: A cabinet with open shelves above and drawers or a cupboard below.

Dutch foot: A simple pad used as the foot on a CABRIOLE LEG.

Ébéniste: A French term for a cabinetmaker.

Ebonized wood: Wood stained black to look like ebony; also called *bois noir* in French. Used frequently on Victorian oriental-style cabinets and for the trim on Biedermeier furniture.

Egg-and-dart moulding: A classic design made up of alternating egg-like ovals and dart shapes, said to symbolize life and death, and carved onto quarter-round or half-round moulding.

Elbow chair: See CARVER CHAIR.

Entablature: In Classical architecture, the whole section above the capital of a column, consisting of the ARCHITRAVE, FRIEZE and CORNICE. The term is also applied to the equivalent part of a cabinet or cupboard.

Escritoire: A French term for a FALL-FRONT WRITING CABINET. Usually it refers to one made before 1720 and with a vertical, rather than sloping, front. Many had secret compartments among the drawers and pigeonholes. See also BUREAU and SECRÉTAIRE.

Escutcheon: A shield or emblem upon which a coat of arms or other special devices are emblazoned.

Étagère: A set of shelves, free-standing or attached to a wall, used for displaying objects. It may have glazed doors.

Fall-front writing cabinet: A cabinet in which the front, when open and supported, can be used as a writing desk. The front may be vertical (as on an ESCRITOIRE or a SECRÉTAIRE) or sloping (as on a BUREAU).

Farthingale chair: An armless, wide, upholstered chair especially designed in Elizabethan times to accommodate voluminous skirts.

Fauteuil: French term for an armchair that has open spaces between the arms and seat.

Festoon: Also known as a swag. This design appears on Renaissance as well as Neoclassical furniture, and imitates a loop of drapery or a garland of fruit and flowers.

Fiddle back: A chair splat that is shaped like a fiddle.

Fire screen: A screen to give protection from the heat of a fire. It may be either a POLE SCREEN (an oval or round screen set on a TRIPOD base) or a cheval screen (which consists of a panel enclosed by two uprights, each on a pair of legs). Fire screens were in use from the eighteenth century.

Flambeau: French term for a carved decoration in the shape of a flaming torch.

Flemish scroll: A Baroque form of double SCROLL, where the curve is broken by an angle. It was used on late seventeenth-century chair legs and stretchers.

Fleur-de-lis: A motif representing a stylized lily, consisting of three petals bound together near the bottom. It was once the royal arms of France.

Fluting: Parallel grooved lines on any horizontal or upright surface; the opposite of REEDING, it was particularly popular in Neoclassical furniture.

Fly rail: A folding bracket to support a DROP LEAF of a table.

Foliated: Decoration composed of leaf designs.

Four-poster: A style of bed that originated in medieval times, with four posts, one at each corner, usually supporting a canopy.

Fretwork: A form of decoration used on woodwork (especially with CHINOISERIE) formed from interlaced geometric designs carved into thin wood. Blind fretwork has a backing, often of a contrasting wood or colour; open fretwork does not.

Frieze: In Classical architecture, the middle part of the ENTABLATURE, between the ARCHITRAVE and CORNICE. In furniture, a decorative, wide horizontal band just below a cornice or a table top, also called the apron or the skirt.

Functionalism: In furniture design, an emphasis on efficiency rather than looks.

Gadroon: A curved moulding in an olive or ruffle shape, sometimes used on the edges of table tops or chairs.

Gate-leg table: A form of DROP-LEAF TABLE with rounded, hinged flaps. When lifted, these are supported by gate-like legs that swing out from the centre of the table. Very popular in seventeenth-century Britain, the Netherlands and colonial America.

Gesso: A white substance traditionally made of chalk and size, which is applied to furniture. Once it has hardened, it produces a smooth, porous surface for gilding, painting or lacquerwork. It can be generally cast to make repeating ornamental forms.

Girandole: An ornate candelabrum, or a wall-mirror to which candle sconces, or brackets, are attached.

Glastonbury chair: A Gothic chair with a sloping, panelled back and arms with a drooping curve. First used by the abbots of Glastonbury in the sixteenth century, it was widely copied in the nineteenth century.

Griffin: A chimerical or fanciful beast that was often employed in early Georgian decoration.

Guéridon: A small table with a round top for holding candlesticks.

Guilloche: A continuous figure-of-eight motif used on a band or border. Originally used in Classical architecture, it was popular for furniture decoration from the sixteenth century.

Hadley chest: A type of early American New England DOWER CHEST on four feet with a drawer, decorated with crude carving.

Highboy: An early eighteenth-century American version of the TALLBOY, often on CABRIOLE LEGS and with a broken PEDIMENT or CORNICE mouldings.

High relief: Deep carving found on any plain surface.

Hitchcock chair: American chair with an oval turned top rail and a rush, cane or wooden seat. The chair was usually painted black, and the top rail and back splat were decorated with coloured or gilded flowers, fruit or similar motifs. Named after the designer Lambert Hitchcock, it was produced between 1820 and 1850.

Hoof foot: The end of a leg in the shape of a goat's hoof.

Hoop-back chair: Wooden chair with upholstered seat with a rounded front rail, CABRIOLE LEGS and a back with a rounded top and solid SPLAT; associated with Britain's Queen Anne period.

Inlay: A decorative technique using contrasting woods, and sometimes small pieces of ivory, horn, metal or MOTHER-OF-PEARL, sunk into holes of similar shape cut into another material, usually solid wood.

Intaglio: Incised, or countersunk, decoration made by cutting into the surface of a material.

Intarsia: Italian type of decoration similar to INLAY where a design is sunk into another surface.

Jasperware: A kind of hard biscuit-ware introduced by the Wedgwood company in the eighteenth century. Occasionally used for medallions set into chair backs.

Joinery: The craft of assembling woodwork by means of a DOVETAIL JOINT, tongue-and-groove, MORTISE and TENON, dowels, etc. Joiners make furniture like chairs and tables, more than CASE PIECES.

Key pattern: Also known as Greek key or fret pattern. A repeated design of straight lines at right angles, creating a maze-like effect. It originates from Classical Greek architecture and is often used as a border.

Kidney desk: A small desk or writing table with a curved front that is shaped like a kidney.

Klismos: A chair used by the ancient Greeks and Romans, and revived in the late eighteenth and early nineteenth century. It had a concave, curved back rail and curved legs.

Kneehole desk: A desk with a space through the middle of it, to allow a person's knees to be accommodated comfortably when seated at the desk.

Ladder back: A chair back with horizontal cross rails instead of a splat. The style was adopted by Chippendale and other cabinetmakers of the eighteenth century.

Lattice: Open FRETWORK decoration using criss-crossed lines forming diamonds or squares.

Linenfold: Wood carved to represent vertical folds of drapery. It was popular in the fifteenth and sixteenth centuries on furniture, particularly chests and wardrobe doors, and on wall panelling, and during the nineteenth-century Tudor revival.

Lit en bateau: French term for a distinctive bed with curving ends, popular during the Empire period.

Lolling chair: See MARTHA WASHINGTON CHAIR.

Loo table: A nineteenth-century round pedestal table for playing the card game Loo.

Lotus: Ancient Egyptian motif based on the water lily of the Nile.

Love seat: A SETTEE, or small SOFA, designed for two people.

Lowboy: An eighteenth-century American dressing table, usually with one long drawer and three short ones. It was often made to match a HIGHBOY.

Low relief: Shallow carving on any plain surface.

Lozenge: A diamond-shaped motif or panel.

Lunette: Semicircular shape used to decorate furniture; often filled with ornamental carving or inlaid or painted decoration in the Neoclassical period.

Lyre back: The back of a chair in the form of a lyre, roughly the shape of a horseshoe with outwardly scrolled ends, and a horizontal bar between its arms. Popular in the late eighteenth century.

Marlborough leg: Heavy, straight, grooved leg with a block foot, used by Thomas Chippendale and others in the eighteenth century.

Marquetry: A flush pattern in a veneered surface, produced by inserting contrasting wood veneers and sometimes tortoiseshell, ivory, MOTHER-OF-PEARL or metals.

Martha Washington chair: Late eighteenth-century American armchair with a low upholstered seat, open arms and a high upholstered back. Also known as a lolling chair.

Medallion: A decorative oval or circular plaque, with an ornamental motif inside.

Modillion: A projecting bracket that is used to support a Corinthian cornice. It is also often used as an independent decorative device.

Morris chair: A large Arts and Crafts easy chair with arms usually extending slightly beyond the back, which can be adjusted to various angles. Designed in 1883, it was produced by William Morris's firm and was very popular in both Britain and the United States.

Mortise: A hole cut in wood to take a TENON projecting from another piece.

Rococo console table with elaborate ormolu, by Cuvilliés, c.1739.

Mother-of-pearl: The iridescent inner layer of some shells, pieces of which were inlaid into furniture from the seventeenth century onwards. In the nineteenth century it was a popular inlay in PAPIER MÂCHÉ furniture.

Mounts: Ornamental or utilitarian metalwork such as handles or drawer pulls, used on CASE FURNITURE.

Ogee: A double curve which is convex above and concave below, as in an ogee moulding. An ogee arch is composed of two mirror-image ogees, whose sides come together before curving in the opposite way. Identified with Gothic forms, and used in Neo-Gothic furniture for chair backs, panelling and architectural mouldings. Also often found on the feet of Georgian furniture.

Ormolu: Gilt-bronze decoration or mounts. The name derives from the French term *bronze doré d'or moulu* ('bronze gilded with ground gold'); it is also known as *bronze doré*.

Ottoman: An upholstered bench without a back, often used as a footstool. The name is taken from the Ottoman (Turkish) Empire.

Oxbow front: Reverse SERPENTINE front (ie, concave in the centre, and convex on either side) used in eighteenth-century CASE FURNITURE.

Pagoda: A Chinese or Japanese tower with several storeys, often used as a motif in oriental furniture.

Palmette: Classical motif resembling a palm leaf, used as carved or painted ornament on furniture.

part two: the specifics

Panel: A surface enclosed by a frame. It may be sunk (below the frame), flush (at the same level) or fielded (raised above the frame).

Papier mâché: French term for pulped paper that is mixed with glue and moulded while wet into various shapes; used for light furniture, often japanned and inlaid with MOTHER-OF-PEARL, in the nineteenth century.

Parcel gilt: Partly gilded.

Parquetry: A geometrical MARQUETRY pattern, which often produces a three-dimensional effect.

Patera: A round or oval disc, often surrounding a rosette or other ornament; particularly used in Neoclassical ornament.

Patina: The natural sheen and softening of colour that develops on wood over the years; also the greenish film that forms on bronze through a chemical reaction.

Paw foot: Furniture leg ending in the shape of a paw. Used in ancient Egypt, Greece and Rome, and popular again in Neoclassical furniture.

Pedestal: A supporting base or block for a statue or vase, usually treated with mouldings at the top and a base block at the bottom. Without any mouldings, it is called a plinth.

Pedestal table: A table on a round, centre support which ends in a wide base.

Pediment: In architecture, the triangular space at each exterior end of a Greek temple. In furniture, an ornamental feature on top of a CASE PIECE. It can be 'broken', 'scrolled' or 'segmental'.

Pembroke table: A DROP-LEAF TABLE with oval or rectangular ends, usually with a drawer in the FRIEZE. Called after a Lady Pembroke, it was used in the eighteenth and nineteenth centuries for writing, playing cards, needlework and meals.

Pennsylvania Dutch or German: Furniture made by German settlers ('Dutch' is a corruption of 'Deutsch') in Pennsylvania between 1750 and 1850. Mostly made in softwood, it was painted with colourful folk-art motifs.

Pie-crust table: A small table with its edge carved or moulded with scallops, like the crimped edge of a pie crust. Popular in the eighteenth century.

Pier glass: Large window-height mirror.

Pietre dure: Italian decorative technique, using inlaid semi-precious stones. The technique was used in ancient Rome and then revived during the Renaissance.

Pilaster: Flattened, rectangular column, often with REEDING, superimposed on a surface. Used to decorate the façade rather than for any structural support.

Pillar: Popular term for a column.

Pineapple: Carved pineapple-shaped ornament often found on bedposts on early nineteenth-century American beds, as well as on gateposts and the newel posts of stairs. It symbolized hospitality.

Pinnacle: Small cone-shaped turret, often used in Gothic decoration.

Plaque: Plate or panel inserted into wood; it is usually made of metal, glass or pottery, and treated with some sort of surface enrichment.

Plinth: See PEDESTAL.

Pole screen: Adjustable panel mounted on a vertical pole and used as a FIRE SCREEN.

Pomegranate: Decorative motif, symbolizing fertility.

Poudresse: French term for small table with mirrored lid that covers a space for cosmetics.

Pouffe: French/English term for large, round, stuffed cushion used as a seat; fashionable from early nineteenth century.

Primitive: Early, simple, naïve furniture.

Quatrefoil: An ornamental figure or leaf motif, divided by cusps or featherings into four foils, leaves or lobes. Much used in Gothic decoration.

Quattrocento: The fifteenth century in Italy; Renaissance furniture of the fifteenth century.

Rail: Any horizontal strip forming a portion of a frame in panelling (vertical strips are STILES); also the top member of a chair.

Récamier: French name for a CHAISE LONGUE with curved ends in the Neoclassical style. The name was adopted after the appearance in 1800 of Jacques-Louis David's portrait of Mme Juliette Récamier reclining on a *chaise longue* while receiving visitors.

Reeding: Decoration consisting of parallel, usually vertical, narrow convex mouldings; the opposite of FLUTING. It is often found on chair and table legs. Sheraton, Adam and Duncan Phyfe used it extensively.

Refectory table: A long, narrow table, originally used in dining rooms of monasteries and convents during the Elizabethan era.

Relief: A type of decoration made prominent by raising it from the surface or background of the material. See also HIGH RELIEF and LOW RELIEF.

Repoussé: Embossed relief decoration on metal.

Ribbon back: Chair back designed with pattern of interlacing ribbons, often used by Chippendale.

Rinceau: French term for Classical, ornamental device made of intertwining stalks of ACANTHUS or other scrolling foliage. It is sometimes used in combination with CARTOUCHES.

Roll-top desk: Desk in which the writing table and fittings are enclosed by a curved, slatted panel.

Romayne work: Carved medallion heads or knobs used as furniture ornaments or drawer pulls, and characteristic of the Jacobean and Restoration periods.

Rondel or roundel: Round outline or object in a surface pattern.

Rope bed: Bed with rope laced to the frame to support a mattress.

Rosette: Ornamental motif formed by a series of leaves or petals around a central point.

Roundabout chair: Chair designed to fit into a corner, with a low back on two adjoining sides of a square seat.

Roycroft furniture: American Arts and Crafts furniture produced by the Roycroft community from 1896. Designs were plain and made from ash, oak or mahogany, often with copper fittings, prominent MORTISE and TENON joints and tapering legs.

Rush seat: Rushes plaited to form a chair seat, a style that was common in Europe and America in the eighteenth and nineteenth centuries, especially for country furniture.

Sabre leg: Curved leg in the Classical style, generally with REEDING.

Saddle seat: Chair seat hollowed to resemble a saddle.

Sausage turning: TURNED legs or STRUTS resembling a string of sausages.

Sawbuck table: A table with an X-frame, either plain or scrolled.

Scagliola: Imitation marble surface formed from hardened and highly polished plaster or GESSO and marble fragments. It was used for table tops as well as columns and pilasters.

Scallop: A carved ornament in the shape of a shell that was widely used in Rococo pieces.

Sconce: Ornamental wall bracket, or candle-holder, used for candles or electric light bulbs.

Scoop seat: A chair which has been especially hollowed out in order to fit the human body.

Scroll or scrollwork: A spiral, or convoluted, line used for ornamental purposes, as in an ARABESQUE. A parchment roll used as an ornament.

Scroll foot: A foot in the form of a spiral line.

Scroll pediment: Broken PEDIMENT with each half shaped in the form of a reverse curve and ending in an ornamental scroll.

Seaweed marquetry: MARQUETRY utilizing woods with a figured grain, such as holly or boxwood, to produce patterns resembling seaweed; often used in the William and Mary period and also in the eighteenth century.

Secrétaire: A French term for a FALL-FRONT WRITING CABINET. Usually it refers to one made after 1720 and with a vertical, rather than sloping, front. Many had compartments among the drawers and pigeonholes. See also BUREAU and ESCRITOIRE.

Secretary: Modern term for a FALL-FRONT WRITING CABINET mounted on a chest of drawers or a stand; also called a BUREAU.

Sedan chair: Enclosed eighteenth-century chair, with two poles, usually carried by four men.

Serpentine curve: Undulating curve used for the fronts of commodes, chests or bureaux. The centre curve is convex and the curves on either side concave.

Serving table: A long, narrow table with drawers.

Settee: A seat or bench with a high back, and often with arms, large enough to seat two or more people. Originally it was more formal than a SOFA, but today the terms are sometimes used interchangeably. It was widely in use in Britain from the early seventeenth century to the nineteenth.

Settle: A wooden bench with a back and solid arms, produced from the sixteenth century onwards. Having developed from the chest, it sometimes had a hinged seat for storage (and was then known as a box-settle).

Sgabellow: Italian term for small wooden Renaissance chair with a carved splat back, octagonal seat and trestle supports.

Sgraffito: Italian term for a pattern that is first scratched onto a surface and then coloured.

Shaft: Central portion of a column or pilaster.

Shaker furniture: Simple, functional, nineteenth-century American furniture with tapering legs, swallowtail joints, much prized today for its spare and elegant lines. Usually made in pine, maple, walnut or fruitwoods. Derived from English country furniture, a Shaker chair was a taller, slimmer version of a LADDER BACK chair, often with a practical bar on top from which to suspend a cushion. Well reproduced today.

Shield back: Chair back shaped like a shield; much used in the eighteenth century by Hepplewhite.

Sideboard: Dining-room serving table with a long, flat top and drawers and cupboards underneath. First popularized by the Adam brothers in the 1760s.

Singerie: French term for eighteenth-century design showing monkeys (*singes* in French) at play, usually dressed up and behaving like humans. Popular as CHINOISERIE decoration.

Skirt: See FRIEZE.

Slant-top desk: Another name for a BUREAU.

Slat back: Late seventeenth-century chair with slats – wide, horizontal, ladder rails – between the back uprights, like a simplified LADDER BACK.

Slipper chair: Any short-legged chair with the seat close to the floor.

Sofa: The sofa, which was large enough to recline on and was more upholstered and informal than the SETTEE, gradually took over from the settee during the nineteenth century. Nowadays it is a general term for upholstered seating for two or more people.

Sofa table: Narrow, rectangular table with two front drawers and hinged leaves at either end. Originally put in front of a sofa, it is now generally placed behind it instead.

Spade foot: Rectangular-shaped tapered foot, like a spade.

Spandrel: Arched form bounded by a horizontal and vertical frame, often used by Sheraton for chair backs.

Spanish foot: Foot in the shape of an inward-curving SCROLL.

Spindle: A long, slender rod, ornamented with TURNED mouldings.

Spiral leg: A leg carved in the shape of a rope twist.

Splat: A plain, shaped or carved vertical strip of wood, usually forming the centre of a chair back.

Splayed: A surface canted outwards, or on a slant.

Split spindle: Spindle cut in half lengthwise, so that each half has one flat and one rounded side. Used as applied decoration in seventeenth-century English and American furniture, particularly chests and cabinets.

Spoonback: A chair back shaped to fit the human back.

Stile: The vertical strips of the frame of a panel.

Strapwork: Furniture decoration consisting of narrow bands of wood folded, crossed and sometimes interlaced; popular in the Netherlands in the sixteenth century, and in Elizabethan England.

Stretcher: A brace, or support, horizontally connecting the legs of a piece of furniture.

Stringing: A decorative border for furniture, especially table tops, consisting of a narrow line or lines of wood or metal INLAY.

Sussex chair: A late nineteenth-century chair produced by William Morris, with a LYRE BACK with SPINDLES, a rush seat and EBONIZED WOOD.

Tabouret: French term for a low, upholstered stool made from the seventeenth century onwards.

Tallboy: A small chest of drawers placed on top of a larger one; also known as a chest-on-chest.

Tambour: A desk with a shelved top and sliding panels replacing a glass or grilled front.

Taper leg: A leg that narrows as it reaches the foot.

Tavern table: Small, sturdy rectangular table, usually braced with STRETCHERS, and generally with a drawer or two in the FRIEZE. Used in eighteenth-century taverns.

Tenon: A projection at the end of a piece of wood, intended to fit into a corresponding shape in another piece of wood (MORTISE). Hence 'mortise and tenon' construction.

Tester: Top framework of a canopy bed.

Tilt-top table: Small table with the top hinged to a pedestal base so that it can be tilted up against a wall when it is not in use.

Torchère: Originally a stand that held a candle or lamp; also known as candle-stand. Today, a floor lamp designed to throw light upwards.

Trefoil: Motif with three leaves, or foils, usually contained within a circle. Typical of Gothic decoration.

Tripod: Three-legged stand for a PEDESTAL TABLE.

Triptych: Three-part, hinged mirror or small screen.

Trumeau: Generally, French term for the decorative treatment of the space over a mantelpiece. More specifically, over-mantel panel treatment popular in the Louis XV and XVI periods.

Trumpet leg: A conical leg with a flared end or foot.

Trundle or truckle bed: A low seventeenth-century bed which was rolled under a larger bed. The term is still used today.

Tudor arch: Flat-pointed arch that is characteristic of Gothic and Renaissance decoration.

Tudor rose: Decorative motif compounded of white and red Tudor roses from the Wars of the Roses.

Turning: A type of ornamentation produced by rotating wood on a lathe, and shaping it into various forms with cutting tools.

Veneer: A thin sheet of finishing wood, or other material, applied to a surface for decorative effect.

Wainscot chair: An early seventeenth-century wooden chair with a back panelled like the wainscoting of a wall.

Wardrobe: Developed in the seventeenth century as a cupboard for storing clothes.

Washstand: Adapted for bedroom use after 1750, and consisting of a straight cupboard on four legs with a basin sunk in the top.

Welsh dresser: A cabinet with a large, enclosed storage base and an upper section of open shelves.

Whatnot: A portable, open cabinet with shelves for books, ornaments, etc, developed about 1800. Popular from the Regency period onwards.

Wheat: Carved ornament representing ears of wheat, much used by Hepplewhite.

Windsor chair: Usually oak, elm or yew, with a back of TURNED SPINDLES, plus pegged legs and a wooden or rush seat. Produced from the seventeenth century in Britain, and popular in America from eighteenth century on.

part two: the specifics

SECTION EIGHT

Once you have created a good background, or framework, in a room, you can fill in the final details, which will give the space its particular character. 'God is in the detail' was one of the twentieth-century architect Mies van der Rohe's design aphorisms. Certainly the final detailing makes all the difference between a room that barely holds the attention and one that is distinguished, memorable and idiosyncratic – in other words, truly personal. This is the really fun part, the icing on the cake, when you can choose the accessories which reflect your own and your family's personality and bring a room to life.

The Finishing Touches

Finessing a Room

There are, of course, many aspects to detailing. All the groundwork will already have been done, and this is the stage when it is all finalized and enhanced. The furnishings and finishes need to be completed and then maintained as well as possible. And, finally, the art and objects, flowers and plants, and general accessorizing can be decided upon.

COUNCIL OF IMPERFECTION

There is a fine line between finessing a room – grooming it, as it were – and making it so perfect that it is positively discomforting to look at. Perfect rooms are as irritating as perfect people. The ideal room is one that manages to look both interesting and relaxing; used, but not abused.

Upholstery should look neat and smoothed, probably piped or edged in some way to keep its shape, and cushions should be plumped and well arranged. But that same upholstery should also look deeply comfortable and welcoming – never too pristine to put one's feet up.

ATTENTION TO DETAIL

If curtains are held back with tiebacks, these should be positioned at just the right height for the folds to look graceful. Blinds should be pulled up so that they are straight – it's surprising how many otherwise well-groomed people fail to notice when blinds are crooked.

Carpets, matting or hard flooring should all look as clean as possible. Rugs should not be rucked. Polished wood should be kept polished; marble, glass, perspex and any metals should be free of spots and smears.

Table tops, window sills, mantelpieces, display units and shelves look best with some sense of arrangement, rather than cluttered with papers and paraphernalia all over the place. Plants, collections and art should be carefully chosen and arranged. But above and beyond these concerns, they should not look so well arranged (or artificial) that one is nervous about putting down a glass or a cup for fear of spoiling an artistic effect.

It is good if door furniture matches and paintwork is clean and free of finger-marks. Ultimately, though, a little imperfection here and there is a reminder that people live in and relax in the room, and so is not a bad thing.

This kitchen with its splendid ecclesiastical window is an excellent example of finesse. Surfaces gleam, and everything appears to work as well as it looks, from the range and extractor fan to the drawers and work surfaces. Yet the room does not look too perfect to be used, which is the fate of all too many beautifully planned kitchens. Surely anyone would want to cook here.

part two: the specifics

Accessories

If good lighting, colour schemes, window and floor treatments, and the choice of furniture and upholstery are what make a room comforting, then the paintings and objects, plants and flowers and other embellishments are the elements that make it special, idiosyncratic and memorable. For a truly individual room, the objects must be personal and enjoyed for their own sake. They should have been thought about carefully and put together for some reason, not just to fill the space.

SIMPLICITY VERSUS CLUTTER

There are two schools of thought on the possession and display of objects: the school for simplicity, and the school for clutter. The first approach is typified by just one or two exquisite and interesting pieces, while the second favours an accretion of possessions and collections that can be called, rather aptly, memorabilia.

The trouble about the 'simple' school is that the few beautiful objects really must be beautiful or unusual, or at least made to appear so. The difficulty about the 'cluttered' school is that the collections – or the disparate amassing of objects that amounts to clutter – must be organized to display the possessions to their best advantage. This involves a careful assemblage of texture and shape and colour, for you are virtually creating 'still lifes' in just the same way as a painter or a photographer.

Collections of small objects are far more effective when grouped together, rather than scattered thinly around a room or home. For example, very small objects like shells, pebbles or polished fragments of stones from the beach can be put into bowls or goblets and displayed on window sills or shelves. Slightly larger objects, however different, should be grouped so that they have something in common, like colour, texture or national origin. Alternatively, they can be juxtaposed with larger or smaller objects to create extra interest and balance. Add a plant or some dried flowers, or even a selection of single blossoms in specimen jars for contrast.

If arrangements are grouped on low tables that are also used for books, magazines, glasses and so on, leave space so that the composition will not be ruined by putting down a tray, drink or book. If arrangements are placed on a glass shelf or table,

1 There is clearly an overload of disparate objects on and around this mantelpiece, including two lamps and a candlestick. But they work successfully together because all are in much the same neutral tones, quite apart from each being interesting in its own right.

2 Again, very different objects share the common denominator of colour against the white woodwork and the pale fawn painted wall, though these are carefully spaced.

3 Everything on these neatly arranged shelves has been chosen for its own merit or memories.

lighting them from underneath with an up-light is effective. If they are not on a transparent surface, try lighting them from above with a down-light or spot, to add extra brilliance.

UNUSUAL COLLECTIONS

Collections of ordinary but unexpected objects often make for more memorable rooms than much rarer and more expensive items. Perhaps this is because one is less impressed by the effect of something one knows to be especially good than by that of something one had not necessarily thought about. I can think back with pleasure on massed assemblies of old irons, shoe lasts, medicine bottles and pill jars with their different-coloured glass, eighteenth- and nineteenth-century spectacle cases, old locks and keys, toast racks, wine glass rinsers, pen boxes, card cases, old matchbox cases and tinder boxes, different ivory objects, old hats, old baskets... the list could go on and on.

SCULPTURE

Sculpture will always add distinction to a room. It might be a classical bust, a figurative bronze or an abstract design; it could be Chinese, Oceanic or pre-Columbian. Almost all sculpture, apart from life-size or free-standing pieces, looks better on some sort of plinth, whether it is stone, wood, fibre-glass, marble, plaster or perspex.

I *Here the shelving adds almost as much interest as the objects displayed, which in turn are as interesting for their blocks of colour as for themselves. The whole effect is of some Miró-like abstract, practically floating in the middle of the expanse of white wall.*

2 *Two pieces of primitive art – a shield and a horse – are shown to good advantage against the yellow wall.*

3 *One way to treat those awkward, shallow, horizontal windows is to use them as a back-lit display area. Here a collection of cameras is on show, which can be lit from the front when the daylight fades. Note that even the light – a photographer's lamp – sustains the theme.*

4 *A collection of amethyst glass on glass shelves stretched across a small window is matched by pinky-purple chrysanthemums.*

5 *No one could deny the decorative value of hats hung on a wall. This collection is hung rather rakishly askew to good effect.*

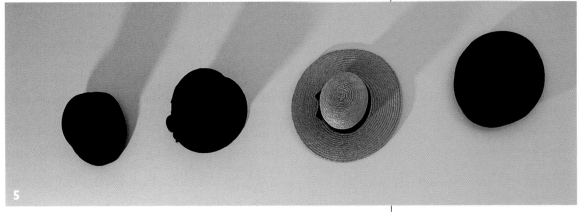

Arranging Art

The schools of thought on hanging art are as varied as the objects on display. Broadly speaking, however, they can be divided into two categories: people who want to make room for their serious collections, and people who want to use their wall space to its most decorative advantage.

People in the first category are always thinking of a wall as a means to an end – a support, a background – and moving paintings around as their collection expands or contracts, or changes direction. These people guard every bit of wall zealously. The second group need to find some unifying factor for their disparate and often undistinguished possessions. This especially applies to first-time house-holders, as well as to new partnerships, where both partners bring their own collections to a new joint home.

tip

IF ONE PAINTING OR PRINT IS MUCH LARGER THAN THE OTHERS, PUT IT AT ONE END OF A GROUPING, RATHER THAN IN THE MIDDLE SURROUNDED BY SMALLER WORKS, WHICH CAN GIVE THE IMPRESSION OF TAILING OFF. BALANCE IT AT THE OTHER END WITH SOMETHING ELSE TALL: A PLANT, A PIECE OF SCULPTURE OR A FLOWER ARRANGEMENT ON A TABLE BELOW.

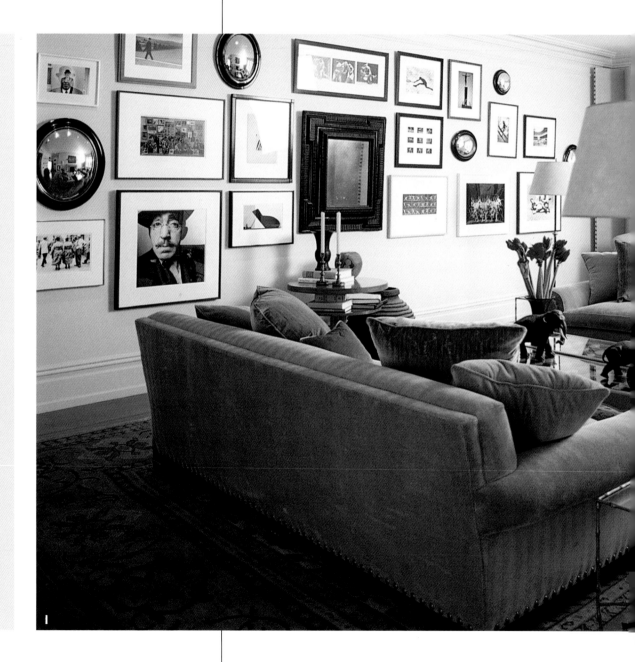

1

UNIFYING A SET

A miscellaneous set of prints can be given a unity it otherwise lacks if each print is given a mount of the same distinctive colour – buff, grey, blue, yellow, deep red or whatever fits the room or space – and is framed with the same material, whether chrome, brass or gilded, silvered or natural wood. Again, an odd assortment of different subjects will have a unity of their own if they share a colour: all sepia tints, or all black and white, or all green, ivory or terracotta.

1 An eclectic collection of different-sized and framed mirrors is hung along with varied prints and photographs, all on wide, white mounts. The varying convex mirrors, with their somewhat distorting reflections, adds a most interesting twist.
2 This collection of ancient Greek images all framed in terracotta and black is hung as a carefully

HANGING HEIGHTS

When there are a lot of different things to hang, try not to hang them too high or too far apart. Do not fix anything so low over a sofa or chair that people will knock their heads on it, and try to hang as much as possible

measured central block of 15, with two smaller groupings of three apiece on adjacent walls. They look especially arresting in an otherwise sparsely decorated, all-white bathroom. Though a bathroom is not an obvious (or always practical) location to hang an art collection, the result is gratifyingly spectacular.

at eye level (taking either sitting or standing levels into account). When there are very large groupings, keep at least the central pieces at eye level. But when the seating in a room consists of low-level couches and chairs, and stools or benches, there is no reason why some paintings, prints or posters should not be hung somewhat lower than usual.

There are certain tenets to follow, which, as always in interior design, are mostly common sense:

- Most artwork stands out on dark walls, although drawings and graphic art look good, even rather serious and gallery-like, on grey and neutral colours.
- If walls are strongly patterned, it is best to give prints and drawings very deep mounts so that the subject is becalmed in an area of its own, and does not get lost in the surrounding background design.
- Before hanging different sizes of pictures, juggle them around on the floor to find the layout that works best with other arrangements in the room and the wall space available.
- Decide on the overall shape of the arrangement and mark out the area on the wall in pencil before you attempt to hang several things together. This will save a lot of unwanted nail holes.
- Vertical arrangements of art will make rooms look taller.
- Horizontal arrangements will make rooms look longer.
- A lot of small works of art can be hung as a block to balance a larger painting or plaque, or as a substitute for a large painting.

2

part two: the specifics

ALTERNATIVE ART

There are plenty of alternatives to conventional art, whether old or current. Framed bits of fabric such as antique lace; square pieces of fabric pinned together like a patchwork; interesting bedspreads or rugs; samples of all manner of things, from different crops to riding crops; ceremonial Chinese and Japanese robes; old plaques; collections of chains; old pieces of jewellery, such as necklaces, earrings and brooches; old advertisements; collections of postcards; book covers – anything, in fact, that can be pinned up and can look decorative or interesting.

- Suspend heavy fabrics on a slim curtain rod hung on hooks. Unless the fabric is very rare, turn over the top to make a casing for the rod.
- Frame lighter fabrics underneath perspex or glass, or stretch them like canvas over thin wood frames.
- Hang smaller items on top of a square of felt, velvet or canvas, again stretched on a frame.

1 *Black-and-white photographs are rested, propped or otherwise fixed against black-painted panelling. The only colour is the touch of green leaves.*

2 *Paper memorabilia is effectively arranged in a long, envelope-like, transparent holder.*

3 *Old sepia prints are similarly propped against the wall on this mantelpiece in a deliberately casual manner. Propping paintings and drawings is often an effective alternative to hanging.*

4 *The ornate but empty picture frame above the carved oak chest shows off the brick wall very nicely. Notice, too, the clever balance of the tall candlestick with the tray, books and balls, and the trug filled with wooden shoe trees.*

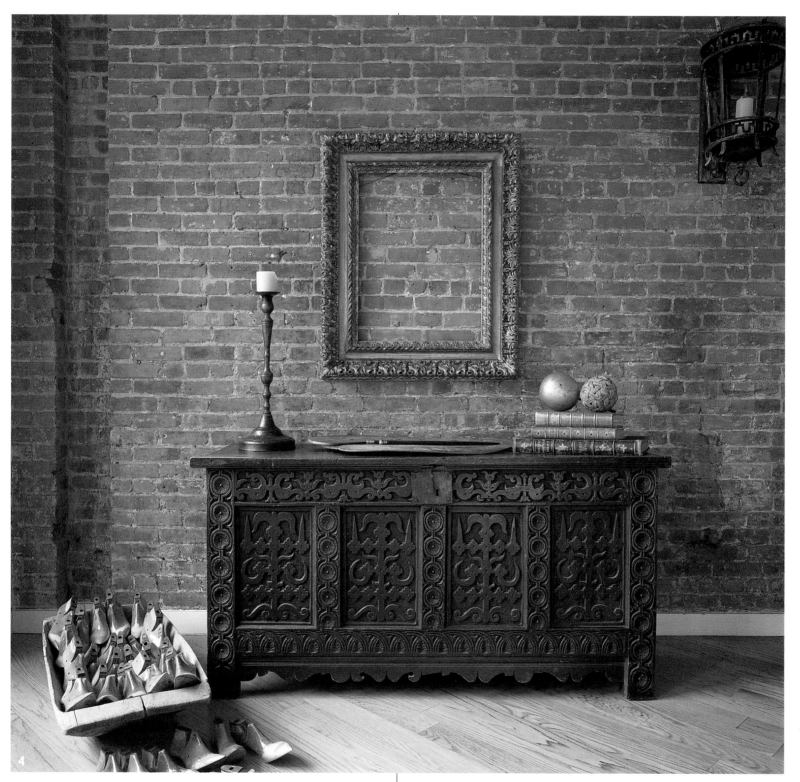

Plants in the Home

I would find it hard not to use plants in a room. Tall plants, wide-spreading plants, clusters of small plants, flowering plants, indoor trees and, of course, flowers all add a new dimension, a liveliness and freshness that are gratifyingly cheap in relation to the pleasure that is given. Moreover, plants, like books, always seem to furnish a room.

There is almost no gap in a room that a plant cannot fill and improve; no piece of furniture that cannot be balanced and made to look better by a spread of leaves, no corner that is not softened by foliage. Conversely, the sight of sick, uncared-for plants is immediately offputting.

LIGHT AND ASPECT

The choice of plants is governed by the amount of light a room gets and its aspect (the direction in which its windows face). If the aspect and light are not right for a plant, no amount of cosseting, fertilizing, spraying and careful watering can prevent its slow demise.

Most people who care for plants maintain that they can tell in a week if the location is appropriate by the gloss on the leaves, and a certain indefinable air of well-being. And if the setting is right, most plants seem to thrive with remarkably little attention, except for repotting as they grow and spread.

USING PLANTS CREATIVELY

Put plants in baskets, stainless steel planters, stone or terracotta pots, Versailles boxes or an urn on a plinth – anything that best suits the prevailing mood of the room. Make a group with plants and sculpture. Mass single flowers in specimen jars and old bottles.

Tall plants and indoor trees make subtle room dividers, and planters can be set on small casters or wheels for moving around easily. I have also seen them massed on shallow trolleys for easier manoeuvrability.

A bushy indoor tree or a well-planted hanging basket set in front of an unshuttered, uncurtained window can make it look completely dressed.

Rows of plants on shelves, strung across awkwardly shaped or placed windows, solve the problem of unity in a minute.

LIGHTING PLANTS

Place up-lights behind plants to throw dramatic shadows onto walls and ceilings, as well as illuminating the foliage on a dull day and at night. Or place small spots so that they shine through the leaves – but be careful not to put them so close that they burn them. Put plants or massed flowers directly under a down-light (again, placed a suitable distance away), for a special brilliance.

Be as generous as possible with anything you have to do with the plant world. Indoor landscaping can be just as exciting, and considerably less work, than the outdoor variety.

1 *Stone jars of grass, twigs of blossom and a paper lampshade make a nicely nuanced contrast of textures.*
2 *The grouping of old suitcases and an oriental statue is greatly enhanced by the oversize basket of scarlet flowers and greenery.*
3 *A huge plant in a pot looks calmly stunning seen through tall double doors. The foreground is softened by a large fern.*

Index

A

accent colour 48, 50, 53
accent lighting 20, 23, 24, 28
accessories
    colour 50–1
    displaying 208–11
    scale and balance 58
acrylic paint 94, 102
Adam, Robert 77, 78, 90, 192
Aesthetic movement 77, 78, 194
aesthetics 12, 14, 183
air-conditioning units 14, 17
alarms 14
America
    period furniture 196–7
    style-periods 77
antique effects 94, 101, 102, 103, 108
antiques 183, 190–203
arched windows 169, 171
architectural details, paper 108
architecture influence 66–8
art
    arranging 212–15
    lighting 26
Art Deco 76, 77, 78
Art Nouveau style 75, 76, 77, 78, 194
Arts and Crafts movement 77, 78, 194,
    197
atmosphere 7, 48–9
Austria 76, 196
Austrian blinds 163, 169, 173

B

background lighting 20, 23, 28
bagging 102
balance 58–9, 68, 71, 148, 181–3, 212
bamboo
    blinds 165
    flooring 141
    furniture 187, 198
barewire 24, 26, 28
Baroque style 73–4, 76, 77, 78, 191
Barry, Joseph B 197
base coat 102
baskets 34, 39
bathroom
    lighting 25
    planning stage 14

storage 38, 39, 40
windows 167
battens 115
Bauhaus 78
bay windows 168–9
Beaux Arts 77, 78
bedroom
    beds 188–9, 200, 202, 203
    curtain fabrics 172
    decorating schedule 17
    furniture arrangement 181
    lighting 24–5
    storage 32–4, 35, 40, 41
    wallpaper 106, 110
Belle époque style 76, 78
Biedermeier style 76, 78, 196
blackboard paint 102
blinds
    Austrian 163, 169, 173
    bamboo 165
    fabric 163–5, 173
    festoon 164, 169, 173
    louvre 165, 169
    matchstick/pinoleum 165
    paper 165
    positioning 206
    pull-up 164, 173
    reverse roller 164
    roller 115, 148, 149, 151, 164, 169, 173
    Roman 164–5, 168, 169, 173
    storage areas 41
    uses 162–3
    Venetian 21, 165, 169, 170
bookshelves 35, 41, 109, 183
borders 104, 106–7, 117
bow windows 168–9
box pleats 158
brick flooring 136
bricks, glass 118
British furniture 190–4
broken-colour technique 102, 103
brushes 102, 103
budget 12, 15, 108, 117, 172

C

café curtains 150, 153, 159, 170
candles 24
cane furniture 187, 199

Carolean style 190
carpet
    see also rugs
    density 124
    fibres 125–6
    grin 124
    maintenance 206
    natural matting 127, 134, 135
    pile 124–5, 135
    texture 124–5
    threshold strip 123
    vocabulary 134–5
    weaves 125, 126
    width 126
case goods 187, 199
cased headings 158, 169–70
casein paint 95, 102, 103
Caucasian rugs 132, 133
ceiling
    colour 47, 92
    decorating schedule 17
    decorative options 90–3
    paint 94
    planning stage 14
    sloping 90, 107, 110
    tenting 115
ceramic tiles 136–7
chair rail 107, 108, 117
children, planning 12, 13, 30
children's rooms
    lighting 25
    storage 35–6
Chinese rugs 132, 133
Chinoiserie 75, 77, 79, 192, 199
Chippendale, Thomas 192, 193, 196
Chronology of style-periods 76–7
circular windows 170, 171
cissing 102
Classical style 70–1, 79, 195
clerestory windows 169, 211
climate
    furniture arrangement 183
    style influence 65–6
clothes, storage 32–4, 40, 41
clutter 208
coir matting 127, 134
collections, display 40, 208–15
Colonial style 77, 78, 79, 196

colour
    and atmosphere 48–9
    balance 44
    board 17
    coordinating 47, 50–2
    contrast 48, 49, 50, 53, 59
    inspiration 42–3
    matching to style 44
    mixing 50–2
    negative design 56, 115
    and pattern 56
    planning 14, 47
    rendering 22, 28
    repetition 59, 93, 119
    and space 47, 106
    texture effect 54
    vocabulary 53
colourwashes 94, 96, 99, 102
combing 99, 102
comfort 12
computer 35, 38
concrete flooring 123, 140
cork flooring 144
cornice poles 153
cornices 47, 49, 71, 92, 95
country style 63, 64, 78, 79, 80
crackle-glaze 101, 102
craft paper 110
craquelure 101, 102
Cromwellian style 77, 79, 190–1
cupboards see period furniture; storage
curtains
    see also blinds; shutters; window
        treatments
    choosing 148–51
    corded 154
    headings 156–9
    insulation 154
    linings/interlinings 154, 157, 160–1, 172
    pelmets 152–3, 155–6
    poles 151, 153
    pull-up 164, 173
    rods 114–15, 153, 169, 170
    sash 169–70
    sheer 150, 153, 156
    storage areas 35, 40, 41
    swags and tails 154–5
    tie-backs 160, 206

top treatments 152–3, 154–9
tracks 154, 169, 174
trims 160–1

D
dado
  painted 99
  wallpaper 104, 107, 108
dark colours 47, 48, 49, 92, 106
daybed 189, 199
daylight 20
De Stijl 79
decorating schedule 17
decorative lighting 20, 23, 24, 26
detail 204, 206
dimmer switch 23, 24, 25, 27, 28
dining room
  chairs 186–7
  furniture arrangement 181, 182
  lighting 24
  storage 37–8
Directoire style 76, 79, 195
disguising techniques 95, 106, 116, 154, 163
distemper 94–5, 102, 103
distressing 102
doors
  borders 106, 107
  hooks 40
  mirrored 116
  planning state 16, 17
  storage units 33–4, 38, 40
  threshold strip 123
  window treatments 169
dormer windows 169
down-lights 23, 24, 27, 28, 29, 170
dragging 96, 97, 99

E
eclectic style 76, 77, 79
Edwardian style 79
Egyptian influences 193, 195
elderly people 12
electrical wiring
  lighting 23–4, 26
  planning stage 14, 16, 17, 35
Elizabethan style 77, 79, 190
Empire style 76, 77, 79–80, 195, 197

emulsion paint 94, 102
enamel paint 94, 102
encaustic tiles 138
entertaining 13
epoxy enamels 94, 102, 118
Etruscan style 80
Europe
  period furniture 194–6
  style-periods 76
eyelet headings 159
eyesores 95

F
fabric
  as artwork 214
  blinds 163–5
  ceiling 90, 92, 115
  colour schemes 51–2
  curtains 172–4
  storage areas 33–4, 40, 41
  upholstered furniture 184–5
  vocabulary 175–7
  wall covering 112–15
  wall hangings 113, 114–15
  wallpaper 104
fashion 62
faux finishes 96, 103, 106, 158
featureless room 68–9
Federal style 77, 80, 197
festoon blinds 164, 169, 173
filing cabinets 38, 40
finessing a room 206–7
finishing touches 206–17
fireplace recesses 32, 34–5, 116
fixed headings 156, 157, 158, 160
flagstones 123, 139
Flemish pleats 157–8
floor lamps 26–7
floor plans 16–17, 58, 183
flooring
  brick 136
  carpet 124–7
  coordinating 47
  concrete 123, 140
  cork 144
  decorating schedule 17
  existing 122
  linoleum 122, 144

maintenance 206
  painted 93, 143
  planning stage 14
  rubber 145
  rugs 128–33
  scale and balance 183
  stone 139
  threshold strip 123
  tiles 123, 136–8, 144
  vinyl 122, 144
  wood 122, 140–3
fluorescent lighting 23, 25
focal point 183
framing projector 26, 28
France
  period furniture 194–5
  style-periods 76
French doors 169, 174
French pleats 156, 157
friezes 107, 108, 200
function 7, 12–13
furnishings
  American furniture 196–7
  arrangement 180–3
  beds 188–9, 200, 202, 203
  British furniture 190–4
  cane/wicker/rattan/bamboo 187
  care and maintenance 206
  climate 183
  colour 50–1
  European furniture 194–6
  existing 6, 14, 15, 30, 122, 180
  floor plan 16, 17, 58, 183
  glass 187
  measurements 17, 185
  metal 187
  period furniture 190–203
  plastic 187
  scale and balance 58–9
  upholstered furniture 184–5, 191, 206
  vocabulary 198–203
  wooden 186–7

G
gathered headings 158
Georgian style 77, 80, 192–3, 196
Germany 76, 196
gilding 103, 192

glass
  collections 210, 211
  etched 167, 170
  furniture 187
  maintenance 206
  shelving 35, 38, 40, 150, 167, 170
  stained 167, 170
  walls 169
glass bricks and tiles 118
glazes 96–7, 98, 99, 103
goblet pleats 156–7
Godwin, E W 194
Gothic style 71–3, 76, 77, 80
gouache 96, 103
graining 103, 118
Grand Tour 70, 80
granite flooring 139
graph paper 17
Greek revival style 77, 80, 193, 197
grisaille 100, 101, 108
grout 117, 123
guest beds 189
Gustavian style 76, 80, 196

H
hallway
  colour 47
  lighting 24
  wallpaper 106
halogen bulbs 22–3, 26, 28
hardware
  furniture 187
  maintenance 206
  planning stage 14, 17
headboards 189
heading tapes 156–9
Hepplewhite, George 192–3, 196, 203
high-tech style 80
historical influences 70–83
hold-backs 158, 160
holiday homes 64–5, 68
hooks 40
Hope, Thomas 193
Hubbard, Elbert 197

I
incandescent bulb 22, 24, 28
Indian rugs 132, 133

International style 77, 79, 80
Italian stringing 160, 169

J
Jacobean style 77, 80–1, 190, 196
japanning 103, 191, 193
Jones, Inigo 70

K
kilims 129, 134
kitchen
    furniture arrangement 181, 206
    lighting 25
    storage 36–7, 40, 41

L
lacquering 100–1, 103, 191, 193
lambrequin 156
laminated wood 141–2
lamp 22, 28
Lannuier, Charles-Honoré 197
leather tiles 118
library
    lighting 23–4
    storage 34–5
lifestyle 12
light bulbs 22–3, 27
light colours 47, 48, 49
lighting 20–9
    accessories 208–9
    art 26
    artificial 20, 22–3
    bathroom 25
    bedroom 24–5
    child's room 25
    daylight 20
    decorating schedule 17
    dining room 24
    function 20
    kitchen 25
    living room 23–4
    mirrors 24, 25
    plan 16
    plants 26, 216
    study 23–4
    vocabulary 28–9
lining paper 103
linoleum 122, 144

living room
    curtain fabrics 172
    floor plan 183
    focal point 183
    lighting 23–4
    panelling 119
    seating arrangements 180–1
    storage 30, 34–5, 40
    wallpaper 106
location, style influence 64–5
Louis Quatorze style 76, 81, 194
Louis Quinze style 76, 81, 195
Louis Seize style 76, 81, 195
louvre blinds 165, 169

M
Mackintosh, Charles Rennie 194
Mannerism 81
marble
    faux 96, 103
    flooring 139
matchstick blinds 165
mattresses 188–9
metal furniture 187
milk paint 103
minimalism 81, 208
mirrors
    floor-to-ceiling 116
    furniture 187
    lighting 24, 25
    size 58
Mission style 81, 197
monochromatic schemes 54
mood 7, 48–9
Morris, William 194, 197
mosaic tiles 118, 138, 144
mouldings
    bedrooms 32–3, 34
    borders 106
    ceiling 90, 92
    colour 49, 95
    decorating schedule 17
    friezes 108
    grisaille 101
    panels 108
    period 198, 199, 200, 201, 202
Murphy bed 189
music systems 35, 183

N
Neo-Palladian style 74, 77, 81, 192
Neoclassicism
    furniture 192, 195, 196
    style-period 70–1, 75, 76, 77, 81
newspaper as wall covering 110
non-drip paint 94

O
office
    see also study
    storage 38, 40, 41
oil-based paint 94, 103, 118
ornaments
    finishing touches 208–11
    lighting 26
    storage 35, 38, 40

P
paint
    acrylic 94, 102
    brushes 102
    colourwashes 94, 96, 99, 102
    disguising eyesores 95
    distemper/whitewash 94–5, 102, 103
    epoxy enamels 94, 102, 118
    glazes 96–7, 98, 99, 103
    non-drip 94
    oil-based 94, 103, 118
    special effects 94, 96–101, 122
    textured enamels 94
    vocabulary 102–3
    water-based 94, 102
paintings
    arranging 212–15
    lighting 26
Palladian architecture 70, 77, 81
panels
    fabric 112
    false 95, 101, 106, 108
    using borders 107
    wallpaper 108, 109
    wood 118–19
paper
    see also wallpaper
    architectural details 108
    blinds 165
parquet flooring 122, 141

pattern 55–6, 104, 106, 118–19
pelmets 152–3, 155–6
pencil pleats 158
period furniture 190–203
Persian rugs 130
pets 12
Phyfe, Duncan 197
pianos 183
picture windows 169
pigment 103
pinch pleats 156, 157
pinoleum blinds 165
planning
    aesthetics 14
    budget 15
    decorating schedules 17
    floor plans 16–17, 58, 183
    function 12–13
    practicalities 14
    sample boards 17
    storage 30
plants
    display 216–17
    lighting 26, 216
    by mirrors 116
    scale and balance 58, 182
plaster finish 101
plastic furniture 187
pleated headings 156–8
Plugmold 26
portière rods 169, 170
Postmodernism 71
practicality 12, 14, 183
Prairie School 82
prayer rugs 130, 131
priming 103
print room paper 105, 108
printing 99
proportion 68, 71, 104, 106, 155

Q
quarry tiles 137
Queen Anne style 77, 78, 82, 191–2, 196–7

R
radiators 151, 168, 183
rag-rolling 98–9, 103

ragging 98–9, 99–100, 103
railroading 108
rattan furniture 187
reading lamps 24, 27, 180
Régence style 76, 82, 194
Regency style 77, 82, 193
Renaissance 70, 76, 77, 82, 190
Renaissance Classicism 71
Renaissance Revival 71, 82
Restoration style 77, 82, 191
Rococo style 74–5, 76, 82–3, 192, 194–5
roller blinds 115, 148, 149, 151, 164, 169, 173
Roman blinds 164–5, 168, 169, 173
rubber flooring 145
rugs
    see also wall-hangings
    Caucasian 132, 133
    Chinese 132, 133
    choice 128
    display 214
    Indian 132, 133
    kilims 129, 134
    non-slip backing 122, 123, 128
    oriental 129–33
    Persian 130
    pile 129, 135
    Turkish 131
    Turkoman 133
rush matting 127

S
sample boards 17, 51
sash curtains 169–70
scale and balance 58–9, 68, 181–3, 212
scale plans 17
scalloped headings 159
screens 31, 37–8, 88, 166
sculpture
    display 210
    lighting 26
    scale and balance 58
scumble glaze 97
seagrass 127
sealants
    stone 139
    tile 138
    wood 143

seasonal changes 65–6
seating
    see also window seat
    arrangement 180–1
    period furniture 198, 199, 200, 201, 202, 203
    sofa beds 189
    upholstered furniture 184–5
    wood 186–7
shading 98–9, 101
Shaker style 83, 197
sheer curtains 150, 153, 156, 173, 174
shellac 103
shelving 40–1
    bookshelves 35, 41, 109, 183
    children's room 36
    corners 40, 41
    finishing touches 208–9, 210
    glass 35, 38, 40, 150, 167, 170
    kitchen 36, 37, 40, 41
    across mirrors 116
    across windows 170
Sheraton, Thomas 192, 193, 196
shutters 151, 166–7, 169
sisal 125, 127, 135
sitting room see living room
size glue 103
sketch plans 16–17
skirting boards 95, 106
skylights 169–70
slate flooring 139
smocked heading 158
sofa bed 189
space
    art displays 213
    best use of 13
    and colour 47, 92, 106
    curtain illusions 154, 163
    decorative options 88, 92
    furniture arrangement 181, 183
    mirrors 116
    wallpaper patterns 106
spattering 103
sponging 98–9, 103
sports equipment 40, 41
spotlights 23, 24, 26, 28, 29
stained glass 167, 170
stainers 103

staircase
    lighting 24
    panelling 119
    storage area 38, 41
    wallpaper 106
stencilling 96, 97, 100, 101, 103, 122
Stickley, Gustav 197
stippling 96, 99, 103
stone flooring 123, 139
storage
    bathroom 38, 39
    bedroom 32–4, 41, 187
    dining room 37–8
    improvising 39–41
    kitchen 36–7, 40, 41
    library 34–5
    lighting 25
    living room 30, 34–5
    planning 30
    study 38
    window seat 35, 38, 154
    wooden units 187
strip lighting 20, 22, 23, 24, 25, 26
stripes
    painted 95
    spatial effect 92, 106
Stuart style 190
study
    lighting 23–4
    storage 38
style
    architecture influence 66–8
    Baroque 73–4, 76, 77, 78, 91
    choice 7, 14
    Classical 70–1, 79, 195
    and colour 44
    featureless room 68–9
    Gothic 71–3, 76, 77, 80
    period furniture 190–7
    Renaissance 70, 71, 76, 77, 82
    Rococo 74–5, 76, 82–3, 192, 194–5
    sense of 62
    suitability factor 64–9
    vocabulary 78–83
style-periods 70–83
    chronology 76–7
Sweden 76, 196
swing-arm lamps 27

T
tab headings 158, 159
table lamps 26–7
tables
    coffee 180, 181
    non-wooden 187
    period 198, 199, 200, 202, 203
    skirted 40
    wood 187
task lighting 20, 24, 27, 28
telephone socket 16, 17
television
    position 183
    socket 16, 17, 35
    storage 35, 40
tenting 115
terracotta tiles 137
terrazzo flooring 139
texture
    carpet 124–5
    and colour 44
    and pattern 54, 57
    plaster 101
    wallpaper 104, 115
textured enamels 94
tie-backs 160, 206
tiles
    ceramic 136–7
    cork 144
    encaustic 138
    flooring 123, 136–8, 144
    glass 118
    grout 117, 123
    laying 138
    linoleum 144
    maintaining 138
    mosaic 118, 138, 144
    options 116–18
    painting 94, 118
    quarry 137
    sealants 138
    terracotta 137
    vinyl 144
tissue paper as wall covering 110
tone 44, 53
track lights 24, 26, 28, 29
triangular windows 169
triple pleats 156, 157

trompe l'oeil 88, 89, 90, 97, 103, 108
Troubadour style 72–3, 83
Tudor style 77, 83, 190
tungsten bulbs 22, 28, 29
Turkish rugs 131
Turkoman rugs 133

U
undercoat 103
United States 77, 196–7
up-lights 23, 26, 29, 116, 170
upholstered furniture 184–5, 191, 206

V
valances 152–3, 156–9
varnish 94, 103
vases, concealed lighting 26
Venetian blinds 21, 165, 169, 170
Victorian style 77, 83, 193–4, 197
Vienna Secession 83
vinyl
    flooring 122, 144
    paint 94, 102
    wallpaper 104
vocabulary
    carpet 134–5
    colour 53
    fabric 175–7
    lighting 28–9
    paint 102–3
    period furniture 198–203
    style 78–83

W
wall hangings
    display 214
    fabric 113, 114–15
    focal point 183
    lighting 26
wall-washers 29
walling 112, 114
wallpaper
    architectural details 108
    borders 104, 106–7
    ceilings 92
    expensive 108
    fabric 104, 115
    friezes 108

lining paper 103
newspaper 110
panels 108
patterned 104, 106
textured 104
tissue paper 110
vinyl 104
wrapping paper 110
walls
    see also wallpaper
    art displays 212–15
    decorating schedule 17
    decorative options 88–9, 92, 95
    fabric 104, 112–15
    glass 169
    plain plaster 101
    planning stage 14
    scale and balance 183
    special effects 94, 96–101
    tiling 116–18
wardrobes *see* storage, bedroom
water beds 188–9
water-based paint 94, 102
whitewash/distemper 94–5, 102
wicker furniture 187
William IV style 193
William and Mary style 77, 83, 191, 196
window seat 35, 151, 154, 158, 162, 168
window treatments
    see also blinds; curtains
    arched windows 169, 171
    bay/bow windows 168–9
    choosing 148–51
    circular windows 170, 171
    clerestory windows 170, 211
    corner windows 170
    dormer windows 169
    fabrics 172–7
    French doors 169, 174
    headings 156–9
    linings/interlinings 154, 157, 160–1, 172
    opening-inwards windows 170
    over-sized windows 170
    pelmets 152–3, 155–6
    picture windows 169
    poles 153–4, 169, 174
    radiators 151, 168
    scale and balance 182–3

shaped windows 169, 170
shutters 151, 166–7, 169
side-by-side windows 170
skylights 169–70
small windows 154, 163, 167, 170
swags and tails 154–5
tie-backs 160
top treatments 152–3, 154–9
tracks 153–4, 169, 174
trims 160–1, 172
windows
    borders 106, 107
    decorating schedule 17
    light 20, 21
    planning stage 14, 16, 17
    recessed 151, 167
    shelving 35, 38, 149, 150, 167, 170, 211
    stained glass 167, 170
    storage 35, 41, 154, 167
wine racks 41
wood
    flooring 122, 140–3
    furniture 186–7, 190–7
    graining 103, 118
    panelling 118–19
    sealants 143
woodwork, decorating schedule 17
wrapping paper as wall covering 110

Acknowledgements

PICTURE CREDITS

1 Ken Hayden/Red Cover; 2 Simon Upton (Designer: Marja Walters/Michael Reeves)/Interior Archive; 4 Simon Upton (Designer: Rupert Spira)/Interior Archive; 5 above left Ray Main/Mainstream/Designer: Roger Oates; 5 above right Deidi von Schaewen; 5 centre left Paul Ryan/International Interiors (Designer: James Gager); 5 centre right Edina van der Wyck (Designer: Jenny Armit)/Interior Archive; 5 below Andreas von Einsiedel (Designer: Charles Rutherfoord); 6: Nadia Mackenzie/Interior Archive; 7: Paul Ryan/International Interiors (Designer: Alexander Vetners) ; 8 left Ray Main/Mainstream/Designer: Jasper Conran ; 8 centre Ken Hayden/Red Cover ; 8 right Verne/Houses and Interiors; 9 left Dennis Gilbert/VIEW (Conran Design Group); 9 centre Jake Fitzjones/Houses and Interiors; 9 right Ray Main/Mainstream/Architect: Gregory Phillips; 10 Paul Ryan/International Interiors (Architect: Barnes & Coy); 12:1 Paul Ryan/International Interiors (Designer: Charles Rutherfoord); 12:2 Ray Main/Mainstream; 13:3 Roger Brooks/Houses and Interiors; 14:1 Chris Gascoigne/View (Architects: Lifschutz Davidson); 14-15:2 Roger Brooks/Houses and Interiors; 15:3 Ray Main/Mainstream; 18-19 Verne/Houses and Interiors; 20-21:1 Arcaid/Richard Glover/Architect: Ben Mather; 21:2 Tim Beddow/Interior Archive; 22:1 Deidi von Schaewen; 23:2 Christl Rohl (Owner: Volker Classen)/Interior Archive; 23:3 James Morris/Axiom Photographic Agency; 24:1 Wayne Vincent (Owner: Dykman)/Interior Archive; 24:2 Ray Main/Mainstream/Designer: Lawrence Llewelyn-Bowen; 25:3 Dennis Gilbert/VIEW (Blauel Architects); 26:1 Laura Resen for Lachapelle Representation; 26:2 Ray Main/Mainstream; 27:3 Ray Main/Mainstream/Designer: Jasper Conran; 28: Ray Main/Mainstream; 29: Dennis Gilbert/VIEW (Conran Design Group); 30:1 Christl Rohl (Owner: Pilz)/Interior Archive; 31:2 Ray Main/Mainstream/Architect: Chris Cowper; 32-33:1 Nathan Willock/VIEW (Circus Lofts); 33:2 Paul Ryan/International Interiors (Designer: Caroline Breet); 34:1 Paul Ryan/International Interiors (Designer: Christian Liaigre); 35:2 Andrew Wood (Architect: Spencer Fung)/Interior Archive; 35:3 Robert Harding Syndications/Polly Wreford/GE Magazines: Inspirations; 36:1 Lu Jeffery; 37:2 Heidi Grassley/Axiom Photographic Agency (Architect: Seth Stein); 37:3 Nadia Mackenzie/Interior Archive; 37:4 Verne/G Fiorentino; 38:1 Paul Ryan/International Interiors (Designer: Frances Halliday); 39:2 Andrew Wood (Designer: The Holding Company)/Interior Archive; 40:1 Deidi von Schaewen; 41:2 Robert Harding Syndications/ Tim Imrie/GE Magazines: Inspirations; 42:1 Dennis Gilbert/VIEW; 43:2 James Morris/Axiom Photographic Agency; 44:1 Robert Harding Syndications/Lucinda Symons/GE Magazines: Inspirations; 45:2 Luke White/Axiom Photographic Agency; 46:1 Richard Waite/Arcaid; 47:2 Chris Gascoigne/VIEW (Architect: John Kerr); 48:1 Robert Harding Syndications/Debi Treloar/GE Magazines: Inspirations; 49:2 Robert Harding Syndications/Sandra Lane/GE Magazines: Inspirations; 49:3 Deidi von Schaewen; 50:1 Paul Ryan/International Interiors (Designer: Barbro Grandelius); 51:2 Ray Main/Mainstream; 52:1 Nick Hutton/VIEW; 52:2 Deidi von Schaewen; 53: Ray Main/Mainstream; 54:1 Ray Main/Mainstream/Designer: Roger Oates; 55:2: Deidi von Schaewen; 56:1 Richard Bryant/Arcaid; 57:2 Ray Main/Mainstream; 57:3 Verne/St Peiters; 57:4 Verne/G Pattun; 58:1 Jake Fitzjones/Houses and Interiors; 58:2 Ray Main/Mainstream; 59:3 Ray Main/Mainstream/Designer: Jasper Conran ; 60-61: Ken Hayden/Red Cover; 62:1 Earl Carter/Belle/Arcaid; 63:2 Ianthe Ruthven; 64:1 Ianthe Ruthven; 65:2 Deidi von Schaewen; 66:1 Ken Hayden/Red Cover; 66:2 Ianthe Ruthven; 67:3 Ray Main/Mainstream; 68:1 James Morris/Axiom Photographic Agency; 69:2 Laura Resen for Lachapelle Representation; 69:3 Jonathan Pilkington (Owner: Rotheston)/Interior Archive; 70:1&3 Ben Johnson/Arcaid; 71:2 Ianthe Ruthven; 72:1 Angelo Hornak; 72:2 Deidi von Schaewen; 73:3 John Bethell/Bridgeman Art Library ; 74:1 Richard Bryant/Arcaid; 74:2 Angelo Hornak; 75:3 Andrew Wood (Designer: Nicholas Haslam)/Interior Archive; 78:1 Jeremy Cockayne/Arcaid; 79:2 Mark Fiennes/Arcaid; 79:3 Richard Bryant/Arcaid; 80:1 James Mortimer (Architect: Le Corbusier)/Interior Archive/(FLC/ADAGP, Paris & DACS, London 2000; 81:2 Christie's Images Ltd; 82:1 Ianthe Ruthven/(ARS, New York & DACS, London 2000; 83:2 Angelo Hornak; 84 left Henry Wilson (Designer: Leslie Goring)/Interior Archive; 84 centre Winfried Heinze/Red Cover ; 84 right Simon Upton (Designer: Ann Boyd)/Interior Archive; 85 left Lu Jeffery; 85 centre Laura Resen for Lachapelle Representation; 85 right Andreas Von Einsiedel; 86-87 Andreas von Einsiedel (Designer: Tara Bernerd); 88:1 Mary Gilliatt; 88:2 Verne; 89:3 Laura Resen for Lachapelle Representation; 90:1 Paul Ryan/International Interiors (Designer: Kathy Gallagher); 90:2 Jonathan Pilkington (Designer: Dido Farrell)/Interior Archive; 91:3 Tim Clinch (Designer: Borja Azcarate)/Interior Archive; 92 left: Alan Weintraub/Arcaid; 92:1 Paul Ryan/International Interiors (Designer: Marcel Wotterinck); 93:2 Ray Main/Mainstream; 93:3 Andreas von Einsiedel; 94:1 Andreas von Einsiedel (Designer: Frederic Mechiche); 95:2 Robert Harding Syndications/Lucinda Symons/GE Magazines: Inspirations; 96:1 Brian Harrison/Red Cover; 96:2 Lu Jeffery; 97:3 Julia Pazowski/Houses and Interiors; 98:1 Andrew Wood (Owner: David Quigley)/Interior Archive; 98:2 Winfried Heinze/Red Cover; 98:4 Jeremy Cockayne/Arcaid ; 99:3 Roger Brooks/Houses and Interiors; 100:1 James Morris/Axiom Photographic Agency; 100:2 Andreas von Einsiedel (Designer: Annie Constantine); 100:4 Jonathan Pilkington (Owner: Hinchcliffe)/Interior Archive; 101:3 Richard Waite/Arcaid; 102: Deidi von Schaewen; 105:1 Edina van der Wyck (Designer: Mimmi O'Connell)/Interior Archive; 105: Wayne Vincent (Designer: Dyckman)/Interior Archive; 105:3: Simon Upton (Owner: Christine Davies)/Interior Archive; 106:1 Paul Ryan/International Interiors; 106:2 Andreas von Einsiedel (Designer: Ina Lindemann); 107:3 Mary Gilliatt; 108:1 Mary Gilliatt; 108:2 Andreas von Einsiedel; 109:3 Andreas von Einsiedel; 110:1 Deidi von Schaewen; 110:2: Steve Hawkins/Teresa Ward/Houses and Interiors ; 111:3 Mark Bolton/Red Cover; 112:1 Andreas von Einsiedel (Designer: Michelle Halard); 112:2 Simon Upton (Designer: Sasha Waddell)/Interior Archive; 113:3 Earl Carter/Belle/Arcaid; 114:1 Deidi von Schaewen; 115:2: Ray Main/Mainstream/Designer: Kelly Hoppen; 116:1 James Morris/Axiom Photographic Agency; 117 centre Richard Powers/Redback/Arcaid; 117:2 Verne; 118:1 Tim Beddow (Designer: Bill Amberg)/Interior Archive; 118:2 Tim Clinch (Owner: Handelsmann)/Interior Archive; 119:3 Robert Harding Syndications/Sandra Lane/Inspirations/GE Magazines; 119:4 Simon Butcher/Houses and Interiors; 119:5 Simon Upton/Interior Archive; 120-121 Eduardo Munoz (Designer: Ferruccio Laviani)/Interior Archive; 122:1 Andreas von Einsiedel; 122:3 Simon Upton (Designer: Bill Amberg)/Interior Archive; 123:2 Paul Ryan/International Interiors (Designer: Sasha Waddell); 124: 'Artistry' carpet, by Stoddard/Carla Reid-Adam; 126:1&3 The Carpet Foundation, UK tel: 01562 755568; 126:2&4 Blenheim Carpet Company/Barbara Douglass; 126:5 Natural Flooring Direct/photo: Peter Johnston/Theo Woodham-Smith; 127:6 The Carpet Foundation, UK tel: 01562 755568; 127:7 Woodstock Blenheim by Fired Earth; 127:9 Natural Flooring Direct/photo: Peter Johnston/Theo Woodham-Smith; 127:8: Richard Bryant (Architect: Spencer Fung)/Arcaid; 128: Ken Hayden/Red Cover; 130-131: Christie's Images Ltd; 132-133: Christie's Images Ltd; 134:1 Robert Harding Syndications/Sandra Lane/GE Magazines: Inspirations; 135:2 Blenheim Carpet Company/Barbara Douglass; 136:1 Richard Powers/Redback/Arcaid; 137:2 Simon McBride (Owner: Katy Brown)/Interior Archive; 138:1 Paul Ryan/International Interiors (Designer: Frances Halliday); 139:2 Brian Harrison/Red Cover; 140:1 Winfried Heinze/Red Cover ; 141:2&3 Natural Flooring Direct/Theo Woodham-Smith; 141:4 Alberto Piovano/Arcaid; 142:1 Roger Brooks/Houses and Interiors; 142:2 Andreas von Einsiedel (Designer: M. Antonin); 143:3 Paul Ryan/International Interiors (Designer: Sharone Einhorn); 143:4 Andrew Wood (Owner: Mandy Coakley)/Interior Archive; 144:1 Ray Main/Mainstream; 144:2 James Morris/Axiom Photographic Agency; 145:3 Christopher Drake/Red Cover; 146-147 Henry Wilson (Architect: Voon Yee Wong)/Interior Archive; 148:1 Laura Resen for Lachapelle Representation; 149:2 Houses and Interiors; 149:3 Richard Waite/Arcaid; 150:1 Ray Main/Mainstream; 151:2 Ray Main/Mainstream; 151:3 Winfried Heinze/Red Cover; 151:4 Andreas von Einsiedel; 152:1 Paul Ryan/International Interiors (Designer: Sasha Waddell); 153:2 Ray Main/Mainstream; 153:3 Paul Ryan/International Interiors

(Designer: Victoria Hagan); **153:**: Roger Brooks/Houses and Interiors; **155:1** Andreas von Einsiedel (Designer: Nona von Haeften); **155:2** Laura Resen for Lachapelle Representation; **156:1**: Richard Felber; **157:2** Andrew Wood (Designer: Christine Rucker/The White Co.)/Interior Archive; **157:3** Andreas von Einsiedel (Fabrics and design by 'Les Olivades', France); **158:1** Andreas von Einsiedel; **159:2** Ray Main/Mainstream; **159:3** Winfried Heinze/Red Cover; **159:4** Henry Wilson (Designer: John Plummer)/Interior Archive; **160:1** Paul Ryan/International Interiors (Designer: Jan des Bouvrie); **160:2** Simon Upton (Designer: Colefax and Fowler)/Interior Archive; **160:3** Paul Ryan/International Interiors (Designer: Harriet Anstruther); **161:4** Andreas von Einsiedel (Designer: Annie Constantine); **162:1** Simon Upton (Designer: Carol Thomas)/Interior Archive; **163:2** Lu Jeffery; **164:1** Robert Harding Syndications/Rowland Roques-O'Neill/GE Magazines: Inspirations; **164:2** Ray Main/Mainstream/Architect: Mary Thum ; **164:3** Ray Main/Mainstream; **165:4** Henry Wilson (Designer: Denise Lee)/Interior Archive; **165:5** Laura Resen for Lachapelle Representation; **166:1** Verne/Houses and Interiors; **166:2** Tim Beddow (Architect: Craig Hamilton)/Interior Archive; **167:3**: Nadia Mackenzie (Property: Ivy Cottage)/Interior Archive; **167:4** Henry Wilson (Designer: Ian Dew)/Interior Archive; **167:5** Paul Ryan/International Interiors (Designer: Kastrup & Sjunnesson); **168:1** Andreas von Einsiedel (Designer: Annie Constantine); **169:2** Ray Main/Mainstream; **170:1** Henry Wilson (Designer: Brett Muldoon)/Interior Archive; **170:2**: Paul Ryan/International Interiors (Designer: Sabina Streeter); **170:3** Eduardo Munoz (Architect: Sobejano/Nieto)/Interior Archive; **171:4** Christopher Drake/Red Cover; **171:5** Ray Main/Mainstream; **172:1** Andreas von Einsiedel (Designer: Annie Constantine); **172-173:2** Simon Upton (Designer: John Wright)/Interior Archive; **173:3** Tim Beddow/Interior Archive; **174:1** Erika Lennard; **174:2** Andreas von Einsiedel; **174:3** Christl Rohl (Owner: Mathias Schrunder)/Interior Archive; **176:1** Laura Resen for Lachapelle Representation; **176:2** Tim Beddow (Architect: Craig Hamilton)/Interior Archive; **178:** Paul Ryan/International Interiors (Designer: Lee Mindel); **180:1** Winfried Heinze/Red Cover; **180–181:3** Andreas von Einsiedel (Designer: Reed/Boyd Partnership); **181:2** Winfried Heinze/Red Cover ; **182** Paul Ryan/International Interiors (Designer: Jan des Bouvrie); **185:1** Andreas von Einsiedel (Designer: Mark Weaver); **185:2** Andreas von Einsiedel (Designer: Grant White); **185:3** Tim Beddow (Designer: Kathryn Ireland)/Interior Archvie; **185:4** Brian Harrison/Red Cover; **186:1** Christl Rohl (Owner: Rueter)/Interior Archive; **186:2** Winfried Heinze/Red Cover; **186:3** Bob Smith (Owner: Ricardo)/Interior Archive; **187:4** Paul Ryan/International Interiors (Designer: Sabina Streeter); **188:1** Jake Fitzjones/Houses and Interiors; **188:2** Paul Ryan/International Interiors (Designer: Lee Mindel); **189:3** Andreas von Einsiedel; **189:4** Paul Ryan/International Interiors (Designer: Kathy Moskal & Ken Foreman); **190–191** Christie's Images Ltd; **192–193:** Christie's Images Ltd; **194 above** Christie's Images Ltd; **194 below** Victoria and Albert Museum, London, UK/Bridgeman Art Library; **195** Christie's Images Ltd; **196 above** Mark Fiennes/Arcaid; **196 below** American Museum, Bath, Avon, UK/Bridgeman Art Library; **197 above** Henry Francis Dupont Winterthur Museum, Delaware, USA/Bridgeman Art Library; **197** below: American Museum, Bath, Avon, UK/Bridgeman Art Library; **198** Christie's Images Ltd; **201** Angelo Hornak; **204–205:** www.elizabethwhiting.com; **206– 207:** Andrew Twort/Red Cover; **208:1** Andreas von Einsiedel (Designer: Yves Taralon); **208:2** Andreas von Einsiedel: (Designer: Grant White); **209:3** Wayne Vincent (Designer: Howard Green)/Interior Archive; **210:1&2** Ray Main/Mainstream; **211:3&5** Ray Main/Mainstream; **211:4** Andreas von Einsiedel; **212:1** Laura Resen for Lachapelle Representation; **213:2** Andreas von Einsiedel (Michael Daly); **214:1** Laura Resen for Lachapelle Representation; **214:2** Andreas von Einsiedel (Designer: Grant White); **214:3** Melanie Acevedo; **215:4** Paul Ryan/International Interiors (Designer: G Pensoy); **216:1**: Laura Resen for Lachapelle Representation; **216-217:2** Ray Main/Mainstream; **217:3** www.elizabethwhiting.com.

AUTHOR'S ACKNOWLEDGEMENTS

I first wrote some of the basic material for this course for the enterprising and fast-growing US franchise company, Decor and You. I am most grateful to Karen Powell and Josie Cicerale for their instigation and for their friendship and for allowing material to be incorporated into this venture. It has been a real pleasure to have worked with Caroline Proud, Muna Reyal, Mary Staples, Jo Walton and Alison Wormleighton who made up the team from Conran Octopus and I thank them so much for their sensitivity to, and understanding of, the material and for their enthusiasm. I certainly have to acknowledge the patience, efficiency, enormous hard work and general agreeableness of Lin Prior, who helped so much with the preparations and organisation. And I most particularly want to thank Kate Coughlan, the best magazine editor I have ever had the good fortune to work with, for her belief in me and her support.

Since the course is the sum total of my own experience in a long working life connected with design and journalism, there are certain people – mentors, employers, friends, colleagues, clients – whom I have learnt a great deal from, or have been greatly helped by, or who have been a particular pleasure to work with. In one way or another, they have all contributed to this work, even if quite unknowingly, and I am deeply thankful to them all, some of them, alas, posthumously. In alphabetical order they are: Mike Adams, David Aldridge, Pam and Larry Barnett, Virginia Bredin, Felicity Bryan, Druscilla Beyfus, Alison Cathie, the late Debbie Christian, John, Carole and Brian Collins, Sam Cohn, Ralph and Amanda Congreve, Virginia Lo Faro Cooper, Katie Couric, John Cresswell-Turner, Kurt Dolnier and Allessandra Manning Dolnier, Michael Dunne, Andreas von Einsiedel, Vicky Ellerton, Dick and Judy Felber, Colin Gee, Jane Gelfman, Annie and Christopher Cruice Goodall, David Gough, Sally Griffiths, Mark Griffiths, Lord and Lady Griffiths, Susie Hanmer, Helene (Fesenmaier) Hodgson, D'Arcy and the late John Howell, Winefride Jackson, Carmel and John Jones, Philip Kendell, Jan Kern, Alex Kroll, Liz and Jack Lambert, Judy and Jim Lance, Alex and Eileen Lari, Sarah Tomerlin Lee, Larry Lehman, Stephen Long, Angela (Caccia) and Taffy Lloyd, John Ludovici, Katherine Manisco, the late Billy McCarty, Joy and George McWatters, Jim and Meredith Mercer, Bobbie Middleton, Michael Middleton, Beatrix Miller, Brian Morris, Filippa Naess, Sue and Paul Neale, Liam Neeson, Toby Nuttal, Barbara Plumb, Polly Powell, Helen (Robinson) Preston and the late Desmond Preston, Max Reinhardt, Natasha Richardson, Ray Roberts, Regina Ryan, Antonia Salvato, Jim Seabrook, Harry and Penelope Seidler, Gloria Steinhem, the late Comtesse Rosa Tarnowska, Ladislas Tarnowski, Angela and Wade Thompson, Jane Turner, Dr Steve Udem and Dr Sharon Nathan Udem, Graham Viney, Fred Weiss and Jeanne Wilkins.

The publisher and author would also like to thank Paul Williams for the floor plans on page 16 and the Blenheim Carpet Company (020 7823 5215/ 020 7225 3393) for the photographs on page 126 (no. 2 and 4) and page 135 (no. 2).